Abstracts of the
TESTAMENTARY PROCEEDINGS
of the
PREROGATIVE COURT OF MARYLAND

Volume XXI: 1736-1739

Libers: 30 (pp. 208-486), 31 (pp. 1-32)

by
V. L. Skinner, Jr.

CLEARFIELD

Printed for Clearfield Company by
Genealogical Publishing Company
Baltimore, Maryland
2009

ISBN 978-0-8063-5429-3

Made in the United States of America

INTRODUCTION

Purpose of the Prerogative Court.

The Prerogative Court was the central point for
probate for Provincial Maryland. It was
mirrored after the Prerogative Court of
Canterbury. There was a judge as well as
clerk(s) of the court. Initially, all probate
was brought directly to the Prerogative Court,
located in the Provincial Capital. As the
Province became more populous, all documents
were still to be filed with the Prerogative
Court; however, administration of probate was
delegated to the various county courts. Even
so, there are documents only in the Prerogative
Court and not in the appropriate county, and
vice versa.

Documents filed in the Prerogative Court.

The following documents were filed in the
Prerogative Court: administration bond, will,
inventory, administration accounts, and final
balances. The testamentary proceedings contain
the administration bond and the docket for the
court. If the administrator is lax in filing
documents, then a summons is also recorded.

Equity Court

The Prerogative Court was also the court for
equity cases—resolution of disputes over the
settlement and distribution of an estate. The
case was brought before the judge and could take
several years to resolve. Often depositions
were taken and recorded in the minutes.

Notes on the Abstraction.

1. The left hand column contains the liber/folio
number. The folio numbers are presented just as
they appear in the actual document, e.g., 32a,
78½.

2. The right hand column contains the
abstraction text.

3. Various libers specify a particular session
for the Prerogative Court, e.g., 1678; or,
September Court 1742. This information is
presented as "Court Session:" followed by the

appropriate session. Should no session have
been specified, then the phrase "no date" is
used.

4. An ellipsis (...) is used to indicate a
continuation of the previous information, but no
relevant genealogical information is present.

5. The following symbols are used in the
abstraction:
  ?   difficult to read.
  #   pounds of tobacco.
  !   [sic].

Abbreviations.

The following abbreviations have been used
throughout this abstraction:

AA - Anne Arundel Co.
ACC - Accomac Co.
BA - Baltimore Co.
CE - Cecil Co.
CH - Charles Co.
CR - Caroline Co.
CV - Calvert Co.
dbn - de bonis non
DE - Delaware
DO - Dorchester Co.
ENG - England
FR - Frederick Co.
g - gentleman
GB - Great Britain
HA - Harford Co.
IRE - Ireland
JP - justice of the
    peace
KE - Kent Co. MD
KEDE - Kent Co. DE
LaC - letters ad
    colligendum (for
    temporary
    collection &
    preservation of
    assets)
LoA - letters of

administration
LoD - list of debts
MA - Massachusetts
MD - Maryland
MO - Montgomery Co.
NE - New England or
    "non est"
NEI - "non est
    inventar" (not
    found)
NY - New York
NYC - New York City
p - planter
PA - Pennsylvania
PG - Prince George's
    Co.
PoA - power of
    attorney
QA - Queen Anne's Co.
SM - St. Mary's Co.
SMC - St. Mary's City
SO - Somerset Co.
TA - Talbot Co.
VA - Virginia
WA - Washington Co.
WO - Worcester Co.

This volume is a continuation of the series,
covering 1736 to 1739. The Court is meeting
every 2 months to review the docket, and to take
appropriate actions. Except for spurious
entries, the information is presented in
chronological order, as recorded by the
Register.

30:208 4 October. Charles Hynson (g, KE)
exhibited:
- will of John Reading, constituting
  Sarah Reding executrix. Said Sarah
  was granted administration.
  Sureties: James Corse, Bullman
  Midford. Date: 23 July 1736.
- bond of Sarah Skirven administratrix
  of George Skirven. Sureties: Gideon
  Pearce, Jervis Spencer. Date: 18
  August 1736.
- will of William Comegys,
  constituting Edward Comegys, Jr.
  executor. Said Edward was granted
  administration. Sureties: Daniel
  Pearkins, William Smithers. Date:
  21 September 1736.
- bond of Edward Dicas administrator
  of William Dicas. Sureties: Abraham
  Ambrose, Thomas Piner. Date: 30
  September 1736.
- renunciation of John Hix & Sarah Hix
  on estate of Nathaniel Pearce,
  recommending Mr. Gideon Pearce
  (greatest creditor). Date: 22 March
  1735/6.
- will of Edward Hales, constituting
  Philip Hales executor.
- will of Mary Howard, constituting
  Mathew Howard executor.
- will of John Fling, constituting
  Mary Fling executrix.
- additional inventory of John
  Johnson, Esq.
- inventory of Edward Cozens.
- additional inventory of John
  Fanning.
- inventory of Benjamin Griffith.
- inventory of William Carter.
- inventory of Archibald Cragh.
- inventory of Richard Fulston.
- inventory & LoD of Samuell Gooding.
- inventory & additional inventory of
  Hans Hanson.
- accounts of James Smith & his wife
  Sarah executrix of Alexander
  McGachan.
- accounts of Glanvill Rolph & his
  wife Margaret administratrix of
  William Shield.
- accounts of Elisabeth Ferrell
  executrix of Daniel Ferrell.

- accounts of Thomas Mahone executor of John Fannen.

30:209
- accounts of George Garnett executor of Thomas Garnett.
- accounts of Susanna Johnson acting executrix of John Johnson, Esq.
- accounts of Robert George administrator of Jonathon Garnett.
- accounts of Rebecca Evans administratrix of John Evans.
- accounts of James Stout & his wife Anne administratrix dbn of St. Leger Codd, Esq.
- accounts of Elisabeth Young & Hans Hanson administrators of Hans Hanson.
- additional accounts of William Trew & his wife Hannah executrix of Francis Bodien.
- accounts of William Clark & Amelia Baker executors of Charles Baker.
- accounts of Hannah Carman administratrix of Joseph Carman.

Peter Dent (g, PG) exhibited:
- will of William Clarkson, constituting Elisabeth Clarkson & Thomas Clarkson executors. Said Elisabeth & Thomas were granted administration. Sureties: Christopher Edelen, John Edelen. Date: 25 August 1736.
- bond of Micajah Plummer & Yate Plummer executors of Elisabeth Plummer. Sureties: Samuel Plummer, John Plummer. Date: 25 August 1736.
- bond of Henry Darnall administrator of Capt. William Darnall. Sureties: John Frazer, Zephaniah Wade. Date: 25 August 1736.
- inventory of Leonard Brooke.
- inventory of Joshua Calvert.
- additional inventory of Thomas Holland.
- additional inventory of Samuel Perrie.
- inventory of Peter Knight.
- 2nd additional accounts of Francis King administratrix of William King.
- accounts of William Beanes administrator of Mary Reed.
- accounts of William Beanes

Court Session: 1736

administrator of Peter Knight.
- accounts of John Dawson executor of Mary Dawson.

0:210 Samuel Hanson (g, CH) exhibited:
- bond of Ann Howison administratrix of John Howison. Sureties: Stephen Mankin, James Muncaster. Date: 15 September 1736.
- will of Henry Mudd. Also, bond of Elisabeth Mudd administratrix. Sureties: Ignatius Hagan, Thomas Mudd, Jr. Date: 15 September 1736.
- will of Peter Fernandes.
- inventory of John Capshaw.
- inventory of Charles McDaniel.
- inventory of John Lewin.
- additional inventory of Ignatius Luckett.
- additional accounts of John Barker administrator dbn of James Peele.
- accounts of Notly Maddox administrator of John Lewin.

6 October. Mr. Peter Dent (PG) to examine accounts of:
- Elisabeth Saser administratrix of John Saser (PG).
- Mary Piles executrix of John Piles (PG).

9 October. Exhibited from BA:
- inventory of Thomas Warren.

11 October. John Parrish vs. estate of his father Edward Parrish. Letter to Mr. William Rogers (Register), citing caveat against settling said estate. Said John is one of the executors. Date: 7 October 1736 at Potapsco.

0:211 13 October. Exhibited from PG:
- inventory of Abraham Parkinson.

Exhibited from AA:
- accounts of John Elliot Brown & his wife Elisabeth executrix of George Simmons.

Exhibited from BA:
- accounts of Mary Warren administratrix of Thomas Warren.

Court Session: 1736

Capt. John Pitt (DO) to examine
accounts of:
• Levin Hicks administrator of
  Elisabeth Lemee (DO).

14 October. Exhibited from AA:
• accounts of Thomas Higgens & his
  wife Dorothy assignees of Samuel
  Cottrell (AA, dec'd) administrator
  of John Hobbs.

19 October. Exhibited from SM:
• accounts of Robert Elliot
  administrator of John Whitlowe.

Thomas Aisquith (g, SM) exhibited:
• bond of Mary McWilliams
  administratrix of Thomas McWilliams.
  Sureties: George Forbes, John
  Forbes. Date: 4 August 1736.
• will of John Readman, constituting
  Aaron Haskins executor. Said
  Haskins was granted administration.
  Sureties: Thomas Gardiner, Edmund
  Boling. Date: 4 October 1736.
• bond of Barbara Frazer
  administratrix of John Frazer.
  Sureties: Henry Tucker, Robert
  Henley. Date: 8 October 1736.
• inventory & LoD of Richard Vowles.
• inventory & LoD of Robert Clark.
• inventory & LoD of Jacob Morris.
• inventory & LoD of John Hayes.
30:212 • inventory & LoD of Richard Coade.
• inventory & LoD of Benjamin Gough.
• inventory of James Armstrong.
• accounts of Ann Smithson
  administratrix of Owen Smithson.
• accounts of John Coffeny
  administrator of James Armstrong.
• accounts of Andrew Foy & his wife
  Barbara executrix of Charles
  Calvert.

20 October. Exhibited from BA:
• additional accounts of Elisabeth
  Smith executrix of William Smith.
• bond of Alexander Black
  administrator of William Cockran.
  Sureties (AA): Dr. Charles Carroll,
  Charles Browne. Date: 20 October
  1736.

Court Session: 1736

MM George Buchanan (BA) & Luke Stansbury (BA) to appraise estate of William Cockran (BA). Mr. Thomas Sheredine (justice, BA) to administer oath.

Tench Francis (g, TA) exhibited:
* bond of Frances Pitchfork administratrix of Thomas Pitchfork. Sureties: Robert Lowry, Robert Waddell. Date: 17 August 1736.
* bond of John Reynolds administrator of Mary Cooper. Sureties: Richard Skinner, Lewis Jones. Date: 6 September 1736.
* inventory of John Barwick.
* inventory of Isaac Marling.
* inventory of John Loveday.
* inventory of Philip Kacey.

30:213 21 October. Capt. John Pitt (DO) exhibited:
* will of Samuel Harper. Also, bond of William Harper executor. Sureties: William Thompson, Thomas Whitley. Date: 14 September 1736. Also, renunciation of Sarah Harper widow, recommending her son William Harper.
* inventory of Thomas Haskins in DO & in AA.
* inventory of David Peterkin.
* inventory of Mary Cook.
* accounts of Jane Thompson executrix of John Thompson.
* accounts of Elisha Stevens & his wife Dorothy executors of Francis Beckwith.

Nehemiah King (g, SO) exhibited:
* bond of Thomas Benson executor of Betts Collier. Sureties: Robert Collier, Joseph Wailes. Date: 21 July 1736.
* will of Stephen Ward, constituting Ann Ward executrix. Said Ann was granted administration. Sureties: Francis Lord, Henry Lord. Date: 21 August 1736.
* will of Samuel Horsey, constituting Smith Horsey executor. Said Smith was granted administration. Sureties: Nathaniel Horsey, Henry

Court Session: 1736

Smith. Date: 4 September 1736.
- bond of Robert Hodge administrator
of Ezekiel Denning. Sureties: John
Payte, John Gilleland. Date: 8
September 1736.
- will of John Tounsand. Also, bond
of Littleton Tounsand executor.
Sureties: Francis Porter, William
Porter. Date: 8 September 1736.
Also, renunciation of Rebecca
Tounsend widow, recommending her son
Littleton Tounsend. Date: 9
September 1736.

30:214
- will of John Turpin, constituting
Hannah Turpin & William Turpin
executors. Said Hannah & William
were granted administration.
Sureties: Col. Robert King, Thomas
Mitchell. Date: 5 October 1736.
- inventory of Robert Skeine.
- inventory of John Stevens.
- inventory of Thomas Tate.
- inventory of Peter Cearsey.
- inventory of Richard Harper.
- inventory of John Murry.
- inventory of David Addams.
- accounts of Elinor Bowland executrix
of William Bowland.
- accounts of Magdalen Smith executrix
of William Smith.
- additional accounts of Susanna Noble
executrix of Isaac Noble.
- accounts of Mary Humphries executrix
of Thomas Humphries.

Gabriel Parker (g, CV) exhibited:
- bond of John Brome, Jr.
administrator of Henry Brome.
Sureties: John Brome, Thomas Brome.
Date: 16 September 1736.
- inventory of Thomas Mannying.
- accounts of Mary Bland
administratrix of John McDowell.
- accounts of John Framan executor of
Martha Gardner.

Mr. Nehemiah King (SO) to examine
accounts of:
- Robert Dashiell executor of George
Dashiell (SO).
- Richard Goslee & his wife Tabitha
executrix of John Veunables (SO).

Page 6

Court Session: 1736

- Esther Williams administratrix of
  William White (SO).

23 October. Exhibited from BA:
- 2nd additional accounts of Frances
  Foy executrix of Daniel Johnson.

Mr. Gabriel Parker (CV) to examine
accounts of:
- Elinor Day executrix of Daniel Day
  (CV).

30:215 William Thomas (TA) vs. Richard Giles
one of witnesses to will of Loftis
Bowdle (TA). Sheriff (TA) to summon
defendant to prove said will.

25 October. Charles Hynson (g, KE)
exhibited:
- bond of Richard Edwards executor of
  William Drury. Sureties: Alexander
  Adair, Alexander Crabin. Date: 20
  October 1736.
- inventory of John Reading.
- inventory & LoD of John Hall.
- inventory of William Tidmarsh.
- inventory & LoD of Thomas Maxfield.
- accounts of Wedge Crouch & his wife
  Mary administratrix of William
  Taylor.
- accounts of Humphry Younger executor
  of Mary Anderson.

Mr. William Rumsey (CE) to examine
accounts of:
- Benjamin Pearce & his wife Margaret
  administrators of Henry Ward (CE).
- Margaret Sapenton executrix of
  Nathaniel Sapenton (CE).
- Joseph Price & his wife Jane
  executrix of Philip Barret (CE).
  Additional accounts.
- Robert Money, Jr. & his wife Ruth
  administratrix of William McDowell
  (CE). Additional accounts.

Capt. John Pitt (DO) to examine
accounts of:
- Mary Robson executrix of Charles
  Robson (DO).
- Elisabeth Bramble administratrix of
  John Bramble (DO).

- Elisabeth Kemey executrix of Walter Kemey (DO).

27 October. Mr. William Rumsey (CE) to examine additional accounts of:
- Joshua George one of administrators of James Moody (CE).

30:216 28 October. Exhibited from AA:
- 2nd additional accounts of Elihu Hall (CE) & his wife Elisabeth administratrix of John Chew.

MM James Mouatt (AA), William Sellman (AA), & Walter Phelps, Sr. (AA) to appraise estate of Joseph Howard (AA). Mr. Edward Gaither (justice, AA) to administer oath. MM John Howard & John Hammond (son of Charles) to appraise that part of the estate near Elkridge. Col. Henry Ridgely (justice, AA) to administer oath.

30 October. Exhibited from SM:
- accounts of Robert Hoskins administrator of Thomas Scott.

2 November. Exhibited from AA:
- accounts of William Alexander executor of Robert Alexander, Esq.

5 November. Exhibited from AA:
- inventory of John Ward.

6 November. Exhibited from AA:
- bond of Thomas Gassaway, Jr. administrator dbn of John Brewer. Sureties: Nicholas Gassaway, Joseph Brewer. Date: 6 November 1736.

8 November. Exhibited from PG:
- inventory of William Mockbee.

9 November. Exhibited from AA:
- additional accounts of Alice Powell administratrix of William Powell.

Court Session: 9 November 1736

30:217 Docket:
- R.F. for administrator of Col. Jacob Loockerman (DO) vs. W.C. for

Court Session: 9 November 1736

- Dorothy Loockerman. Libel, answer.
  W.C. for John Lusby (AA) vs. E.J.
  for Thomas Wells & his wife Elinor
  executrix of John Lusby. Libel,
  answer.
- William Cumming, Esq. executor of
  Thomas Facer (AA) vs. M.M. for
  Achsah Woodward administratrix dbn
  of Amos Garrett, Esq. Also, Edmund
  Jenings, Esq. & John Galloway
  attorneys-in-fact for Elisabeth Ginn
  & the executors of Mary Woodward.
  Libel, answer, interrogations,
  depositions.
- John Edmondson (TA) vs. Richard
  Francis, Esq. for Jacob Loockerman
  executor of Jacob Loockerman (TA).
  Sheriff (DO) to summon defendant to
  render accounts. Summons to
  plaintiff to show cause for
  complaint.

30:218
- Sheriff (SO) to summon John Whaley &
  his wife widow of John Darby (DO) to
  take LoA. Attachment rendered to
  sheriff.
- Sheriff (DO) to summon Comfort
  Hopkins widow of John Hopkins (DO)
  to take LoA.
- W.C. for John Phillips & his wife
  Ann (PG) vs. B.Y. for Nicholas
  Downing & his wife Elisabeth
  executrix of John Clarvo. Libel,
  answer
- Sheriff (SO) to summon Nathaniel
  Horsey & Sarah Horsey to show cause
  why they conceal estate of William
  Horsey (SO).
- Sheriff (KE) to summon Mary Raisens
  executrix of Thomas Raisens (KE) to
  take LoA.

30:219
- William Thomas (TA) vs. Richard
  Giles one of witnesses to will of
  Loftis Bowdle (TA). W. Thomas
  (sheriff, TA) to summon defendant to
  prove said will.

Court Session: 1736

12 November. Peter Dent (g, PG)
exhibited:
- bond of James Smallwood, Thomas
  Smallwood, & Pryor Smallwood

administrators of Benjamin
Smallwood. Sureties: Humphry Bury,
William Nelson (CH). Date: 5
November 1736.
• will of Robert Skinner, constituting
Nathaniel Skinner executor.
• inventory of Robert Magruder.

Exhibited from AA:
• inventory of Joseph Howard.

17 November. Exhibited from AA:
• inventory of Edmund Evans.

30:220 23 November. Mr. Samuel Hanson (CH) to
examine accounts of:
• Virlinda Sanders administratrix of
Thomas Sanders (CH).
• Thomas Marshall administrator of
Elisabeth Fendall (CH).
• Ann Capshaw administratrix of John
Capshaw (CH).
• William Coombes & William Mackatee
executors of Katherine Ensey
administratrix of John Ensey (CH).

Mr. Nehemiah King (SO) to examine
accounts of:
• Abigail Tomlinson & Solomon
Tomlinson executors of Samuel
Tomlinson (SO).
• Isaac Addams administrator of David
Addams executor of Thomas Addams,
Sr. (SO).
• Katherine Layfield & George Layfield
executors of Thomas Layfield (SO).
• Thomas Handy & Samuel Handy
executors of Samuel Handy (SO).

26 November. Gabriel Parker (g, CV)
exhibited:
• will of Jesse Jacob Bourne. Also,
bond of Alice Bourne administratrix.
Sureties: Isaac Rawlings, Daniel
Rawlings. Date: 4 November 1736.
• inventory of Burden Crosby.
• accounts of Elinor Day executrix of
Daniel Day.

29 November. Peter Dent (g, PG)
exhibited:
• inventory of Thomas Summersett.

Court Session: 1736

- accounts of Mary Piles executrix of John Piles.

30 November. Exhibited from PG:
- additional accounts of George Buchanan administrator of Capt. Hugh Arbuthnott.

30:221 1 December. Capt. John Pitt (DO) exhibited:
- inventory of George Drew.
- inventory & LoD of William Shipley.

3 December. Exhibited:
- renunciation of Mary Humphrys on estate of Justinian Barwell (AA), recommending Dr. Charles Carroll (Annapolis). Date: 3 December 1736. Witness: William Rogers.

6 December. James Earle (g, QA) exhibited:
- will of William Swift. Also, bond of John Swift executor. Sureties: Richard Harrington, Jr., Jeremiah Jadwin. Date: 26 July 1736. Also, renunciation of Thomas Swift (p, son), recommending his brother John Swift. Date: 24 July 1736. Witnesses: Redmond Fallin, Jeremiah Jadwin.
- bond of Lilley Burroughs administratrix of William Burroughs, Jr. Sureties: William Burroughs, George Burroughs, Michael Bateman. Date: 1 November 1736.
- will of James McClean, constituting Ann McClean executrix. Said Ann was granted administration. Sureties: John Earle, Richard Collins. Date: 15 November 1736.
- bond of Anna Maria Hemsley administratrix of William Hemsley. Sureties: Richard Tilghman, Esq., Richard Tilghman, Jr., James Earle. Date: 12 October 1736.

30:222
- will of Mary Lee. Also, executors renunciation.
- inventory of William Carman.
- inventory of Alice Murphey.
- inventory of John Bath.
- inventory of John Droughton.

Page 11

Court Session: 1736
- inventory of James Barkhust.
- inventory & LoD of Samuel Wright.
- accounts of Elisabeth Mathews administratrix of William Mathews.
- accounts of Francis McKown & his wife Sarah administrators of John Falcom.

Charles Hynson (g, KE) exhibited:
- will of Francis Wickes.
- inventory of David Thomas.
- inventory of Henry Hosier.
- inventory of Darby Shehawn.
- inventory of Benjamin Hopkins.
- additional accounts of Frederick Hanson & Jane Knowlman executors of George Hanson.

7 December. Mr. Thomas Aisquith (SM) to examine accounts of:
- Ann Hayes executrix of John Hayes (SM).
- Thomas Gardiner administrator of Elisabeth Cole (SM). Additional accounts.

Mr. Tench Francis (TA) to examine accounts of:
- Mary Sherwood administratrix of Hugh Sherwood (TA).
- Henry Clift & his wife Elisabeth executrix of James Dudley (TA).

Mr. William Rumsey (CE) to examine accounts of:
- Sarah Touchstone administratrix of Henry Touchstone (CE).

30:223 Mr. Charles Hynson (KE) to examine additional accounts of:
- Samuel Wickes surviving executor of Charles Galloway (KE).

8 December. Samuel Hanson (g, CH) exhibited:
- will of Ann Gwinn, constituting Robert Yates, Joseph Gwinn, & Benjamin Gwinn executors. Said executors were granted administration. Sureties: John Harris, Richard Mastin. Date: 2 October 1736.

- bond of John Groves administrator of Mathew Groves. Sureties: John Scrogen, Notley Maddox. Date: 5 November 1736.
- inventory of Edward Davis, Sr.
- inventory of Thomas Wheeler.
- inventory of John Fairfax.
- additional inventory of Elisabeth Fendall.
- inventory of Robert Hanson, Jr.
- additional accounts of John Phillpott administrator of Rev. Esdra Theodore Edzard.
- accounts of Rachel Darnall administratrix of John Darnall.
- accounts of Mary Burroughs administratrix of Thomas Burroughs.
- accounts of William Vincent & his wife Sarah administratrix of John Dixon.

Mr. James Earle (QA) to examine accounts of:
- John Hayes, Jr. & his wife Sarah executrix of Edward Wright, Jr. (QA).
- Benjamin Elliott & his wife Mary executrix of Workman Harris (QA). Additional accounts.
- Jane Barkhurst administratrix of James Barkhurst, Jr. (QA).
- Mary Wright executrix of Samuel Wright (QA).

Mr. Peter Dent (PG) to examine accounts of:
- Leonard Wheeler, Francis Wheeler, Clement Wheeler, & Ignatius Wheeler executors of Francis Wheeler (PG).
- Susannah Ray administratrix of George Ray (PG).
- Benjamin Smith & his wife Mary executrix of Benjamin Stimpson (PG). Additional accounts.
- Leonard Marbury & Luke Marbury executors of Francis Marbury (PG). Additional accounts.
- Amy Groome executrix of Richard Groome (PG).

30:224 Elisabeth Thomas executrix of Thomas Thomas (CH) was granted continuance.

Court Session: 1736

Mr. Samuel Hanson (CH) to examine accounts of:
- Mary Parker administratrix of Abraham Parker (CH).
- Henry Trueman executor of Sarah Howard (CH).
- Mary Cawood executrix of Stephen Cawood (CH).

17 December. Michael Macnemara (g, AA) exhibited:
- bond of Sarah Robinson administratrix of Peter Robinson. Sureties: William Hammond, William Fairbrother. Date: 31 January 1735.
- bond of Elisabeth Ward administratrix of John Ward. Sureties: William Coale, Richard Franklin. Date: 7 May 1736.
- bond of Margaret Child administratrix of Henry Child. Sureties: Philip Thomas, John Darnall, William Wilson. Date: 21 May 1736.
- will of Samuel Young, Esq., constituting Richard Young (CV), Samuel (CV), & Joseph Young (CE) executors. Said executors were granted administration. Sureties: John Andrews, Levin Hill. Date: 7 July 1736.
- bond of Thomas Lusby administrator of Lawrence Garey. Sureties: Henry Ridgley, Jr., Robert Lusby. Date: 27 August 1736.
- bond of Mary Mercer administratrix of Dr. David Mercer. Sureties: Michael Macnemara, Edward Fottrell. Date: 17 September 1736.
- will of Jane Sanders, constituting William Cotter executor. Said Cotter was granted administration. Sureties: John Watkins, John Gassaway. Date: 17 November 1736.

30:225 20 December. Thomas Aisquith (g, SM) exhibited:
- will of John Leigh, constituting Dorothy Leigh executrix. Said Dorothy was granted administration. Sureties: William Cavenaugh, John Hicks. Date: 15 October 1736.

Court Session: 1736

- will of John Burroughs, constituting John Burroughs & Benjamin Burroughs executors. Said executors were granted administration. Sureties: John Seager, Meverill Lock. Date: 2 November 1736.
- bond of Esther Wattson administratrix of John Wattson. Sureties: John Price, John Welch. Date: 8 November 1736.
- will of John Bullock, constituting Catherine Bullock executrix. Said Catherine was granted administration. Sureties: John Graves, Jr., William Biggs, Jr. Date: 17 November 1736.
- bond of Samuel Cammel administrator of John Hutson. Sureties: William Jones, Anthony Smith. Date: 22 November 1736.
- will of Robert Taylor, constituting Mary Taylor executrix. Said Mary was granted administration. Sureties: Timothy Tolle, James Taylor. Date: 22 November 1736.
- nuncupative will of James Bissco. Also, bond of Jonathon Bissco administrator. Sureties: Benjamin Williams, George Craghill. Date: 6 December 1736.
- will of Elisabeth Williams, constituting Benjamin Williams executor. Said Benjamin was granted administration. Sureties: William Harrison, Jonathon Bissco. Date: 6 December 1736.
- inventory & LoD of James Angel.
- inventory & LoD of James King.
- inventory & LoD of James Simmonds.
- accounts of Ann Hill executrix of John Hill.
- accounts of Randolph Morris administrator of John Pomroy.
- accounts of Ann Wimsett administratrix of John Wimsett.
- accounts of Joseph Chunn administrator of Jane Price.
- accounts of John Alvey administrator of Richard Bullock.
- 2nd additional accounts of William Deacon, Esq. & his wife Mary administratrix of Joseph

Vansweringen.
- accounts of John Hinkson & his wife Ann administratrix of Mallygo Oryon.
- accounts of Ann Farthing administratrix of William Maria Farthing.

30:226
- accounts of Nicholas Green & his wife Susannah administratrix of Jacob Vandeaver.
- 4th additional accounts of William Deacon, Esq. & his wife Mary executrix of Jeremiah Adderton.
- accounts of Katherine Waughop & James Waughop executors of Thomas Waughop.

22 December. Tench Francis (g, TA) exhibited:
- will of William Elbert, constituting Frances Elbert executrix. Said Frances was granted administration. Sureties: John Davis, Thomas Russell. Date: 1 November 1736.
- will of James Horney, constituting Margaret Horney & James Horney executors. Said executors were granted administration. Sureties: Aaron Higgs, Samuel Kininmont, Andrew Kininmont. Date: 1 November 1736.
- renunciation of Margaret Horney & James Horney executors of James Horney executor of Solomon Horney, on estate of said Solomon. Date: 1 November 1736.
- inventory of Loftis Bowdle.
- inventory of William Jones.

30:227 23 December. Exhibited from AA:
- inventory of Joseph Howard at Elkridge.

24 December. William Rumsey (g, CE) exhibited:
- bond of Sarah Othoson administratrix of Garret Othoson. Sureties: John Penington, Kinwin Wroth. Date: 6 December 1736.
- bond of William Douglas administrator of Joseph King. Sureties: Walter Scott, Jr., John McDermot. Date: 1 November 1736.

- inventory of John Thompson.
- inventory & LoD of Thomas Bavington.
- inventory of Peter Bouchelle.

28 December. Gabriel Parker (g, CV)
exhibited:
- bond of Thomas Reynolds
  administrator of James Cooley.
  Sureties: James Heighe, John
  Prindowell. Date: 30 November 1736.

4 January. MM James Mouatt (AA), Peter
Galloway (AA), & Nehemiah Birkhead (AA)
to appraise estate of Samuel Chew in AA.
Mr. Nicholas Maccubbin (justice, AA) to
administer oath. MM Sabrett Sollers
(CV), Richard Hall (CV), & Benjamin
Hance (CV) to appraise his estate in CV.
Mr. Roger Boyce (justice, CV) to
administer oath. MM Richard Caswell
(BA), Thomas Bond (BA), & Isaac Webster
(BA) to appraise his estate in BA. Mr.
Humphry Wells Stokes (BA) to administer
oath. MM Robert Story (CE), Edward
Jackson (CE), & John Williams (CE) to
appraise his estate in CE. John Copson,
Esq. to qualify said appraisers.

30:228 6 January. Exhibited from AA:
- will of John Coutanceau
  (Northumberland Co. VA), by William
  Taite (g). Also, depositions.

John Lusby vs. Thomas Wells & his wife
Elinor executrix of John Lusby (AA).
Sheriff (AA) to summon Levin Hill (AA),
Thomas Watkins (AA), Henry Bateman (AA),
& John Shivers (AA) to testify for
plaintiff.

7 January. Humphry Wells Stokes (g, BA)
exhibited:
- codicil of Bryan Taylor to will made
  in ENG. Also, bond of Richard
  Caswell administrator. Sureties:
  William Dallam, John Taylor (Land of
  Nod). Date: 10 December 1736.
- bond of Frances Mason executrix of
  John Mason. Sureties: Thomas Sligh,
  John Roberts. Date: 5 October 1736.
- bond of Philip Jones, Jr.
  administrator of William Rose.

Court Session: 1736

Sureties: John Rattenbury, Jacob
Rowles. Date: 29 November 1736.
• will of Simon Gregory. Also, bond
of Caleb Pennell one of executors.
Sureties: Isaac Webster, John
Roberts. Date: 13 October 1736.
The other executors live in PA:
Thomas Bab, Andrew More, Samuel
Williams.
• inventory of John Crockett.
• inventory of Samuel Lowe.
• inventory & LoD of Thomas Tolley,
Jr.
• inventory of Jonas Hewling.
• inventory of Richard Stevenson.
• accounts of George Buchanan
administrator of Richard Stevenson.
• accounts of James Boreing
administrator of Thomas Boreing.

Court Session: 11 January 1736

30:229   Docket:
• Richard Francis, Esq. procurator for
Jacob Loockerman administrator of
Col. Jacob Loockerman (DO) vs.
William Cumming, Esq. procurator for
Dorothy Loockerman.
Text of libel. Mentions: will of
dec'd, bequeathing to his wife
(defendant), her thirds; residue of
estate of his son John Loockerman,
his son Nicholas Loockerman, his son
Govert Loockerman, & his son Thomas
Loockerman.
30:230   Jacob Loockerman (son of dec'd) died
in July 1731. Appraisers of estate
of said Col.: Dr. William Murray,
Capt. Thomas Woollford.
30:231   Said Dorothy is guardian to her son
Thomas Loockerman.
30:232   Mentions: Peter Taylor (sheriff,
DO).
30:233   Text of answer.
30:234   Mentions: Mr. William Beckingham
attorney for plaintiff.
30:235-6   ...
30:237   Ruling: matter set forth is not a
testamentary matter. Dismissed,
with costs.
• W.C. for John Lusby (AA) vs. E.J.
for Thomas Wells & his wife Elinor

Court Session: 11 January 1736

executrix of John Lusby. Zach.
Maccubbin (sheriff, AA) to summon
Levin Hill (AA), Thomas Watkins
(AA), Henry Bateman (AA), & John
Shivers (AA) to testify for
plaintiff. Said Shivers is in NE.
• William Cumming, Esq. executor of
Thomas Facer (AA) vs. Michael
Macnemara procurator for Achsah
Woodward administratrix dbn of Amos
Garrett, Esq. Also, Edmund Jenings,
Esq. & John Galloway
attorneys-in-fact for Elisabeth Ginn
& executors of Mary Woodward.
Libel, answer, interrogatories,
depositions. MM Charles Cole
(merchant, Annapolis) &
30:238   John Lomas (merchant, Annapolis)
deposed for plaintiff. Edmond
Jenings, Esq. is procurator for
William Woodward & Mary Holmes. Mr.
Richard Francis is procurator for
said Elisabeth Ginn. Zach.
Maccubbin (sheriff, AA) to summon
Vachel Denton (AA), Charles Carroll,
Esq. (AA), & Richard Young to
testify for plaintiff.
• Ruling for all Plenary Causes.
30:239 • John Edmondson (TA) vs. Richard
Francis, Esq. for Jacob Loockerman
executor of Jacob Loockerman (TA).
Sheriff (DO) to summon defendant to
render accounts. Plaintiff to show
cause of his complaint.
30:240   Ruling: Struck off.
• Sheriff (SO) to summon John Whaley &
his wife widow of John Darby (SO) to
take LoA.
• Sheriff (DO) to summon Comfort
Hopkins widow of John Hopkins (DO)
to take LoA.
• W.C. for John Philips & his wife Ann
(PG) vs. B.Y. for Nicholas Downing &
his wife Elisabeth executrix of John
Clarvo. Libel, answer.
• Sheriff (SO) to summon Nathaniel
Horsey & Sarah Horsey to show cause
why they conceal estate of William
Horsey (SO).
30:241 • Sheriff (KE) to summon Mary Raisins
executrix of Thomas Raisins (KE) to
take LoA.

Page 19

Court Session: 11 January 1736

- William Thomas (TA) vs. Richard Giles one of witnesses to will of Loftis Bowdle (TA). Sheriff (TA) to render attachment to defendant.
- Coroners (SO) to render attachment to sheriff (SO) for contempt in not returning summons for John Whaley & his wife widow of John Darby (SO).
- Coroners (SO) to render attachment to sheriff (SO) for contempt in not returning summons for Nathaniel Horsey & Sarah Horsey (SO).

30:242
- Coroners (KE) to render attachment to sheriff (KE) for contempt in not returning summons to Mary Raisins executrix of Thomas Raisins (KE).

Court Session: 1736

12 January. Exhibited from AA:
- bond of William Taite (g) administrator of John Coutanceau (Northumberland Co. VA). Sureties: William Cumming, Esq. (Annapolis), Dr. George Stewart (Annapolis). Date: 12 January 1736.

25 January. John Gresham (g, KE) exhibited:
- bond of John Cleaver & his wife Elisabeth executors of John Spencer. Sureties: Vincent Hatcheson, Morgan Hurt. Date: 15 August 1735.
- will of Mary Anderson, constituting Humphry Younger executor. Said Younger was granted administration. Sureties: Francis Meekes, Robert Meekes. Date: 4 August 1735.
- bond of Robert Green administrator of Richard Davis. Sureties: Bowles Green, James Smith, Jr. Date: 8 November 1735.

30:243
- bond of Mary Taylor administratrix of William Taylor. Sureties: William Hurt, Wedge Crouch. Date: 7 August 1735.
- bond of Elisabeth Hanson & Hans Hanson administrators of Hans Hanson. Sureties: Robert Green, Stephen Glanvill. Date: 11 September 1735.
- will of Rev. Mr. Richard Sewell.

Also, executors renunciations.
- will of James Combs, constituting Philip Kennard executor.
- will of Evan Evans, constituting his wife Sarah executrix.
- will of William Bayley, constituting Philip Kennard executor.
- nuncupative will of Joseph Francis.
- nuncupative will of William Drury.
- inventory of John Spencer.
- inventory of Mary Anderson.
- inventory of Richard Normansell.
- inventory of Peter Dozen.
- inventory of Abraham Milton.
- inventory of Thomas English.
- inventory of Harmanus Schee.
- inventory of John Burrows.
- inventory of Patrick Gault.
- additional inventory of St. Leger Cod, Esq.
- inventory of Richard Jarman.
- inventory of John Fanning.
- inventory of George Gleaves.
- inventory & LoD of Charles Baker.
- inventory of Joseph Carman.
- accounts of William Trew & his wife Hannah executrix of Francis Ludolph Bodien.
- accounts of William McClane administrator of Richard Jerman.
- accounts of Capt. Ebenezar Blackiston executor of Nicholas Joce.
- accounts of James Galloway administrator of Patrick Gault.
- accounts of Fran. Barney & Robert Meeks administrator dbn of Nicholas Waterman.
- additional accounts of James Stout & his wife Anne administrators dbn of St. Leger Cod, Esq.

27 January. Mr. Humphry Wells Stokes (BA) to examine additional accounts of:
- Frances Hale executrix of Nicholas Hale (BA).

30:244 2 February. MM Peter Galloway (AA) & Samuel Smith (AA) to appraise estate of Mr. Samuel Chew in AA. MM Richard Hall (CV), Benjamin Hance (CV), & Sabret Sollers (CV) to appraise his estate in

CV.

8 February. Exhibited from AA:
- inventory of Murdock Dowling.

10 February. Capt. John Pitt (DO) to
examine accounts of:
- Thomas Layton & his wife Alice &
  William Nutter administrators of
  William Nutter (DO).

Summons to Joseph Ennalls executor of
William Ennalls (DO) to render
additional accounts.

11 February. Mr. Tench Francis (TA) to
examine accounts of:
- John Richardson & his wife Jane
  administratrix of Patrick Mullican
  (TA).
- Grace Harwood administratrix of
  Peter Harwood, Jr. (TA).

Francis Hall (PG) vs. Charles Digges
administrator of Nicholas Lowe, Esq.
(SM). Sheriff (PG) to summon defendant
to render additional accounts.

30:245 12 February. Capt. John Pitt (DO)
exhibited:
- bond of Bartholomew Ennalls, Sr.
  administrator of John Morristen.
  Sureties: Thomas Ennalls, George
  Griffith. Also, renunciation of Ann
  Morristen widow, recommending Capt.
  Bartholomew Ennalls. Witnesses: B.
  Ennalls, John Pitt. Also,
  renunciation of George Morristen,
  recommending Capt. Bartholomew
  Ennalls. Date: 13 December 1736.
  Witness: John Pitt.
- bond of Dr. William Murray
  administrator of Richard Tull.
  Surety: Henry Ennalls. Date: 14
  December 1736. Also, renunciation
  of Robert Beaucham, Isaac Beaucham,
  & Sarah Beaucham, recommending Dr.
  Murray. Date: 21 May 1736.
  Subscribers are: husband of dec'd's
  mother, brother & sister of
  half-blood.
- additional inventory of Daniel Cox.

- inventory of Samuel Harper.
- accounts of Ann Cox executrix of Daniel Cox.

30:246 Capt. John Pitt (DO) to examine accounts of:
- Hannah, Patrick, & Thomas Brahaun executors of Patrick Brahaun (DO).

17 February. Francis Linthicum (AA) vs. estate of Thomas Linthicum (AA). Deposition of Rebecca Linthicum, witness to said will, before Michael Macnemara (g).

18 February. Samuel Hanson (g, CH) exhibited:
- will of James Boyce, constituting Solomon Nicholls executor. Said Nicholls was granted administration. Sureties: Richard Lewis, Dennis Dowen. Date: 2 February 1736.
- bond of Edmond Devene administrator of James Proffee. Sureties: Robert Hanson, James Smallwood, Sr. Date: 15 December 1736.
- bond of Sarah Bruce administratrix of John Bruce. Sureties: Francis Ware, John Winter. Date: 10 January 1736.
- bond of Benoni Harrison administrator of Charles Montoe. Sureties: Thomas Hudson, William Groves. Date: 2 February 1736.
- will of William Whitter, constituting Ann Whitter executrix.
- nuncupative will of Juliana Semmes, exhibited by Ignatius Semmes legatee.
- inventory of John Howison.
- inventory of Henry Mudd.
- accounts of Mary Manning executrix of John Manning.
- accounts of Anne Mason administratrix of Col. George Mason.
- accounts of Benjamin Bateman administrator of Mary Bateman.
- accounts of Jane Caphaw administratrix of John Caphaw.
- accounts of Elisabeth Stramat administratrix of Peter John Baptist

Court Session: 1736

Stramat.
- accounts of Elisabeth Hodgson & Johannah Hodgson executrix of Richard Hodgson.
- accounts of Mary Cawood executrix of Stephen Cawood.

30:247
- accounts of Thomas Marshall administrator of Mrs. Elisabeth Fendall.
- accounts of William Coombes & William Maggatee executors of Catherine Ensey administratrix of John Ensey.

21 February. Capt. Robert North, Samuel Smith, & Luke Trotton to appraise estate of Mr. Richard Galloway in BA.

Mr. Peter Dent (PG) to examine accounts of:
- Elinor Deveron executrix of William Deveron (PG).

Gabriel Parker (g, CV) exhibited:
- will of John Dodson. Also, bond of James Dodson & Joseph Wooden administrators. Sureties: John Lavell, James Freeman. Date: 7 February 1736.
- inventory of Jesse Jacob Bourne. Also, widow's election by Alice Bourne. Date: 26 November 1736.
- inventory of Henry Brome.
- accounts of James Heighe executor of George Beck.
- accounts of Charles Somerset Smith administrator of Richard Hudson.

30:248
23 February. Exhibited from BA:
- inventory of Johanna Hall.

Exhibited from SM:
- accounts of James Mills administrator of Elisabeth Willis.

24 February. Exhibited from BA:
- inventory of George Drew.

25 February. Exhibited from AA:
- accounts of John Gassaway executor of Elisabeth Larkin.

Peter Dent (g, PG) exhibited:
- will of John Edgar, constituting William Eilbeck executor. Said Eilbeck was granted administration. Sureties: Capt. John Stoddert, Mr. Richard Tubman. Date: 12 January 1736/7.
- will of John Jones, constituting Anne Jones executrix. Said Anne was granted administration. Sureties: Clement Wheeler, Henry Jones. Date: 7 February 1736/7.
- bond of Elisabeth Cloyd administratrix of Robert Cloyd. Sureties: James Atcheson, Leonard Marbury. Date: 1 February 1736/7.
- bond of Nathaniel Skinner executor of Robert Skinner. Sureties: Robert Whitaker, Owen Ellis. Date: 24 November 1736.
- bond of Thomas Odell administrator of Sarah Coomes. Sureties: Henry Odell, Ninian Mariarte. Date: 25 November 1736.

30:249
- bond of John Stoddert administrator of William Stoddert. Sureties: William Eilbeck, Henry Ward. Date: 12 January 1736/7.
- inventory of Sarah Coomes.
- inventory of William Clarkson.
- inventory of Elisabeth Plummer.
- accounts of Thomas Marshall administrator of Thomas Summerset.
- accounts of Amey Groome executrix of Richard Groome.

1 March. Exhibited from CV:
- additional accounts of Martha Lyngan executrix of Thomas Lyngan.

Exhibited from SM:
- additional accounts of Robert Hopkins administrator of Thomas Scott.

2 March. Exhibited from AA:
- additional accounts of Sarah Burgess, Samuel Burgess, & John Burgess executors of Edward Burgess.

4 March. Sheriff (AA) to summon (N) Pearce widow of William Pearce (London

Court Session: 1736

Town, AA) to take LoA.

5 March. Exhibited from AA:
- accounts of Edmond Kelley & his wife Elinor administratrix of Murdock Dowlin.

Court Session: 8 March 1736

30:250 Docket:
- W.C. for John Lusby (AA) vs. E.J. for Thomas Wells & his wife Elinor executrix of John Lusby. Libel, answer, depositions. Zach. Maccubbin (sheriff, AA) summoned John Shivers (AA) to testify for plaintiff & Ezekiel Gillis (AA) to testify for defendant.
- William Cumming, Esq. executor of Thomas Facer (AA) vs. M.M. for Achsah Woodward administratrix dbn of Amos Garrett, Esq. Also, Edmond Jenings, Esq. & John Galloway attorneys-in-fact for Elisabeth Ginn & executors of Mary Woodward. Libel, answer, interrogatories, depositions. Zach. Maccubbin (sheriff, AA) summoned to testify for plaintiff: Jane Bell (AA),

30:251 Vachel Denton (AA), Charles Carroll, Esq. (AA), & Samuel Smith (AA). Summons to Richard Young (CV) to testify for plaintiff.
- Sheriff (SO) to summon John Whaley & his wife widow of John Darby (SO) to take LoA.
- Sheriff (DO) to summon Comfort Hopkins widow of John Hopkins (DO) to take LoA.
- W.C. for John Phillips & his wife Ann (PG) vs. B.Y. for Nicholas Downing & his wife Elisabeth executrix of John Clarvo. Libel, answer.
- Sheriff (SO) to summon Nathaniel Horsey & Sarah Horsey to show cause why they conceal effects of William Horsey (SO).

30:252 - Sheriff (KE) to summon Mary Raisins executrix of Thomas Raisins to take LoA.
- William Thomas (TA) vs. Richard

Page 26

Court Session: 8 March 1736

> Giles one of witnesses to will of
> Loftis Bowdle (TA). Sheriff (TA) to
> render attachment to defendant.
> Said Giles could not come in the
> winter season without hazarding his
> health.
> - Coroners (SO) to render attachment
>   to sheriff (SO) for not returning
>   summons to John Whaley & his wife
>   widow of John Darby & Nathaniel
>   Horsey & Sarah Horsey (SO).
>   Mentions: Mr. Henry Ballard as one
>   of the coroners.

30:253
> - Coroners (KE) to render attachment
>   to sheriff (KE) for not returning
>   summons to Mary Raisins executrix of
>   Thomas Raisins (KE).
> - Zach. Maccubbin (sheriff, AA) to
>   summon (N) Pearce widow of William
>   Pearce (London Town, AA) to take
>   LoA. NEI. Summons to be re-issued
>   to her as (N) Austin wife of Henry
>   Austin (AA).
> - Sheriff (DO) to summon Joseph
>   Ennalls executor of William Ennalls
>   (DO) to render additional accounts.
> - Francis Hall (PG) vs. Charles
>   Digges (PG) administrator of
>   Nicholas Lowe, Esq. (SM). Sheriff
>   (PG) to summon defendant to render
>   additional accounts.

Court Session: 1736

30:254
8 March. Thomas Aisquith (g, SM)
exhibited:
- bond of Christopher Shener
  administrator of John Sweetman.
  Sureties: Thomas Kirby, Sr., Patrick
  Lenord. Date: 14 December 1736.
- bond of Sarah Broughton
  administratrix of Daniel Broughton.
  Sureties: Andrew Eaton, William
  Flower. Date: 31 January 1736.
- bond of John Baptes Anderson
  administrator of Margaret Anderson.
  Sureties: William Jones, Richard
  Brewer. Date: 1 February 1736.
- bond of Thomas Graves administrator
  of William Bullock. Sureties: John
  Graves, Jr., William Jones. Date: 1
  February 1736.

Court Session: 1736

- inventory & LoD of John Watson.
- inventory & LoD of Robert Taylor.
- accounts of John Thompson & his wife Mary administratrix of Thomas Battson.
- accounts of Mary Miller administratrix of Nicholas Feilder.

Exhibited from AA:
- accounts of Thomas Gassaway, Jr. administrator dbn of John Brewer.

Exhibited from PG:
- additional accounts of Samuel & Robert Pottenger executors of John Pottenger.

9 March. Exhibited from AA:
- bond of Dr. Charles Carroll administrator of Justinian Barwell. Sureties: George Thorp, John Lomass (Annapolis). Date: 9 March 1736.

30:255 11 March. Exhibited from AA:
- LoD on estate of William Bladen, Esq., by Benjamin Tasker, Esq. administrator.

12 March. Exhibited from AA:
- receipt to John Elliett Browne from Thomas Jones & his wife Mary for her portion of her father's estate, as 2nd daughter of George Simmes (AA). Date: September 1736, BA.
- receipt to John Elliett Browne from John Farmer & his wife Sophia for her portion of her father's estate, as 4th daughter of George Simmons (AA). Date: September 1736, BA.
- receipt to John Elliott Browne from James Pickering & his wife Elisabeth for her portion of her father's estate, as 3rd daughter of George Simmons (AA). Date: 9 November 1736.
- receipt to John Elliott Browne from George Simmons for his portion of his father George Simmons estate. Date: 21 February 1736/7.
- receipt to John Elliott Browne from Roger Crudgenton & his wife Dinah for her portion of her father's

Page 28

estate, as eldest daughter of George Simmons (AA). Date: 9 November 1736.

18 March. Mr. Peter Dent (PG) to examine accounts of:
- John Dunn administrator of James Read (PG).
- Mary Norris executrix of Dr. John Norris (PG).
- John Boyd administrator of Isaac Hyde (PG). Additional accounts.

30:256 22 March. Mr. Peter Dent (PG) to examine 2nd additional accounts of:
- Mary Offutt administratrix of William Offutt (PG).

Nehemiah King (g, SO) exhibited:
- will of Thomas Benson, constituting Mary Benson executrix. Said Mary was granted administration. Sureties: Robert Dashiells, Francis Parsons. Date: 17 January 1735/6.
- will of Cumfort Benton, constituting Isaac Costin executor. Said Costin was granted administration. Sureties: John Shockley, Randall Smullin. Date: 17 November 1736.
- bond of Katherine Donelson administratrix of John Donelson. Sureties: James Martin, Addam Bell. Date: 18 December 1736.
- bond of Mary Hall administratrix of Alexander Hall. Sureties: Richard Chambers, Whittington King. Date: 18 December 1736.
- bond of William Holland administrator of John Singleton. Sureties: Robert Nairne, Caleb Milbourne. Date: 8 February 1736/7.
- bond of Sarah Fisher administratrix of Bartley Fisher. Sureties: Richard Chambers, Underwood Rencher. Date: 16 February 1736/7.
- will of Andrew Scott, exhibited by Day Scott legatee.
- inventory of Edward Vigros.
- inventory & LoD of William Turvill.
- inventory of Samuel Roach.
- inventory of Jonathon Shaw.
- inventory of James Lindow.

- inventory of Samuel Horsey.
- inventory of John Donelson.
- inventory of Ezekiel Denning.
- additional inventory & LoD of John Linch.
- inventory of Burr Outerbridge.
- additional inventory of Thomas Layfield.
- inventory of Stephen Ward, Sr.
- accounts of John Scarborough administrator of Richard Pennewell.
- accounts of Robert Dashiell executor of George Dashiell.

30:257
- accounts of John Williams & his wife Jane administratrix of William White.
- accounts of Richard Gasle & his wife Tabitha executrix of John Vennables.
- accounts of Thomas & Samuel Handy executors of Samuel Handy.
- accounts of Isaac Addams administrator of Thomas Addams.
- accounts of Abigail & Solomon Tomlinson executors of Samuel Tomlinson.
- accounts of George Layfield & James Breeman & his wife Katherine executors of Thomas Layfield.
- accounts of Capell King executor of Benjamin King.

Court Session: 1737

4 April. Capt. John Pitt (DO) exhibited:
- bond of Elisabeth Paul administratrix of Nicholas Paul. Sureties: Richard Webster, Sr., Thomas Walker. Date: 4 January 1736.
- bond of William Murray administrator of Thomas Ramesy. Surety: Henry Ennalls. Date: 7 February 1736. Also, renunciation of Andrew Ramesy father, recommending Dr. Murray (greatest creditor). Also, renunciation of James Ramesy brother, recommending Dr. Murray (greatest creditor). Also, renunciation of William Grainger. Date: 4 February 1736.

30:258
- bond of Mary Uscears administratrix

of John Uscears. Sureties: Owen
Ward, Thomas Thompson. Date: 7
March 1736.
- bond of Peter Taylor, Sr.
administrator of John Alling.
Surety: Joseph Alford. Date: 4
March 1736. Also, renunciation of
Ann Alling, recommending Peter
Taylor (greatest creditor). Date: 2
February 1736. Witness: Walter
Stevens.
- inventory of Clare Mackeel.
- additional inventory of Joseph
Nicholls.
- accounts of William Shaghunsy
administrator of James Griffin.
- accounts of Levin Hicks
administrator of Elisabeth Lemee.
- accounts of Mary Robson
administratrix of Charles Robson.
- accounts of Elisabeth Bramble
administratrix of John Bramble.
- accounts of Elisabeth Kimey
executrix of Walter Kimey.

7 April. Mr. Samuel Hanson (CH) to
examine accounts of:
- Mary Parker administratrix of
Abraham Parker (CH).
- William Coombes & William Maggatee
executors of Catherine Ensey (CH).
- Anne Gardiner executrix of Francis
Gardiner (CH).
- Francis Meek administrator of John
King (CH).
- Sarah Fowke executrix of Gerrard
Fowke (CH).
- John Theobalds & his wife Elisabeth
one of executors of Daniel Jennifer
(CH). Additional accounts.

30:259 8 April. Mr. Tench Francis (TA) to
examine additional accounts of:
- Robert Newcom & his wife Anne
administratrix of John Price (TA).

11 April. Peter Dent (g, PG) exhibited:
- Mr. Thomas Odell has LoA on estate
of Sarah Coomes as greatest
creditor, her son John Pearce
declining. Since then, Dr. Hasswell
has married a daughter. Date: 22

February 1736.

James Earle (g, QA) exhibited:
- bond of Daniel Griffith administrator of Thomas Barber. Sureties: John Coursey, Geo. Jackson. Date: 12 December 1736.
- bond of Albert Johnson administrator of Henry Johnson. Sureties: John Andrews, Solomon Seney. Date: 12 December 1736. Also, renunciation of Mary Johnson, recommending Alburt Johnson son of said Henry. Date: 8 December 1736. Witnesses: Aug. Thompson, John Berry.

30:260
- bond of Mary Cox administratrix of Lazarus Cox. Sureties: John Miller, John Clayland. Date: 14 December 1736.
- bond of Solomon Clayton administrator of Thomas Poole (butcher). Sureties: Edward Brown, Matthew Mason. Date: 28 February 1736/7. Also, renunciation of Sarah Poole widow. Date: 9 February 1736. Witnesses: Joseph Gough, Jane Rokey.
- bond of Mary Kemp administratrix of richard Kemp. Sureties: Thomas Newton, William Harbert. Date: 7 March 1736/7.
- will of Dr. William Edwards (chirurgeon). Also, bond of Nicholas Broadaway administrator. Sureties: John Carpenter, John Ryley. Date: 22 December 1736. Also, renunciation of Sarah Edwards widow. Date: 30 November 1736. Witness: William Hopper.
- will of Daniel Walker, constituting John Walker executor. Said John was granted administration. Sureties: James Williams, John Williams. Date: 28 March 1737.
- renunciation of Lylly Manson widow of John Manson (joyner). Date: 6 December 1736.

30:261
- renunciation of Margaret Wise widow of Richard Wise (planter). Date: 4 April 1737.
- inventory of John Rowles.
- inventory of William Pinder.
- inventory of Solomon Wright.

- inventory of Henry Johnson.
- additional inventory of James Barkhurst.
- inventory of William Burroughs.
- inventory & LoD of James Mcclean.
- inventory of John Smith.
- inventory of Thomas Barber.
- additional inventory & LoD of William Pinder.
- inventory of Lazarus Cox.
- accounts of Solomon Clayton administrator of William Owens.
- accounts of John Hays, Jr. & his wife Sarah executrix of Edward Wright, Jr.
- accounts of Jane Barkhurst administratrix of James Barkhurst.

12 April. Mr. Charles Hynson (KE) to examine accounts of:
- William Massey & his wife Elisabeth administratrix of Archibald Cragh (KE).
- John Waltham administrator of William Waltham (KE).
- Robert Green administrator of Richard Davis (KE). Additional accounts.
- Samuel Barton & his wife Martha administratrix of Francis Lewis (KE). Additional accounts.

30:262 Mr. Samuel Hanson (CH) to examine additional accounts of:
- Barbara Allen administratrix of Joseph Allen (CH).

Exhibited from AA:
- bond of Rachel Norwood administratrix of John Norwood. Sureties: Thomas Todd, John Dorsey, Jr. Date: 12 April 1737.

15 April. Humphrey Wells Stokes (g, BA) exhibited:
- bond of Nicholas Day administrator of Sarah Day. Sureties: Josias Hendon, Thomas Amos. Date: 28 December 1736.
- bond of Redmon Dearing administrator of William Connell. Sureties: William Rogers, Josias Hendon.

Date: 12 January 1736.
- accounts of William Lowe administrator of George Groves.
- additional accounts of Frances Haile executrix of Nicholas Haile.

18 April. Mr. Nehemiah King (SO) to examine accounts of:
- Aaron Tillman, Ann Gibbins, & Thomas Gibbins executors of John Gibbins, Sr. (SO).
- James Anderson & his wife Rebecca administratrix of David Brown (SO).
- Ann Ward executrix of Stephen Ward (SO).
- Thomas White administrator of John White (SO).

22 April. Mr. Peter Dent (PG) to examine additional accounts of:
- Benjamin Smith & his wife Mary executrix of Benjamin Stimpton (PG).

26 April. Tench Francis (g, TA) exhibited:
- will of George Collisson, constituting Elisabeth Collisson executrix. Said Elisabeth was granted administration. Sureties: Daniel Landman, Robert Sands. Date: 6 December 1736.
- bond of John Carslake administrator of Solomon Horney. Sureties: Richard Skinner, George Garey. Date: 23 November 1736.
- bond of John Guy Williams administrator of Isaac Tunney. Sureties: Dennis Hopkins, Michael Fletcher. Date: 9 December 1736.
- bond of Lambert Shield administrator of William Sheild. Sureties: Francis Armstrong, William Stacey, Edward Harding, Jr., John Walker. Date: 22 December 1736.
- bond of Hannah Maclendon administratrix of James Maclendon. Sureties: John Reynolds, James Higgins. Date: 27 February 1736.
- will of Isaac Dixon. Also, bond of Robert Harwood administrator. Sureties: Peter Harwood, John Stevens, James Wilson the younger.

30:263

Court Session: 1737

Date: 14 March 1736.
- bond of John Loockerman administrator of John Hendrick. Sureties: Robert Newcom, Thomas Spry. Date: 28 march 1737.
- renunciation of James Ratcliff, James Wilson, Jr., Joseph Atkinson, & Joseph Bartlet executors of Isaac Dixon. Date: 14 March 1736. Witness: John Tilghman.
- inventory of Thomas Pitchfork.
- additional inventory of Annion Williams.
- inventory of Mary Wilds.
- inventory of Mary Cooper.
- inventory of George Collisson.
- accounts of William Thomas & Trustram Thomas administrators of Walter Riddle.
- accounts of Henry Clift & his wife Elisabeth executrix of James Dudley.

Mr. Thomas Aisquith (SM) exhibited:
- will of Robert Phillips. Also, bond of Mary Phillips administratrix. Sureties: John Culverhouse, George Beverly, Jr. Date: 7 March 1736.
- bond of Martha Vansweringen administratrix of Joseph Vansweringen. Sureties: John Baker, Jonathon Bissco. Date: 21 March 1736.
- inventory & LoD of Charles Mills.
- inventory of Lawrence Gally.
- inventory & LoD of John Redman.
- inventory & LoD of Elisabeth Williams.
- inventory & LoD of James Bissco.
- inventory & LoD of William Walker.
- inventory & LoD of Capt. John Leigh.
- inventory of John Huttson.
- inventory & LoD of Daniel Broughton.
- inventory & LoD of John Sweetman.
- inventory of Mary Mullon.
- inventory of John Burroughs, Sr.
- accounts of Mary Tolley administratrix of Thomas Tolley.
- additional accounts of Thomas Gardiner administrator of Elisabeth Cole.
- accounts of Ann Hayes executrix of

30:264

Page 35

John Hayes.
- accounts of John Talton administrator of James Talton.
- accounts of James Kirk executor of Mary Kirk.
- accounts of Joseph Kirk administrator of Mary Mullon.

2 May. Peter Dent (g, PG) exhibited:
- bond of John Murdock administrator of Capt. John Martindall. Sureties: Thomas Middleton, Thomas Middleton, Jr. Date: 1 March 1736/7.
- will of Robert Clyd, constituting Elisabeth Clyd executrix.
- additional inventory of William Marshall.
- inventory of William Stoddert.
- accounts of Leonard, Francis, Ignatius, & Clement Wheeler executors of Francis Wheeler.
- additional accounts of John Boyd administrator of Isaac Hyde.
- accounts of John Dunn administrator of James Read.

30:265 3 May. Exhibited from AA:
- inventory of Nathaniel Chew.
- inventory of Mary Chew.

Gabriel Parker (g, CV) exhibited:
- will of William Hickman, constituting Margaret Hickman executrix. Said Margaret was granted administration. Sureties: Benson Bond, Thomas Ireland, Jr. Date: 16 April 1737.
- will of John Betenson, constituting Samuel Stallings & Joseph Stallings executors. Said executors were granted administration. Sureties: Jacob Stallings, Thomas King. Date: 29 April 1737.
- bond of Priscilla Ladyman administratrix of William Ladyman. Sureties: John Brady, John Grover. Date: 2 April 1737.
- inventory of Elisabeth Turner.

Samuel Hanson (g, CH) exhibited:
- will of James Keen, constituting

Court Session: 1737

Nicholas Keene executor. Said
Nicholas was granted administration.
Sureties: William Maconchie, Joseph
Clements. Date: 6 April 1737.

- bond of Anne Whitter executrix of
William Whitter. Sureties: Ralph
Gwinn, John Brookes. Date: 6 April
1737.
- will of Zachariah Wade. Also, bond
of Charity Wade administratrix.
Sureties: John Courts, Charles
Courts. Date: 2 March 1736.
- will of William Penn, constituting
William Penn executor. Sureties:
Mark Penn, Notley Maddox. Date: 14
March 1736.
- bond of John Theobalds administrator
of Henry Coody. Sureties: Thomas
Hawkins, Edward Clements. Date: 16
February 1736.
- bond of Mary Haw administratrix of
Daniel Haw. Sureties: Thomas Swann,
Henry Trueman. Date: 18 February
1736.
- bond of Bathia Higton administratrix
of John Higton. Sureties: Marmaduke
Semmes, Sr., John Biggs. Date: 3
March 1736.
30:266 - bond of William Cage administrator
of Richard Lloyde. Sureties: Edward
Ford, Richard Mastin. Date: 5 March
1736.
- bond of Priscilla Newman
administratrix of John Newman.
Sureties: John Courts, John Harris,
Jr. Date: 14 March 1736.
- bond of Stephen Mankin administrator
of John Maccoy. Sureties: James
Carroll, Patrick Kerrick. Date: 6
April 1737.
- will of Eleanor Sanders,
constituting William Robertson &
Margaret Ward executors.
- inventory of Ann Gwinn.
- inventory of Matthew Groves.
- accounts of Verlinda Sanders
administratrix of Thomas Sanders.
- accounts of Henry Trueman executor
of Sarah Howard.

4 May. Capt. John Pitt (DO) exhibited:
- bond of Thomas Ennalls, Sr.

administrator of William Layton.
Sureties: Joseph Ennalls,
Bartholomew Ennalls, Sr.   Date: 23
April 1737.   Also, renunciation of
Thomas Layton brother, recommending
Thomas Ennalls, Sr.   Date: 14 April
1737.   Witnesses: J. Ennalls,
Benjamin Whayland.
- inventory & LoD of Andrew Simmons.
- inventory of Richard Tull.
- inventory & LoD of Nicholas Paul.
- accounts of Thomas Armsby & his wife
  Sarah administrators of Andrew
  Simmons.
- accounts of Thomas Layton & his wife
  Alice & William Nutter
  administrators of William Nutter.
- accounts of Hannah Brahawn, Patrick
  Brahawn, & Thomas Brahawn executors
  of Patrick Brahawn.

30:267   Capt.   John Pitt (DO) to examine
accounts of:
- Mary Peterkin & Nathaniel Manning
  executors of David Peterkin (DO).
- Mary Peterkin & Nathaniel Manning
  administrators of Mary Cooke (DO).
- John Hayward executor of Francis
  Hayward (DO).
- Mary Money administratrix of Francis
  Money (DO).

6 May.   Mr.   Peter Dent (PG) to examine
2nd additional accounts of:
- Mary Offutt administratrix of
  William Offutt (PG).

Mr.   Nehemiah King (SO) to examine
accounts of:
- Panther Laws administrator of Robert
  Sheen (SO).
- Bell Maddux executor of Thomas
  Maddux (SO).
- Sarah Outten executrix of John
  Outten (SO).
- Listian Alexander surviving executor
  of William Alexander (SO).
- Elisabeth Rhoads executor of Timothy
  Rhoads (SO).
- William Cearsey administrator of
  Peter Cearsey (SO).
- William Turvile administrator of

Court Session: 1737

William Turvile (SO).
- Robert Austin administrator of Edward Fowler (SO).
- Katherine Steward administratrix of William Steward (SO).
- Elisabeth Nicholson administratrix of John Nicholson (SO).
- Isaac Costin executor of Cumfort Benton (SO).
- John Davis & his wife Elisabeth executrix of John Magee (SO).
- Robert Dashiels executor of George Dashiels (SO). Additional accounts.
- James Mumford executor of Thomas Mumford (SO). Additional accounts.

Mr. Gabriel Parker (CV) to examine accounts of:
- Samuel Young & his wife Rebecca executrix of Thomas Cockshutt (CV).
- Richard Roberts executor of Robert Roberts (CV).

4 May. Mr. Robert Ritchie as attorney for James Thompson brother & executor of Thomas Thompson (DO) vs. MM (N) Woolford & (N) Trippe. Caveat against accounts being passed.

30:268 7 May. Mr. Humphry Wells Stokes (BA) to examine accounts of:
- Thomas Hutchins & Nicholas Hutchins executors of Thomas Hutchins (BA).
- Patrick Lynch administrator of Jonas Hewling (BA).
- Christopher Shepherd executor of Rowland Shepherd (BA).

Mr. Thomas Aisquith (SM) to examine accounts of:
- Dennis Burn & his wife Ann administratrix of William Houlton (SM).
- Jane Gough executrix of Benjamin Gough (SM).
- Grace Galle executrix of Lawrence Galle (SM).
- John Medly Thompson & his wife Elinor administratrix of John Boules (SM).
- Ann Vowles administratrix of Richard Vowles (SM).

Page 39

Court Session: 1737

9 May. Exhibited from CE:
* will of Joseph Young, Esq.,
  constituting Araminta Young
  executrix.

Charles Hynson (g, KE) exhibited:
* bond of John Thomas & his wife
  Hannah executrix of John Ence.
  Sureties: Thomas Hepbourn, Henry
  Truelock. Date: 30 April 1736.
* will of Rebecca Evans, constituting
  Edward Comegys & Thomas Wilkins
  executors. Said Comegys & Wilkins
  were granted administration.
  Sureties: James Pinar, Joseph
  Garnett. Date: 1 January 1736.
* will of Joseph Everett, constituting
  Katherine Everett executrix. Said
  Katherine was granted
  administration. Sureties: John
  Williams, Jackson Griffith. Date:
  30 April 1737.
* bond of Edward Beck administrator of
  John Murray. Sureties: William
  Early, Benjamin Ricaud. Date: 2
  February 1736.
* bond of William Trew administrator
  of James Norman. Sureties: William
  Clark, Joseph Mason. Date: 7
  February 1736. Also, renunciation
  of Mary Howard on estate of her
  former husband, recommending William
  Trew. Date: 25 January 1736/7.
* renunciation of John Rowlls & Ann
  Rouls, recommending Edward Diceas.
  Appraisers: Mr. Willmore, James
  Piner. Date: 16 September 1736.
  Witness: Thomas Allfree.
* will of William Davis, constituting
  Mary Davis & Elisabeth Davis
  executrices.
* inventory of William Davis.
* inventory of George Skirven.
* inventory of Nathaniel Pearce.
* additional inventory of Samuel
  Gooding.
* additional inventory of William
  Waltham.
* inventory of John Murray.
* accounts of Robert Green
  administrator of Richard Davis.
* additional accounts of Samuel Wicks

30:269

Page 40

Court Session: 1737

surviving administrator of Charles
Galloway.
- accounts of John Waltham
  administrator of William Waltham.

9 May. Mr. Samuel Hanson (CH) to
examine accounts of:
- Robert Yates, Joseph Gwinn, &
  Benjamin Gwinn executors of Anne
  Gwinn (CH).
- John Stramat & his wife Anne
  executrix of William Williams (CH).
- Henry Acton, Sr. & his wife Anne &
  John Chandler executors of John
  Chandler (CH).
- Mary King administratrix of Robert
  King (CH).

Court Session: 10 May 1737

Docket:
- W.C. for John Lusby (AA) vs. E.J.
  for Thomas Wells & his wife Elinor
  executrix of John Lusby. Libel,
  answer, depositions.
30:270 • William Cumming, Esq. executor of
  Thomas Facer (AA) vs. M.M. for
  Achsah Woodward administratrix dbn
  of Amos Garrett, Esq. Also, Edmund
  Jenings, Esq. & John Galloway
  attorneys-in-fact for Elisabeth Ginn
  & executors of Mary Woodward.
  Libel, answer, interrogatives,
  depositions.
- Sheriff (SO) to summon John Whaley &
  his wife widow of John Darby (SO) to
  take LoA.
- Sheriff (DO) to summon Comfort
  Hopkins widow of John Hopkins (DO)
  to take LoA.
- W.C. for John Phillips & his wife
  Anne (PG) vs. B.Y. for Nicholas
  Downing & his wife Elisabeth
  executrix of John Clarvo. Libel,
  answer.
- Sheriff (SO) to summon Nathaniel
  Horsey & Sarah Horsey to show cause
  why they conceal estate of William
  Horsey (SO). Exhibited letter from
  John Horsey (one of sons of said
  William) citing that he is
  satisfied. Struck off.

30:271 • Sheriff (KE) to summon Mary Raisins
executrix of Thomas Raisins (KE) to
take LoA.
• William Thomas (TA) vs. Richard
Giles one of witnesses to will of
Loftis Bowdle (TA). J. Goldsborough
(sheriff, TA) to render attachment
to defendant to prove said will.
Said Richard is not in his
bailywick.
• coroners (SO) to render attachment
to sheriff (SO).
• Mr. William Ringgold (coroner, KE)
to render attachment to William
Harris (sheriff, KE). Discontinued.

30:272 • Zach. Maccubbin (sheriff, AA) to
summon (N) Austin wife of Henry
Austin late widow of William Pearce
(AA) to take LoA.
• sheriff (DO) to summon Joseph
Ennalls executor of William Ennalls
(DO) to render additional accounts.
• Francis Hall (PG) vs. Charles
Digges (PG) administrator of
Nicholas Lowe, Esq. (SM). Richard
Lee (sheriff, PG) to summon
defendant to render additional
accounts.

Court Session: 1737

30:273 10 May. At the request of Trustram
Thomas (TA) & Thomas Ennalls (DO),
affirmation of Solomon Birkhead, one of
witnesses to will of Andrew Skinner
(TA), was exhibited.

Mr. Tench Francis (TA) to examine
accounts of:
• John Nicholls & his wife Mary (DO)
executrix of Mark Noble (TA).

12 May. Exhibited from CE:
• bond of Araminta Young executrix of
Joseph Young, Esq. Sureties: Thomas
Johnson, Jr. (CE), Samuel Young
(CV), Robert Gordon (Annapolis),
William Cumming (Annapolis). Date:
12 May 1737.

Maj. John Davidge, William Chapman,
Thomas Baldwin, John Bullen, & John

Court Session: 1737

Lomas to appraise estate of Joseph
Young, Esq. in AA.

13 May. Michael Fletcher (TA) vs.
Risdon Bozman (TA) executor of Mary
Knowles (QA). Sheriff (TA) to summon
defendant to prove said will.

16 May. Nehemiah King (g, SO)
exhibited:
• will of Richard Hill, constituting
  Charles Rackliff executor. Said
  Rackliff was granted administration.
  Sureties: Capell King, John Pope.
  Date: 16 March 1736/7.
• will of Joseph Wailes, constituting
  Helenor Wailes executrix. Said
  Helenor was granted administration.
  Sureties: George Irving, Abraham
  Cordery. Date: 31 March 1737.
• will of James Dashiells. Also, bond
  of Joseph Dashiells one of
  executors. Sureties: Benjamin
  Townsend, George Dashiells, Jr.
  Date: 25 April 1737. Also,
  renunciation of Bridget Dashiells,
  recommending said James.

30:274 • bond of Anne Nelson administratrix
  of John Nelson. Sureties: William
  Moor, Thomas Shiles. Date: 7 March
  1736/7.
• bond of Alexander Buncle
  administrator of Francis Ellit.
  Sureties: John Scarborough, David
  Murra. Date: 16 March 1736/7.
• bond of John Deal administrator of
  William Stevenson. Sureties: Thomas
  Coffin, William Nilson. Date: 7
  April 1737.
• bond of John Fleming administrator
  of Robert Carney. Sureties: Solomon
  Long, Samuel Long. Date: 23 April
  1737.
• bond of Peris Chapman administrator
  of John Hunter. Sureties: John
  Horsey, Randal Macclester. Date: 30
  April 1737.
• bond of George Gale administrator of
  John Follows. Sureties: David
  Wilson, Samuell Willson. Date: 10
  May 1737.
• will of Joy Hobbs,, constituting

Page 43

Absalom Hobbs executor.
- inventory of John Turpin.
- inventory & LoD of Comfort Benton.
- accounts of James Train administrator of John Crofford.
- accounts of Sarah Brown (alias Sarah Shaw) administratrix of Jonathon Shaw.
- additional accounts of Arthur Cunningham & his wife Barbara administratrix of Joseph Kenning.

17 May. Mr. Peter Dent (PG) to examine 2nd additional accounts of:
- Richard Marsham Waring executor of Marsham Waring (PG).

18 May. Exhibited from AA:
- bond of Benjamin Lawrence administrator of John Lawrence. Sureties: Henry Howard, Levin Lawrence. Date: 18 May 1736.

30:275 19 May. Mr. James Earle (QA) to examine accounts of:
John Browne & Matthew Browne executors of Mary Browne (QA).

21 May. William Rumsey (g, CE) exhibited:
- nuncupative will of James Forster. Also, bond of Aaron Latham acting executor. Sureties: Richard Thompson, John Kankey. Date: 8 April 1737. Also, renunciation of Thomas Johnson, Jr. executor of estate of James Foster. Date: 17 December 1736.
- bond of Hester Warner administratrix of Richard Warner. Sureties: John McManus (p), Benjamin Childs (p). Date: 10 January 1736.
- bond of Mary Hukill administratrix of John Hukill. Sureties: William Husband, Richard Elwood. Date: 26 January 1736.
- bond of Thomas Bouldin administrator of Jane Clarke. Sureties: Robert Patton, Andrew Alexander. Date: 22 February 1736.
- bond of Rachel Pennington administratrix of Robert Pennington.

Court Session: 1737

Sureties: John Campbell, Thomas
Jones. Date: 2 May 1737.
- inventory of Thomas Burge.
- inventory of Garratt Othoson.
- inventory of Richard Warner.
- additional accounts of Joseph Price
  & his wife Jane executrix of Philip
  Barrett.
- accounts of Tarance Graham & his
  wife Margarett (late Margaret
  Sapenton) executrix of Nathaniel
  Sapenton.
- additional accounts of Robert Money,
  Jr. & his wife Ruth administratrix
  of William McDowell.
- accounts of Benjamin Pearce & his
  wife Margarett administrators of
  Henry Ward.
- accounts of Benjamin Pearce
  administrator of Robert
  Goldsborough.
- accounts of John Baldwin
  administrator of John Rosser.

30:276
- accounts of Sarah Touchstone
  administratrix of Henry Touchstone.
- accounts of John Holland
  administrator of John Thompson.
- additional accounts of Elisabeth
  John administratrix of Joshua John.
- additional accounts of Francis
  Herron & his wife Frances
  administratrix of John Walker.

21 May. Exhibited from QA:
- 2nd additional accounts of Daniel
  McClean & his wife Jane
  administratrix of Hans Hamilton.

At the request of John Moale (BA), Roger
Mathews, one of witnesses to will of
Anthony Bale (BA), deposed regarding
said will.

24 May. Mr. Humphry Wells Stokes (BA)
to examine accounts of:
- Edward Thorp & his wife Catherine
  executrix of Thomas Cullin (BA).

25 May. Humphry Wells Stokes (g, BA)
exhibited:
- bond of Thomas Taylor administrator
  of William Cox. Sureties: William

Page 45

Wiley, John Daugheday. Date: 22
April 1737. Also, renunciation of
Mary Cox widow, recommending Mr.
Thomas Taylor (g, BA). Date: 30
March 1737. Witnesses: John Wood,
Abbraham Vaune.
- inventory of Anne Hall.
- inventory of Robert Gardiner.
- inventory & LoD of Luke Raven.
- accounts of Temperance Barton
  executrix of James Barton.

30:277 Roger Peele for self & his 2 brothers
Robert & Samuel Peele vs. William Peele
(AA) administrator of Samuel Peele (AA)
& administrator of Robert Peele (AA).
Sheriff (AA) to summon defendant to
render answer.

Mr. William Rumsey (CE) to examine
additional accounts of:
- Joshua George & Sarah Moody
  administrators of Capt. James Moody
  (CE).

Mr. Tench Francis (TA) to examine
accounts of:
- Sarah Loveday administratrix of John
  Loveday (TA).
- Frances Williams executrix of Ennion
  Williams (TA).
- James Holton & his wife Martha &
  William Harding executors of Joseph
  Harding (TA).
- Nathaniel Grace, Jr. executor of
  William Grace (TA).
- Thomas Winchester & his wife Tabitha
  executrix of Isaac Marling (TA).
- Margaret Horney & James Horney on
  estate of Solomon Horney (TA), after
  receiving inventory.
- Mary Sherwood administratrix of Hugh
  Sherwood (TA).
- John Edmondson executor of James
  Edmondson (TA).

Mr. William Rumsey (CE) to examine
accounts of:
- Peter Bowyer & his wife Hester
  executrix of John Lewis (CE).

Court Session: 1737

26 May. Mr. Nehemiah King (SO) to
examine accounts of:
- Catherine Stewart administratrix of
  William Stewart (SO).
- Isaac Morris executor of Elisabeth
  Davis (SO).
- Elisabeth Robbins, Bodwin Robbins, &
  Thomas Robbins executors of Thomas
  Robbins (SO). Additional accounts.

30:278 Mr. Charles Hynson (KE) to examine
accounts of:
- Katherine Normansell administratrix
  of Richard Normansell (KE).
- Anne Thomas administratrix of David
  Thomas (KE).
- Hannah Hosier executrix of Henry
  Hosier (KE).

Mr. Humphrey Wells Stokes (BA) to
examine accounts of:
- Josias Middlemore executor of
  Richard Jenkins (BA).

27 May. Mr. William Rumsey (CE) to
examine accounts of:
- Joseph Rich administrator of Daniel
  Jobson (CE).
- Sarah Othoson administratrix of
  Garret Othoson (CE).
- Laurence Galshiott & Cornelius Cook
  executors of James McCabe (CE).

Abigail Ryan widow of Cornelius Ryan
(KE) vs. Henry Truelock (KE). Sheriff
(KE) to summon defendant to prove said
will.

28 May. Mr. James Earle (QA) to
examine accounts of:
- Margaret Pinder executrix of William
  Pinder (QA).
- Nathaniel Scott executor of Abraham
  Oldson (QA).

1 June. Joseph Allen (son of Joseph
Allen (CH, dec'd)) vs. Barbara Allen
administratrix of said dec'd. Sheriff
(CH) to summon defendant to render
answer.

30:279 Exhibited from AA:
- bond of Philip Smith & William Chapman administrators of Philip Smith (merchant, London). Sureties: Mordecai Hammond (AA), Zachariah Maccubbin (AA), Richard Gist (BA), Turner Wootton (PG). Date: 1 June 1737.

2 June. Exhibited from PG:
- additional accounts of James Edmonston administrator of Ninian Edmonston. Also, additional inventory.

7 June. Exhibited from AA:
- inventory & LoD of William Cromwell.

10 June. John Hillery (PG) vs. Philip Dowell & John Dowell executors of Philip Dowell (AA). Sheriff (CV) to summon defendants to render additional accounts.

14 June. Exhibited from AA:
- accounts of Edward Thursby & his wife Ann administratrix of Abraham Parkinson.

Mr. Charles Hynson (KE) to examine accounts of:
- Elinor Gooding executrix of Samuell Gooding (KE).
- Anne Blakiston executrix of William Blakiston (KE).

15 June. Exhibited from AA:
- accounts of John Watkins administrator of Ann Disney administratrix of James Disney.

Robert Gordon, Esq. one of sureties on estate of John Cromwell (AA) vs. William Worthington & his wife Hannah executrix of said Cromwell. Sheriff (AA) to summon defendants to render accounts.

30:280 16 June. Capt. John Pitt (DO) to examine accounts of:
- William Harper executor of Sarah Harper (DO).

Court Session: 1737

Exhibited from AA:
• inventory of John Norwood.

17 June. Michael Macnemara (g, AA)
exhibited:
• will of Samuel Chew, constituting
  Henrietta Maria Chew & Philip Thomas
  executors.

20 June. Exhibited from AA:
• bond of Henrietta Maria Chew
  executrix of Samuel Chew. Sureties:
  Philip Thomas, Samuel Chamberlain,
  Robert Lloyd. Date: 18 June 1737.
  Also, renunciation of Philip Thomas
  (AA) one of executors. Date: 17
  June 1737.

23 June. Exhibited from PG:
• additional accounts of Martha Waring
  & Thomas Waring administrators of
  Basil Waring.

25 June. Exhibited from BA:
• will of Charles Daniel, constituting
  Rachell Daniel executrix.

30:281 27 June. Gabriel Parker (g, CV)
        exhibited:
• , will of Jonathon Cay, constituting
  Dorothy Cay executrix. Said Dorothy
  was granted administration.
  Sureties: John Hungerford, William
  Sharples, Ellis Slater. Date: 6
  June 1737.
• bond of Aaron Williams administrator
  dbn of William Ladyman. Sureties:
  John Grover, William Winnall. Date:
  7 June 1737.
• inventory of John Dottson.
• inventory of James Cooley.
• accounts of William Card one of
  administrators of Matthew Gardner.

Humphrey Wells Stokes (g, BA) exhibited:
• bond of Walter Dallas administrator
  of Edward Evans. Sureties:
  Christopher Durbin, Jacob Wright.
  Date: 14 June 1737.
• will of Joseph Allen, constituting
  Elisabeth Allen executrix.
• will of Richard Jones, Sr.,

Page 49

Court Session: 1737

exhibited by Richard Jones, Jr. one
of executors.
- Elisabeth Stone, constituting John
Sampson & James Bagford executors.
- inventory of William Rose.
- inventory & LoD of John Demmitt.
- inventory & LoD of William Connell.
- accounts of Daniel Shaw
administrator of Ann Hall.
- accounts of Philip Jones
administrator of William Rose.

Mr. Peter Dent (PG) to examine accounts
of:
- Sarah Magruder executrix of Robert
Magruder (PG).

30:282 29 June. Mr. Gabriel Parker (CV) to
examine additional accounts of:
- John Beckett & his wife Priscilla
executrix of Richard Johns (CV).

1 July. Peter Dent (g, PG) exhibited:
- inventory of John Edgar.
- inventory & LoD of Capt. John
Martindale.
- inventory of John Jones.
- inventory of Benjamin Smallwood.
- 2nd additional accounts of William
Magruder administrator of Rupert
Butler.
- accounts of Mary Norris executrix of
Dr. John Norris.
- additional accounts of Benjamin
Smith & his wife Mary executrix of
Benjamin Stimton.

2 July. Mr. Humphrey Wells Stokes (BA)
to examine additional accounts of:
- Mary Warren administratrix of Thomas
Warren (BA).

6 July. Exhibited from AA:
- will of Peter Shipley, constituting
Richard Shipley executor. Said
Richard was granted administration.
Sureties: James Barnes, Adam
Shipley. Date: 6 July 1737.

7 July. Exhibited from AA:
- 2nd additional accounts of John
Burgess surviving executor of John

Page 50

Stifin.

Mr. Thomas Aisquith (SM) to examine additional accounts of:
- Catherine Waughop & James Waughop executors of Thomas Waughop (SM).

30:283 8 July. Mr. Gabriel Parker (CV) to examine accounts of:
- Joshan Mannyng executrix of Thomas Mannyng (CV).

Exhibited from BA:
- inventory of William Cockran.

11 July. Exhibited from AA:
- accounts of Thomas Hall & his wife Katherine executrix of John Conaway.

Exhibited from PG:
- 4th additional accounts of Col. Joseph Belt & his wife Margery administratrix of Thomas Sprigg.

Samuel Hanson (g, CH) exhibited:
- bond of William Campell administrator of John White. Sureties: William Theobalds, John Theobalds. Date: 25 April 1737.
- bond of Robert Doyne & his wife Jane administrators of Joseph Sanders. Sureties: William Cooper, Joseph Doyne. Date: 4 May 1737.
- inventory of John Bruce.
- inventory of James Keen.
- inventory of Charles Montoes.
- inventory of James Boyce.
- inventory of Dr. John Haw.
- inventory of John McCoy.
- inventory of John Newman.
- inventory of William Penn.
- inventory of Richard Lloyd.
- inventory of John Higton.
- accounts of Sarah Fowke executrix of Gerrard Fowke.
- accounts of Ann Parker administratrix of Abraham Parker.
- additional accounts of Barbara Allen administratrix of Joseph Allen.

30:284 Docket:
- William Cumming procurator for John
  Lusby (AA) vs. Edm. Jenings
  procurator for Thomas Wells & his
  wife Elinor executrix of John Lusby.
  Text of libel. Plaintiff (p) is one
  of children of said dec'd (p).
  Mentions: certain of his legatees:
  son John Negro Charles, daughter
  Rachel Negro Jenny (girl), 3
  children Samuel & Mary & Ellenor
  Negro Bess (woman), executrix: wife
  Ellenor. Said dec'd left: widow, 5
  sons, 3 daughters.

30:285 Said widow married Thomas Wells (p,
  AA). Said Rachel died before
  receiving her share; also Mary,
  Ellinor,

30:286 Mentions: Nich. Maccubbin (sheriff,
  AA), Zach. Maccubbin (sheriff, AA).

30:287 Text of answer.

30:288 Mentions: summons to Levin Hill
  (AA), Thomas Watkins (AA), Henry
  Bateman (AA), John Shivers (AA).
  Said Shivers is NEI.
  - Levin Hill (Quaker, AA) affirmed
    on 12 January 1736.
  - Thomas Watkins deposed on 12
    January 1736.

30:289 Also, summons to Ezekiel Gillis
  (AA).
  - John Shivers deposed on 12 March
    1736.
  - Ezekiel Gillis (AA) deposed on
    12 March 1736.

30:290 Ruling: plaintiff.
- William Cumming, Esq. executor of
  Thomas Facer (AA) vs. M.M. for
  Achsah Woodward administratrix dbn
  of Amos Garrett, Esq. Also, Edmond
  Jenings, Esq. & John Galloway
  attorneys-in-fact for Elisabeth Ginn
  & executors of Mary Woodward.
  Libel, answer, interrogatories,
  depositions. Summons to: Samuel
  Smith (AA), Jane Bell (AA), Richard
  Young (CV).
- Summons to John Whaley & his wife
  widow of John Darby (SO) to take
  LoA.

30:291 • Summons to Comfort Hopkins widow of
  John Hopkins (DO) to take LoA.

Court Session: 12 July 1737

- W.C. for John Phillips & his wife Jane (PG) vs. B.Y. for Nicholas Downing & his wife Elisabeth executrix of John Clarvo. Libel, answer, general replication.
- William Harris (sheriff, KE) to summon Mary Raisins executrix of Thomas Raisins (KE) to take LoA.
- William Thomas (TA) vs. Richard Giles one of witnesses to will of Loftis Bowdle (TA). Sheriff (TA) to render attachment to defendant.
- Coroners (SO) to render attachment to sheriff (SO).
- Sheriff (AA) to summon (N) Austin, wife of Henry Austin, late widow of William Pearce (AA) to take LoA.

30:292
- Sheriff (DO) to summon Joseph Ennalls executor of William Ennalls (DO) to render additional accounts.
- Francis Hall (PG) vs. Charles Digges administrator of Nicholas Lowe, Esq. (SM). Sheriff (PG) to summon defendant to render additional accounts.
- William Cumming for Roger Peele for self & his 2 brothers Robert & Samuel Peele (AA) vs. E.J. for William Peele administrator of Samuel & Robert Peele. Libel. Zach. Maccubbin (sheriff, AA) summoned defendant. Defendant filed an answer. Plaintiff filed a certificate of his father's marriage.
- Michael Fletcher (TA) vs. Risdon Bozman (TA) executor of Mary Knowles (QA)> Sheriff (TA) to summon defendant to prove said will.
- Abigail Ryan widow & executrix of Cornelius Ryan (KE) vs. Edmund Jenings, procurator for Henry Truelock (KE). William Harris (sheriff, KE) to summon defendant to show cause why said will should not be proved.

30:293
Said Truelock filed a subsequent will, constituting said Truelock executor. Notice sent to plaintiff.
- E.J. for Joseph Allen (CH) vs. W.C. for Barbara Allen administratrix of Joseph Allen. Libel. George Dent

Court Session: 12 July 1737

(sheriff, CH) to summon defendant to render answer. Answer filed.
- John Hilleary (PG) vs. Philip & John Dowell executors of Philip Dowell (AA). Sheriff (CV) to summon defendant to render additional accounts. Additional accounts exhibited. Discontinued.
- Robert Gordon, Esq. one of sureties on estate of John Cromwell (AA) vs. William Worthington & his wife Hannah executrix of said Cromwell. Zach. Maccubbin (sheriff, AA) to summon defendants to render accounts.

Court Session: 1737

30:294 14 July. James Earle (g, QA) exhibited:
- will of John Knowles. Also, bond of Risdon Bozman administrator. Sureties: William Jump, Sr., William Price. Date: 21 April 1737.
- will of John Leonard, Sr., constituting John Leonard, Jr. executor. Said executor was granted administration. Sureties: William Bell, John Cooper, Jr. Date: 24 May 1737.
- will of John Sparkes, constituting Cornelia Sparkes executrix. Said Cornelia was granted administration. Sureties: George Elliott, John Merridith. Date: 28 May 1737.
- bond of Margaret Pinder administratrix of Richard Wise. Sureties: William Bruton, John Woodal. Date: 18 April 1737.
- bond of Tamer Thomasman administratrix of James Thomasman. Sureties: Matthew Docwra, Nathaniel Read. Date: 2 May 1737.
- bond of Margaret Pickering administratrix of Robert Pickering. Sureties: John Downes, Sr., John Emerson. Date: 4 May 1737.
- bond of William Roth & his wife Mary administrators of Thomas Day. Sureties: John Hammond, Henry Coursey. Date: 6 June 1737.
- will of Charles Seth, constituting Elisabeth Seth & John Seth

Page 54

Court Session: 1737

executors.
- inventory of Dr. William Edwards.
- inventory of William Hemsley.
- inventory & LoD of Richard Kemp.
- inventory of Edward Chetham.
- inventory of William Swift.
- additional inventory of Mary Brown.
- inventory of Daniel Walker
- accounts of Diana Tippen administratrix of William Tippen.

15 July. Mr. James Earle (QA) to examine accounts of:
- Sarah Chetham executrix of Edward Chetham (QA).
- Mary & William Hampton executors of Thomas Hampton (QA).
- Jane Swift administratrix of John Ayres (DO).
- Robert Blunt & his wife Mary executrix of Samuel Wright (QA).
- William Joyner executor of John Roberts (QA).
- Margaret & Jacob Boon executors of William Boon (QA).
- Nicholas Broadaway administrator of William Edwards (QA).
- Benjamin Elliott & his wife Mary executrix of Thomas Harris (QA). Additional accounts.

30:295

Exhibited from AA:
- additional accounts of Philip & John Dowell (CV) executors of Philip Dowell.

19 July. MM Richard Caswell (BA) & Gilbert Crockett (BA) to appraise estate of Philip Smith (BA).

20 July. Exhibited from PG:
- bond of Jane Offutt administratrix of William Offutt. Sureties: Samuel Magruder 3rd, William Wallace. Date: 20 July 1737.

Mr. Edward Fottrell vs. Richard Young (CV) & Samuel Young (CV) surviving executors of Col. Samuel Young (AA). Sheriff (CV) to summon defendants to render inventory.

Exhibited from BA:
- accounts of William Savory administrator of James Maxwell.

22 July. Exhibited from BA:
- 2nd additional accounts of Rebecca Hawkins widow of James Cobb.
- additional accounts of Rebecca Hawkins executrix of John Hawkins.

25 July. Exhibited from AA:
- accounts of Abigail Burkett administratrix of Edmund Evans.

30:296 Gabriel Parker (g, CV) exhibited:
- bond of Elisabeth Gover administratrix of Robert Gover. Sureties: Samuel Gover, Richard Johns (Fuller). Date: 2 July 1737.
- inventory of William Hickman.
- 3rd additional accounts of John Beckett & his wife Priscilla executrix of Richard Johns.

26 July. Exhibited from AA:
- will of Elisabeth Orgin. Also, bond of James Donaldson & his wife Bridget guardians of Mary Johnson her daughter.

27 July. Capt. John Pitt (DO) exhibited:
- bond of Garey Warner administrator of William Thomas. Sureties: Charles Beckwith, John Pullin. Date: 18 May 1737. Also, renunciation of Ann Bradly, recommending Mr. Garey Warner. Date: 16 May 1737. Witness: Mary Medford. Also, renunciation of Alexander Standly, recommending Garey Warner. Date: 17 May 1737. Witness: John Summers. Also, renunciation of Simon Thomas, recommending Garey Warner. Date: 17 May 1737. Witness: John Summers.
- bond of Mary Granger administratrix of John Granger. Sureties: Jacob Pattison, St. Leger Pattison. Date: 15 June 1737.
- bond of Mary Summers administratrix of John Summers. Sureties: Jacob

Pattison, John Robson.   Date: 17
June 1737.
- inventory of John Uscears.
- accounts of John Nicolls & his wife
Mary executrix of Mark Noble.
- accounts of Kezia Morain
administratrix of Jonathon Morain.

30:297 - 1st additional accounts of Isaac
Meekins executor of James Meekins.

Exhibited:
- receipt of Benjamin Harris from
Benjamin Hance & George Harris
surviving trustees of his father
Benjamin Harris.   Date: 14 March
1736.   Witnesses: John Mackall, Jr.,
John Games.

30 July.   Exhibited from AA:
- accounts of John Dorsey
administrator of Pleasance
Wainwright.

3 August.   Tench Francis (g, TA)
exhibited:
- bond of William Bennett
administrator of Thomas Tennant.
Sureties: Richard Aldern, John
Valiant.   Date: 16 April 1737.
- bond of Rachel Wrightson
administratrix of John Wrightson.
Sureties: William Lamden, William
Webb Haddaway.   Date: 18 April 1737.
- bond of Elisabeth Quinn
administratrix of John Quinn.
Sureties: Francis Neall, John Webb.
Date: 27 June 1737.
- additional inventory of Peter
Harwood, Jr.
- 2nd additional inventory of Thomas
Martin.
- inventory of Isaac Tunny.
- inventory & LoD of James McClendon.
- inventory of William Sheild.
- inventory of Isaac Dixon.
- additional inventory of George
Collison.
- inventory of John Wrightson.

30:298 - accounts of Grace Harwood
administratrix of Peter Harwood, Jr.
- accounts of Thomas Winchester & his
wife Tabitha executrix of Isaac

Marling. Also, debt of Francis
Isgate.
- accounts of Sarah Loveday
administratrix of John Loveday.
- accounts of Samuel Harwood & his
wife Frances executrix of Ennion
Williams.
- accounts of James Holton & his wife
Martha & William Harding executors
of Joseph Harding.
- accounts of Mary Sherwood
administratrix of Hugh Sherwood.

5 August. Exhibited from PG:
- 2nd additional accounts of George
Buchanan administrator of Hugh
Arbuthnot.

8 August. Bartholomew Ennalls (DO) vs.
estate of Col. Thomas Ennalls (DO).
Exhibited depositions of John Hayward &
Margrett Eccleston two of witnesses to
said will.

Capt. John Pitt (DO) exhibited:
- bond of Rebecca Courson
administratrix of Thomas Courson.
Sureties: Thomas Canner, Marmaduke
Handly. Date: 29 July 1737.
- bond of Elisabeth Smart
administratrix of Richard Smart.
Sureties: Thomas Ennalls, Sr.,
Edward Trippe, Sr. Date: 30 July
1737.
- will of Richard Pearson, exhibited
by Noah Pearson his son & legatee.
- additional inventory & LoD of
Francis Money.
- 2nd additional accounts of John
Charlscroft & his wife Elisabeth
administrators of Morriss Mackemys.
- accounts of Mary Peterkin &
Nathaniel Manning executors of David
Peterkin.
30:299 • accounts of Mary Peterkin &
Nathaniel Manning administrators of
Mary Cooke.
- accounts of Mary Money
administratrix of Francis Money.
- 1st additional accounts of Kezia
Moraine administratrix of Jonathon
Moraine.

- accounts of John Hayward executor of Francis Hayward.

Thomas Aisquith (g, SM) exhibited:
- will of Maj. Nicholas Sewall, constituting Charles Sewall executor. Said Charles was granted administration. Sureties: Clement Sewall, William Cavenough. Date: 30 June 1737.
- will of William Asbestone, constituting Mary Asbestone executrix. Said Mary was granted administration. Sureties: Joseph Kirk, Joseph FitzJeffery. Date: 4 July 1737.
- bond of Elisabeth Wiseman administratrix of Robert Wiseman. Sureties: Francis Hopewell, Mark Heard. Date: 19 May 1737.
- bond of Ann Balley administratrix of John Balley. Sureties: James Thompson, Richard Raper. Date: 8 June 1737.
- inventory & LoD of John Smith.
- inventory & LoD of John Frazer.
- inventory & LoD of Robert Phillips.
- inventory & LoD of Thomas Hunt.
- inventory & LoD of John Bullock.
- inventory & LoD of William Bullock.
- inventory of Joseph Vansweringen.
- additional inventory of Owen Smithson.
- inventory of William Houlton.
- additional accounts of Ann Smithson administratrix of Owen Smithson.
- accounts of Joseph FitzJeffery administrator of James Simmons.
- accounts of John Fanning & his wife Mary administrators of Philip Tipet.
- accounts of Jane Gough executrix of Benjamin Gough.
- accounts of Grace Galle executrix of Laurence Galle.
- accounts of Ann Vowles administratrix of Richard Vowles.
- accounts of John Medly Thompson & his wife Elinor administratrix of John Bould.
- accounts of Dennis Burn who married Ann Houlton administratrix of William Houlton.

30:300   Gabriel Parker (g, CV) exhibited:
- will of Thomas Cox, constituting Mary Cox executrix. Said Mary was granted administration. Sureties: William Holland, Parker Young. Date: 20 July 1737.
- will of William Day, constituting Rebecca Day executrix. Said Rebecca was granted administration. Sureties: Robert Day, Thomas Johnson. Date: 1 August 1737.
- inventory of John Betenson.

Mr. Gabriel Parker (CV) to examine accounts of:
- Elinor Elt & Robert Elt executors of Elisabeth Turner (CV).

Petition of John Williams & his wife Esther (SO) administratrix of William White. Stevens White, father of said William, made his will in 1718, constituting his wife Catherine, Thomas Howard, & Col. William Whittington executors. Said Catherine White & Thomas Howard renounced administration. No accounts have been exhibited. Bond on estate of Stevens White assigned to petitioner.

Exhibited from DO:
- additional accounts of Hugh Handly & his wife Susannah & Owen Ward executors of John Summers.
- additional accounts of Bartholomew Ennalls & his wife Elisabeth executrix of William Taylor.

Exhibited from SO:
- additional accounts of Joseph Dashiell & his wife Sarah administratrix of Thomas Dashiell.

Exhibited from PG:
- accounts of Micajah & Yate Plummer executors of Elisabeth Plummer.

30:301   19 August. Exhibited from SO:
- accounts of Joseph Dashiel executor of James Dashiell surety on estate of Christopher Dashiel.

Court Session: 1737

Exhibited from AA:
- accounts of Nathaniel Stinchcomb & his wife Ann administrators of John Burley, Jr.

Peter Dent (g, PG) exhibited:
- bond of Deborah Boyd administratrix of Abraham Boyd. Sureties: Thomas Lancaster, Henry Hall. Date: 29 June 1737.
- bond of John Prather, Jr. administrator of Catherine Prather. Sureties: Thomas Scott, Edward Prather. Date: 30 June 1737.
- bond of Michael Jones administrator of David Jones. Surety: Matthew Markland. Date: 13 July 1737.
- accounts of William Hitcherson executor of Margaret Locklin.
- 2nd additional accounts of Mary Offutt executrix of William Offutt.
- accounts of Sarah Magruder executrix of Robert Magruder.

Mr. Peter Dent (PG) to examine accounts of:
- Sarah Moore on behalf of Henry Moore executor of Henry Moore (PG).

10 August. Exhibited from AA:
- additional accounts of Thomas Higgins & his wife Dorothy assignees of Samuel Cotterell administrator of John Hobbs.
- additional accounts of Thomas Harrison & his wife Dorcas executrix of Francis Hardisty.

12 August. Humphrey Wells Stokes (g, BA) exhibited:
- bond of Elisabeth Miles administratrix of Evan Miles. Sureties: Henry Rhoads, Thomas Donawen. Date: 26 June 1737.
- bond of Sarah Hanson administratrix of Benjamin Hanson. Sureties: William Hollis, Samuel Griffith. Date: 26 June 1737.
- bond of Sarah Robinson & Benjamin Bond administrators dbn of Robert Robertson. Sureties: Mathew Beck, Joshua Starkey. Date: 16 July 1737.

30:302
- inventory of Sarah Day.
- inventory of William Cox.
- inventory of Simon Gregory.
- inventory & LoD of John Lea.
- inventory & LoD of Richard Jenkins. Also, additional inventory.
- additional accounts of Mary Warren administratrix of Thomas Warren.
- accounts of Edward Thorpe & his wife Catherine executrix of Thomas Cullin.
- accounts of Thomas Hutchins & Nicholas Hutchins executors of Thomas Hutchins, Sr.

Exhibited from AA:
- bond of Mathew Elliot administrator of Mary Richardson. Sureties: Nicholas St. Lawrence, James Sanders. Date: 12 August 1737.
- additional accounts of Thomas Hall & his wife Katherine executrix of John Conaway.

15 August. Nehemiah King (g, SO) exhibited:
- bond of Absalom Hobbs executor of Joy Hobbs. Sureties: Benjamin Mitchell, Joy Hobbs. Date: 21 May 1737.
- will of Teague Donahoe, constituting Sarah Donahoe executrix. Said Sarah was granted administration. Sureties: Charles Riggin, James Tounsend. Date: 22 June 1737.
- bond of Day Scott executor of Andrew Scott. Sureties: Robert King, Sr., John Horsey. Date: 28 July 1737.
- bond of Jane Handy administratrix of Thomas Handey. Sureties: Samuel Long, Thomas Tull, Sr. Date: 3 June 1737.
- bond of Dunkin Murray administrator of John Williams. Surety: Robert King, Sr. Date: 6 June 1737.
- bond of Elinor Taylor administratrix of Walter Taylor. Sureties: John Newbold, John Lay. Date: 22 June 1737.
- inventory of Thomas Benson.
- inventory of George Betts Collier.
- inventory of John Nellson.

Court Session: 1737

30:303

- inventory of James Dashiell, Jr.
- inventory of Alexander Hall.
- inventory of William Horsey.
- inventory of William Stevinson.
- accounts of Thomas Marshall & his wife Jane administratrix of Abraham Haith.
- accounts of Thomas White administrator of John White.
- accounts of Aaron Tillman, Anne Gibbens, & Thomas Gibbens executors of John Gibbins, Sr.
- accounts of Robert Austin administrator of Edward Foulars.
- 2nd accounts of Robert Dashiel executor of George Dashiels.
- accounts of Elisabeth Rhoads executrix of Timothy Rhoads.
- accounts of Bell Maddux executor of Thomas Maddux.
- accounts of Panther Laws administrator of Robert Skeen.
- accounts of Nicholas Kelley & his wife Sarah administrators of Edward Vigrose.
- accounts of John White administrator of John Beauchamp.
- additional accounts of Elisabeth Robins, Bowdoin, & Thomas Robins executors of Thomas Robins.
- accounts of Isaac Morris executor of Elisabeth Davis.
- accounts of Ann Ward executrix of Stephen Ward.
- accounts of James Anderson & his wife Rebecca administratrix of David Brown.
- accounts of Elisabeth Hopkins (alias Elisabeth Nicholson) administratrix of John Nicholson.
- accounts of Sarah Outon (alias Sarah Kellam) executrix of John Outon.
- accounts of John Davis & his wife Elisabeth executrix of John Magee.
- accounts of Listian Alexander surviving executor of William Alexander.
- accounts of Robert Taylor administrator of Hope Taylor.
- accounts of William Cearsey administrator of Peter Cearsey.
- accounts of Isaac Costin executor of

Page 63

Cumfort Benton.

16 August. Tench Francis (g, TA) exhibited:
- bond of Jacob Bromwell administrator of Jacob Cole. Sureties: John Lurtey, Nicholas Glen. Date: 5 August 1737.
- additional inventory of Mary Cowper.
- accounts of Nathaniel Grace executor of William Grace.

Mr. Humphrey Wells Stokes (BA) to examine accounts of:
- Josias Middlemore executor of Richard Jenkins (BA).
- Alice Lea administratrix of John Lea (BA).

30:304 Mr. James Earle (QA) to examine accounts of:
- John Alley, Jr. administrator of Thomas Richardson (QA).

Mr. Charles Hynson (KE) to examine accounts of:
- James Stout & his wife Ann administratrix dbn of St. Leger Codd, Esq. (KE). 3rd additional accounts.
- Thomas Hynson & William Hynson executors of Margaret Murphey (KE). Additional accounts.

Mr. Thomas Aisquith (SM) to examine accounts of:
- John Angel executor of James Angel (SM).
- George Vaudery & William Bond executors of Thomas Hunt (SM).
- John Dossey who married Ann Cooper administratrix of Mary Cooper (SM).
- Theodorus Jordan & his wife Elisabeth administratrix of Charles Mills (SM).
- George Vaudery & his wife Jane executrix of John Morrett (SM).

Mr. Nehemiah King (SO) to examine accounts of:
- Stephen Hopkins administrator of Jane Hopkins (SO).

Court Session: 1737

Mr. Samuel Hanson (CH) to examine accounts of:
• Eleanor Hunter (late Eleanor Glashon) administratrix of John Glashon (CH).

Capt. John Pitt (DO) to examine additional accounts of:
• Edward Cock & Richard Frame executors of Major Frame (DO).

Tench Francis (TA) to examine accounts of:
• Elisabeth Rathell executrix of John Rathell (TA).
• Thomas Metcalfe & his wife Mary administratrix of Richard Holmes (TA).
• Thomas Martin administrator of Thomas Martin (TA).
• Elisabeth Collisson executrix of George Collisson (TA).
• Isaac Dobson & his wife Hannah administratrix of James Powell (TA).
• Isaac Dobson & Anne Erwin executors of William Dobson (TA). Additional accounts.

30:305 20 August. Mr. Gabriel Parker (CV) to examine accounts of:
• John Broome, Jr. administrator of Henry Broome (CV).
• James Dodson & Joseph Wooden administrators of John Dodson (CV).
• Dorothy Cay executrix of Jonathon Cay (CV).

22 August. Exhibited from PG:
• additional accounts of Priscilla Crabb executrix of Ralph Crabb.

23 August. Exhibited from AA:
• accounts of George Plater, Esq. & Onorio Razolini (g) executors of Rebecca Calvert, who were likewise administrators of Charles Calvert, Esq.

Mr. Peter Dent (PG) to examine additional accounts of:
• Mary Reiley executrix of Bryan Reiley (PG).

Court Session: 1737

25 August. Exhibited from AA:
- additional inventory of Charles Calvert, Esq.

27 August. Samuel Hanson (g, CH) exhibited:
- bond of Susanna Bennett administratrix of Isaac Bennett. Sureties: Alexander Hawkins, Peter Harraut. Date: 27 June 1737.
- bond of William Robson executor of Eleanor Sanders. Sureties: William Millstead, John Blanchett. Date: 6 July 1737.
- bond of Elisabeth Williams administratrix of James Williams. Sureties: Hugh Currick, Walter Fearson. Date: 6 July 1737.
- bond of Thomas Haile administrator of Alexander Lashley. Sureties: Francis Glass, William Penn. Date: 18 July 1737.

30:306
- inventory of John Rogers.
- inventory of Joseph Sanders.
- inventory of John White.
- inventory of Peter Hays.
- additional inventory of John King.
- accounts of Henry Acton who married Ann Chandler (dec'd) & John Chandler executors of John Chandler.
- accounts of William Coombes & William Mackatee executors of Catherine Ensey.
- accounts of Charles Courts administrator of John Rogers.
- accounts of John Stromat & his wife Ann executrix of William Williams.
- accounts of Ann Howison administratrix of John Howison.
- accounts of William Campbell administrator of John White.
- Joseph Foxley & his wife Elisabeth administratrix of Peter Hays.

Henry Wright (PG) one of sureties on estate of Richard Moore (AA) vs. Margaret Moore, Samuel Preston Moore, & Mordecai Moore executors of said Richard. Sheriff (AA) to summon defendants to render accounts.

Court Session: 29 August 1737

Docket:
- Philip Key, Esq. procurator for William Cumming, Esq. (Annapolis) executor of Thomas Facer (shoemaker, AA) vs. M. Macnemara procurator for Achsah Woodward administratrix dbn of Amos Garrett, Esq. Also, Edmund Jenings, Esq. & John Galloway attorneys-in-fact for Elisabeth Ginn & executors of Mary Woodward.

30:307   Text of libel. Mentions: libel by Thomas Facer against Amos Woodward (merchant, Annapolis); will of Amos Garrett, bequeathing to his kinsman Thomas Facer (brother to Henry Facer); Elenor Chinton (widow); John Baldwin; said Woodward is nephew of said Garrett; will of said Thomas Facer, bequeathing to Mrs. Achsa Woodward wife of Mr. Amos Woodward;
30:308   sisters of said Garrett -
30:309   said Elisabeth Ginn & Mary Woodward. Nich. Maccubbin (sheriff, AA) summoned defendant. Text of answer.
30:310   ...
30:311   Exhibited copy of will of Amos Garrett dated 4 September 1714. Cites that he is son of James & Sarah Garrett (St. Olives Street, Southwark, ENG). Mentions:
          - Robert Hewett (overseer),
          - his 2 sisters, brother-in-law, nephews, nieces,
30:312   - children (under age 17) of his sister Mary Woodward,
          - sister Elisabeth Ginn,
          - mother Sarah Garrett,
          - brother-in-law Henry Woodward,
          - cousin Henry Facer & Elisabeth wife of Seth Garrett - 1 acre in Annapolis.
30:313   - kinsman Thomas Facer (shoemaker, AA, brother to said Henry) - Lot #82.
          - cousin James Garrett (son of Seth Garrett (hatmaker, St. Olives Street, Southwark near London) - Lots #15 & #17.
          - William Monrow.
          - kinswoman Martha Eltington (aunt of said James Garrett) - Lot

#21.
- Robert Quary.
- kinsman James Facer (son of Thomas & Martha Facer (Rugby, ENG)) - Lot #31.
- Alexander Dehinoyosia.
- Sarah Hickcock & William Bruner.
- niece Elisabeth Woodward (daughter of Henry & Mary Woodward) - "Middle Neck" 300 acres in CE.

30:314
- niece Mary Woodward (daughter of Henry & Mary Woodward) - pt. "Middle Neck" 150 acres in CE, "Dryer's Inheritance" 254 acres in BA, 1/2 "Littleton" 226 acres in BA, "Robins Camp" 100 acres in BA, "Canons' Delight" 110 acres in BA, "Land of Goshen" 260 acres in BA.
- Hezekiah Hayns.
- nephew William Woodward (son of Henry & Mary Woodward) - "Gillingham" 400 acres in BA, "Davis Pasture" 200 acres in BA, "Kendall's Delight" 250 acres in BA, "The Enlargement" 400 acres in BA, "Hall's Palace" 300 acres in BA, "Sewells Increase" 100 acres in AA, pt. "Sewells Increase" 150 acres in AA, pt. "Sewells Increase" 250 acres in AA, "Chilton" 40 acres in AA, "Addition" 50 acres in AA,

30:315
Lots #33 & #34.
- niece Hannah Woodward (daughter of Henry & Mary Woodward) - "Maiden Fancy" 580 acres in PG, "Great Brushey Neck" 150 acres in AA, "Sumerlands Lott" 60 acres in AA, "Woodcocks Nest" 30 acres in AA, "Clarks Purchase" 70 acres in AA, "Range" 384 acres in AA,
- nephew Amos Woodward (son of Henry & Mary Woodward) - pt. "Roger Grey" alias "Gentle Craft" 100 acres in AA, "Swan Neck" 250 acres in AA, "Addition" 25 acres in AA, "Grimes Enlargement" 187 acres in AA, "Grimes Stone" 100 acres

in AA, "Brutons Hope" 40 acres in AA, Lots #42 & #43. Mentions: Mary Newell, Thomas Andrews, John Freeman.

30:316 — nephew Garrett Woodward (son of Henry & Mary Woodward) – "Hackleberry Forest" 114 acres in AA, "Hicory Ridge" 262 acres in AA, "One Third Timber Neck" 101 acres in AA, "Charles Hills" 51 acres in AA, "Todds Range" 120 acres in AA, "Majors Choice" 100 acres in BA. Mentions: Sarah Norwood widow of Samuel Norwood, Benjamin Fordham, Cornelius Howard. Also, pt. "Charles Hills" 50 acres in AA, "Timber Neck" 101 acres in AA, Lots #46 & #104. Mentions: Ann Noads, Richard Evans.

— mother Sarah Garrett – "Medcalfs Chance" 80 acres in AA, "Medcalfs Mount" 70 acres in AA, "Honest Mans Lott" 110.5 acres in AA, pt. "Howards & Porters Range" 150 acres in AA, pt. "Hereford" 26.5 acres in AA, "Mill Land" 100 acres in AA, moyety of "Norwoods Fancy" 210 acres in AA, "Providence" 200 acres in AA, "Half Solomons Hill" 50 acres in AA, pt. "Greys Sands" 19 acres in AA, "Canaan" 120 acres in AA, "Sturtons Rest" 110 acres in AA, "Millford & Taylors Lott" 300 acres in AA,

30:317 Lots #45, #61, #62, #63.

— Minister & Vestry of Parish Church of St. Ann's – land bought of Samuel Dorsey & John Pettycoat, "Wyatts Range" 225 acres in AA, "Clarks Enlargement" 165 acres in AA, residue to "Clarks Enlargement" 100 acres in AA, "Howards Interest" 150 acres in AA, pt. "Upper Taunton" 166 acres in AA, "Burntwood" 100 acres in AA, "Dorseys Addition" 50 acres in AA, pt. "Vennings Inheritance" 50 acres in AA, "Ridgeleys

Court Session: 29 August 1737

	Beginning" 40 acres in AA, "Howards Mount" 80 acres in AA, "Woodyard" 150 acres in AA, "Bare Ridge" 100 acres in AA, pt. "Upper Taunton" 114 acres in AA, "Burntwood Common" 50 acres in AA. Mentions: Robert Hewett (overseer).
30:318	...
30:319	Nich. Maccubbin (sheriff, AA) summoned: Mary Carroll (AA), Charles Cole (AA), Jane Bell (AA), Col. Samuel Young (AA). Pereg. Ward (sheriff, CE) summoned: Col. Joseph Young, Esq. (CE). Mentions: Zach. Maccubbin (sheriff, AA).
30:320	Petition of John Galloway & Edmund Jenings attorneys-in-fact for Elisabeth Ginn (GB) & William Woodward & Mary Holmes executors of Mary Woodward. Text of answer. Richard Francis, Esq. procurator for John Galloway & Edmund Jenings, Esq. attorneys.
30:321-322	...
30:323	Text of Interrogatories on behalf of William Cumming.
30:324	- Richard Young (clerk, CV), age 40, deposed. - John Lomas (bookkeeper, Annapolis), age 43, deposed.
30:325	Mentions: Mr. William Bates.
30:326	- Charles Cole (merchant, Annapolis), age over 40, deposed.
30:327	- Charles Carroll, Esq. (Annapolis), age 35, deposed. - Mrs. Mary Carroll (widow, Annapolis), age 58, deposed. Mentions: her husband Charles Carroll, Esq. (dec'd).
30:328	- Vachel Denton (merchant, Annapolis), age 40, deposed. Mentions: John Young. - Jane Beall (spinster, AA), age 48, deposed.
30:329	Signed: Jane Bell. - Joseph Young, age 39, deposed. Mentions: his brother John Young who wrote said will, William McCubbin, Robert Hewett,

30:330   Mary Large.
            Text of Interrogatories on behalf of
            Elisabeth Gin, William Woodward, &
            Mary Holmes. Mentions: Sarah
            Garrett (mother of Amos Garrett),
30:331   John Beall, Esq. (AA, dec'd).
            Exhibited letter from Amos Woodward
            to his aunt (N) Ginn. Mentions:
            Amos Garrett died 8 March 1727/8,
30:332   said Amos' mother. Date: 28 March
            1728.
30:333   -   Richard Young (clerk, CV), age
                40, deposed. Mentions: his
                brother John Young who wrote
                said will, said Garrett had a
                mother living in ENG.
            -   John Lomas (bookkeeper,
                Annapolis), age 43, deposed.
30:334   Mentions: John Young (son of
                Col. Samuel Young) who wrote
                said will.
            -   Charles Cole (merchant,
                Annapolis), age over 40,
                deposed.
30:335   Mentions: said Garrett died 8
                March 1727/8, John Beall, Esq.
                (AA, dec'd).
            -   Charles Carroll, (Annapolis),
                age 35 deposed.
30:336   -   Mrs. Mary Carroll (widow,
                Annapolis), age 58, deposed.
                Mentions: said Garrett's mother
                died 2-3 years before his death.
            -   Vachel Denton (merchant,
                Annapolis), age 40, deposed.
30:337   -   Jane Beall (spinster, AA), age
                48, deposed.
30:338   ...
30:339   Text of letter from William Woodward
            to his brother Amos Woodward. Date:
            12 April 1732 at London. Proved by
            oaths of Capt. John Carpenter & Mr.
            John Lomas. Mentions: Capt. Hurt.
            Text of letter from William Woodward
            to his brother Amos Woodward. Date:
            23 June 1732 at London. Proved by
            oaths of Capt. John Carpenter & Mr.
            John Lomas. Mentions: Capt. Peat,
            said William's wife gave birth to a
            boy, Capt. Sinners, Capt. George
            Vuriell,
30:340   Henry Tyrea, Capt. West, Capt.

Court Session: 29 August 1737

30:341
30:342

Davidson & his wife, Capt. Hoxton,
Capt. Watts.
...
Ruling: plaintiff. LoA to said
Achsah Woodward is declared null &
void. At the request of Edmund
Jenings, Esq., transcripts from AA
Co. Court Records were annexed.
Mentions: land purchased by Amos
Garrett from:
- Richard Rawlings & his wife
  Deborah pt. "Long Venture" 150
  acres on 26 May 1715.
- John Wood "Cockey's Addition"
  130 acres on 14 June 1715.
- Joseph Winstanley & his wife
  Elisabeth Lot #64 on 9 July
  1715.
- William Philip Reas Lot #13,
  except for part sold to James
  Carroll, on 4 October 1715.

30:343
- Timothy Swallyivant & his wife
  Catherine "Iniskern" 133 acres
  on 5 March 1715.
- Susannah Johnson (alias Susannah
  Raymond) "Friends Choice" 100
  acres, "Sheperds Range" 100
  acres, "Marsh's Forest" 60 acres
  on 17 August 1716.
- Hannah Eager "Feethold" 135
  acres, "Deep Creek Neck" 50
  acres on 5 October 1716.
- John Brown 1/2 "Ranters Ridge"
  207.5 acres on 18 April 1717.
- Thomas Jobson "Smith's Range"
  112 acres, "Hopkins Forbearance"
  142 acres, "Little Piney Next"
  80 acres on 22 March 1716.
- Charles Carroll "Brownstone" 100
  acres, "Brown & Clark" 50 acres,
  "Hopewell" 30 acres,
  "Middleland" 40 acres, "Tylors
  Lot" 100 acres, "Piney Neck" 100
  acres, "The Contest" 100 acres,
  land of Ann Jobson on 3 July
  1717.
- Timothy Swillyivant & his wife
  Katherine release of equity of
  "Redemption of Iniskern" on 4
  May 1717.
- Benjamin Howard & his wife
  Katherine "Howard's Search" 121

           acres on 12 November 1717.

- Alexander Warfield "Peirpoints Lot" 207 acres on 7 October 1719.
- Hannah Eager release of "Foothold" & "Deep Creek" on 10 December 1719.
- Peter Galloway & his wife Elisabeth Lot #98 on 5 March 1719.
- Robert Cross & his wife Hannah "Friendship" 160 acres on 14 April 1720.
- Robert Thomas Lot #23 on 9 November 1720.
- William Rowles & his wife Ann pt. "Swann Neck" 125 acres, land of John Smith bought of William Crouch on 14 January 1720.
- Henry Merreday & his wife Sarah pt. "Broad Creek" 100 acres, "Swan Cove" 50 acres on 11 November 1721.
- Alexander Smart & his wife Margaret Lot #74 on 28 October 1721.
- Michael Jenifer & his wife Mary pt. "Roper Gray" 200 acres on 25 June 1722.
- Thomas Rencher attorney for Robert Edny & his wife Ann "Cuckholdspoint" 100 acres on 3 August 1722.
- Henry Sewell & his wife Mary "Sewells Fancy" 300 acres on 15 September 1722.
- John Buckingham & his wife Hannah "Baker's Delight" 40 acres, "Lunns Addition" 55 acres on 4 April 1723.
- Dr. Alexander Fraser pt. Lot #74 on 13 April 1723.
- Richard Young Lot #100 on 6 May 1724.
- Rachel Freeborn "Millford" 400 acres on 31 August 1726.
- William Grimes & his wife Ann release of "Sheperds Grove" & "Sheperds Chance" 300 acres on 20 November 1727.

Lands conveyed by said Garrett to:
- Sarah Stephens pt. "Brown's

30:344

Court Session: 29 August 1737

> > Increase" 100 acres on 10 August
> > 1716.
> > - John Brown pt. of several
> >   tracts, "Clink" 200 acres on 5
> >   June 1719.
> > - Thomas Bordley, Esq. pt.
> >   "Providence".

Court Session: 1737

30:345 30 August. Exhibited from TA:
- will of Michael Howard, Esq. Also,
  renunciation of Daniel Dulany, Esq.
  & Walter Carmichaell executors.

31 August. Mr. Thomas Aisquith (SM) to
examine accounts of:
- John Dossey & his wife Ann
  administratrix of Mary Cooper (SM).

William Robison one of sureties on
estate of James Little (BA) vs. Thomas
Farlow & his wife Elisabeth (late
Elisabeth Little) administratrix of said
James. Sheriff (BA) to summon
defendants to render accounts.

9 September. Kenelm Chezeldine (SM) vs.
estate of Kenelm Chezeldine (SM).
Thomas Boult, one of the witnesses to
said will, deposed regarding said will.

30:346 Exhibited from AA:
- additional accounts of Jerome
  Plummer & his wife Margaret
  administratrix of Henry Child, Jr.

10 September. Exhibited from DO:
- will of Robert Ritchie, constituting
  Walter Dallas executor.

Exhibited from TA:
- bond of Charles Browne administrator
  of Michael Howard, Esq. Sureties:
  William Cumming (Annapolis), Michael
  Coulter (CE). Date: 10 September
  1732.

Court Session: 13 September 1737

Docket:
- Sheriff (SO) to summon John Whaley &

Page 74

his wife widow of John Darby (SO) to take LoA.

- Jacob Hindman (sheriff, DO) to summon Somfort Hopkins widow of John Hopkins (DO) to take LoA. NEI.
- W.C. for John Phillips & his wife Ann (PG) vs. B.Y. for Nicholas Downing & his wife Elisabeth executrix of John Clarvo. Libel, answer, general replication, rejoynder.

30:347 Sheriff (KE) to render attachment to Mary Raisins executrix of Thomas Raisins (KE) to take LoA.

- William Thomas (TA) vs. Richard Giles one of witnesses to will of Loftis Bowdle (TA). J. Goldsborough (sheriff, TA) to render attachment to defendant to prove said will. Exhibited "cepi corpus". Said Giles proved said will. Discontinued.
- Coroners (SO) to render attachment to sheriff (SO) for not returning summons to John Whaley.
- Sheriff (AA) to summon (N) Austin wife of Henry Austin late widow of William Pearce (AA) to take LoA.
- Jacob Hindman (sheriff, DO) to summon Joseph Ennalls executor of William Ennalls (DO) to render additional accounts.
- Francis Hall (PG) vs. Charles Digges (PG) administrator of Nicholas Lowe (SM). Richard Lee (sheriff, PG) to render attachment to defendant to render additional accounts.

30:348 Said Digges deposed that there are vouchers from ENG & other vouchers that he has not been able to procure. Also, he has paid the representatives of said dec'd, their full share. Discontinued.

- Michael Fletcher (TA) vs. Risdon Bozman (TA) executor of Mary Knowles (QA). Sheriff (TA) to summon defendant to prove said will. Said Bozman has proved said will. Discontinued.
- W.C. for Roger Peele for self & his 2 brothers Robert & Samuel Peele (AA) vs. E.J. for William Peele

administrator of Samuel & Robert Peele. Libel, answer Witnesses to be examined: Thomas Burton, Ichabod Plaisted, John Higginson, Samuel Barnard, Esq. of Salem in New England.

- Richard Francis, Esq. procurator for Abigail Ryan widow of Cornelius Ryan (KE) vs. Edmund Jenings, Esq. procurator for Henry Truelock (KE). Sheriff (KE) to summon defendant to show cause why the will of said dec'd, constituting plaintiff executrix, should not be proved. Defendant exhibited a subsequent will, constituting defendant executor.
- E.J. for Joseph Allen (CH) vs. W.C. for Barbara Allen administratrix of Joseph Allen. Libel, answer.

30:349 • Robert Gordon, Esq. one of sureties on estate of John Cromwell (AA) vs. William Worthington & his wife Hannah executrix of said Cromwell. Sheriff (AA) to summon defendant to render accounts.

- Mr. Edward Fottrell vs. Richard Young & Samuel Young surviving executors of Col. Samuel Young (AA). Sheriff (CV) to summon defendants to render inventory.
- Mr. Henry Wright (PG) one of sureties on estate of Richard Moore (AA) vs. Margaret Moore, Samuel Preston Moore, & Mordecai Moore executors of said Richard. Sheriff (AA) to summon defendants to render accounts.
- William Robison one of sureties on estate of James Little (BA) vs. Thomas Farlow & his wife Elisabeth (late Elisabeth Little) administratrix of said James. William Hammond (sheriff, BA) to summon defendants to render accounts.

Court Session: 1737

30:350   14 September. William Thomas (TA) vs. Richard Giles one of witnesses to will of Loftis Bowdle (TA). Said Giles

Court Session: 1737

deposed.

15 September. Exhibited from AA:
* will of Thomas Hughes, constituting Mary Hughes & Thomas Hughes executors.
* inventory of Justinian Barwell.

Exhibited from DO:
* bond of Walter Dallas executor of Robert Ritchie. Sureties: William Ghiselin (g, Annapolis, AA), Richard Tootell (sadler, Annapolis, AA). Date: 15 September 1737.

16 September. James Earle (g, QA) exhibited:
* bond of Joseph Wickes administrator of George Birch. Sureties: Jacob Winchester, Francis Bright. Date: 23 July 1737.
* bond of Elisabeth Seth executrix of Charles Seth. Sureties: William Coursey, John Emory, Jr. Date: 25 July 1737.
* will of James Gould, constituting Richard Gould executor. Said Richard was granted administration. Sureties: James Brown, Nicholas Broadaway. Date: 29 August 1737.
* will of John Roe, constituting Martha Roe, Thomas Roe, & Edward Roe executors. Said executors were granted administration. Sureties: James Barwick, Henry Covington. Date: 15 August 1737.
* will of Mary Knowles, constituting Risdon Bozman executor. Said Bozman was granted administration. Sureties: William Price, Matthew Mason. Date: 24 August 1737.
* inventory & LoD of James Thomasman.
* inventory of George Burch.
* inventory of Robert Pickering.
* inventory of Richard Wise.
* inventory of John Leonard, Sr.
* inventory of John Sparkes.
* inventory of Thomas Day.
* accounts of William & John Carman executors of William Carman, Sr.
* accounts of Robert Blunt & his wife Mary executrix of Samuel Wright.

30:351

Page 77

Court Session: 1737

- additional accounts of Benjamin Elliot & his wife Mary executrix of Workman Harris.
- accounts of Margaret Pinder executrix of William Pinder.
- additional accounts of Nathaniel Scott executor of Abraham Oldson.
- accounts of Mary & William Hampton executors of Thomas Hampton.

19 September. Mr. James Earle (QA) to examine accounts of:
- Anna Maria Hemsley administratrix of William Hemsley (QA).
- Esther Baynard, John Baynard, & George Baynard executors of Thomas Baynard (QA).
- William Austin administrator of William Austin (QA). Additional accounts.

Mr. Charles Hynson (KE) to examine accounts of:
- Thomas Mohone executor of John Fanning (KE). Additional accounts.
- Ann Griffith & Jackson Griffith executors of Benjamin Griffith (KE).
- James Price & his wife Sarah executrix of John Reading (KE).
- Elinor Chipley & John Chipley (KE) administrators of William Chipley (DO).

26 September. William Rumsey (g, CE) exhibited:
- bond of Sarah Bass administratrix of John Bass. Sureties: Thomas Johnson, Sr., Powell Poleson. Date: 15 June 1737.
- **30:352** bond of John Winterbury administrator of Henry Register. Sureties: James Wroth, Francis Bonner. Date: 18 June 1737.
- will of Peter Numbers, constituting Catherine Numbers executrix. Said Catherine was granted administration. Sureties: Robert Money, Sr., James Wroth. Date: 27 June 1737.
- bond of Mary Price administratrix of Hyland Price. Sureties: Thomas Pearce, John Sutton. Date: 29

Page 78

August 1737.
- will of William Pennington, constituting Mary Pennington executrix.
- will of Henry Johnson.
- inventory of John Hukill.
- inventory of Joseph King.
- inventory & LoD of Robert Pennington.
- inventory, LoD & additional inventory of Dominick Carroll.
- inventory of John Bass.
- accounts of John Kankey & Edward Johnson administrators of Thomas Wamsley.
- accounts of John Underhill & his wife Ann administratrix of Robert Dutton.
- accounts of Laurence Galshiott & Cornelius Cook executors of James McCabe.
- accounts of Peter Bowyer & his wife Hester executrix of John Lewis.
- accounts of John Bavington administrator of Thomas Bavington.
- accounts of Sarah Othoson administratrix of Garrett Othoson.
- accounts of Joseph Rich administrator of Daniel Jobson.

29 September. Samuel Hanson (g, CH) exhibited:
- codicil of John Watts to will made in ENG. Also, bond of Andrew Scott administrator. Sureties: George Scott (PG), Charles Neale (CH). Date: 7 September 1736.
- inventory of Zachariah Wade.

30:353 Charles Hynson (g, KE) exhibited:
- will of Robert Mansfield, constituting Robert Mansfield & Samuel Mansfield executors. Said executors were granted administration. Sureties: Philip Hudson, William Walls. Date: 7 May 1737.
- will of John Johnson, constituting Mary Johnson executrix. Also, widow's election. Said Mary was granted administration. Sureties: Augustine Thompson (QA), Thomas

Smyth (KE). Date: 28 May 1737.
- will of William Blakistion, constituting Ann Blakiston executrix. Also, widow's election. Said Ann was granted administration. Sureties: Ebenezar Blakiston, James Ringgold. Date: 28 May 1737.
- bond of Mary Rasin executrix of Thomas Rasin. Sureties: William Trew, Daniel Perkins. Date: 11 June 1737.
- bond of Mary Sewell administratrix of Rev. Mr. Richard Sewell. Sureties: Daniel Perkins, Joseph Gleaves. Date: 1 August 1737. Also, renunciation of P. Kennard. Date: 29 July 1737.
- bond of James Moore & Lambert Wilmer executors of Simon Wilmer. Sureties: James Smith, Charles Hynson. Date: 6 September 1737.
- inventory of William Comegys.
- inventory & LoD of James Norman.
- inventory of Alexander Johnson.
- inventory & LoD of William Blakiston.
- additional inventory of David Thomas.
- inventory & LoD of Robert Mansfield.
- inventory of Joseph Everett.
- inventory of Thomas Rasin.
- inventory of John Inch.
- accounts of William Massey & his wife Elisabeth administratrix of Archibald Cragh.
- additional accounts of Robert Green administrator of Richard Davis.
- accounts of David Hall executor of William Carter.
- accounts of Ann Thomas administratrix of David Thomas.
- **30:354** accounts of Benjamin Parsons executor of Margaret Arano.
- accounts of Hannah Hosier executrix of Henry Hosier.
- accounts of Ann Blakiston executrix of William Blakistion.
- accounts of Elinor Gooding executrix of Samuel Gooding.

3 October. Humphrey Wells Stokes (g, BA) exhibited:

Court Session: 1737

- bond of Elisabeth Lloyd executrix of Theophilus Jones. Sureties: John Lloyd (husband of said Elisabeth), Thomas Coale, William Dallam. Date: 29 September 1737.
- bond of Margaret Painter administratrix of Edward Painter. Sureties: Ford Barnes, Thomas Mitchell, Sr. Date: 26 August 1737.
- will of John Hall, Esq., constituting Edward Hall, John Hall, & Parker Hall executors.
- inventory of Evan Miles.
- accounts of John Serjent & his wife Elisabeth administrators of Thomas Gostwick.
- accounts of Josias Middlemore executor of Richard Jenkins.

6 October. Peter Dent (g, PG) exhibited:
- bond of Thomas Dorsett & John Smith administrators of James Hoy. Sureties: Walter Brooke, Thomas Hodgkin. Also, renunciation of Tabitha Hoye, recommending Mr. Thomas Dorsett & John Smith. Date: 30 September 1737.
- will of Sarah Clagett, constituting Mary Clagett executrix.
- 2nd additional accounts of Richard Marsham Waring executor of Marsham Waring.
- accounts of Sarah Moore administratrix of Henry Moore, on behalf of Henry Moore (minor) executor.

30:355 7 October. Capt. John Pitt (DO) exhibited:
- bond of Rebecca Wall administratrix of Thomas Wall. Sureties: Noah Pearson, James Madsley. Date: 10 August 1737.
- will of James Paulson, constituting Ann Paulson executrix. Said Ann was granted administration. Sureties: Thomas Cooke, Jr., Charles Beckwith. Date: 10 August 1737.
- inventory of John Grainger.
- inventory of William Thomas.
- inventory of John Summers.

- inventory of John Morriston.
- accounts of William Harper executor of Samuel Harper.
- accounts of Thomas Diass administrator of Henry Diass.
- 1st additional accounts of John Cannon administrator of Andrew Majors.
- accounts of Capt. Bartholomew Ennalls administrator of John Morriston.

11 October. Exhibited from AA:
- inventory of Peter Shipley.
- will of John Ashman. Also, renunciation of executors. Also, bond of George Ashman & John Ashman administrators. Sureties: John Willmott (BA), William Cromwell (AA), John Cromwell (AA), John Bailey (BA). Date: 11 October 1737.

13 October. Exhibited from BA:
- bond of Rachel Darnell executrix of Charles Darnell. Sureties (AA): John Orrick, William Worthington, Jr., Thomas Henderson, Josiah Slade. Date: 13 October 1737.

14 October. Exhibited from PG:
- accounts of Thomas Lancaster administrator of Isaac Lansdale.

17 October. Exhibited from BA:
- accounts of Charles Ridgely executor of Richard Huett.

30:356 Thomas Aisquith (g, SM) exhibited:
- bond of Justinian Teneson administrator of William Gibson. Sureties: Thomas Shanks, John Boult. Date: 21 September 1737.
- bond of Thomas Skillirn administrator of John Magrah. Sureties: Daniel Burney, Peter Garrett. Date: 21 September 1737.
- bond of Robert Gordon administrator of Arthur Hamilton (Liverpoole). Sureties: Richard Cooper, James Mills. Date: 2 August 1737.
- inventory & LoD of Thomas McWilliams.

Court Session: 1737
- inventory of Charles Slye.
- inventory of John Bailey.
- inventory & LoD of Nicholas Sewall.
- inventory & LoD of Robert Wiseman.
- inventory & LoD of William Asbeston.
- accounts of John Manning & his wife Victorious administratrix of William Larrance.
- accounts of Catherine Peney administratrix of John Peney.
- additional accounts of Catherine Waughop & James Waughop executors of Thomas Waughop.

21 October. Exhibited from PG:
- 3rd additional accounts of Richard Marsham Waring executor of Marsham Waring.

Mr. Tench Francis (TA) to examine accounts of:
- Rachel Wrightson administratrix of John Wrightson (TA).

22 October. Exhibited from QA:
- inventory of John Knowles.

30:357 Tench Francis (g, TA) exhibited:
- additional inventory & LoD of James Powell.
- inventory of John Hendrick.
- additional inventory & LoD of William Dobson.
- inventory & LoD of John Mulliken.
- inventory, LoD, & additional inventory of Solomon Horney.
- accounts of Isaac Dobson & his wife Hannah administratrix of James Powell.
- accounts of John Reynolds administrator of Mary Cooper.
- accounts of Thomas Martin administrator of Thomas Martin.
- additional accounts of Isaac Dobson & Anne Erwin executors of William Dobson.
- accounts of Elisabeth Rathell executrix of John Rathell.
- accounts of Alexander Jordan & his wife Margaret & James Horney executors of James Horney executor of Solomon Horney.

James Smith, Robert Roberts, & Joseph Nicholson, as sureties on estate of Richard Normansell (KE), were granted administration on said estate. James Harris, Esq. (KE) to administer oath.

24 October. Exhibited from DO:
• 2nd additional accounts of Elisabeth Jarrard executrix of James Jarrard.

Exhibited from PG:
• bond of Henry Enoch administrator of Samuel Finnly. Sureties: John Upton, John Perren. Date: 24 October 1737.

Gabriel Parker (g, CV) exhibited:
• inventory of William Ladyman.
• inventory of Rev. Jonathon Cay.
• accounts of Richard Roberts executor of Robert Roberts.
30:358 • accounts of Joshan Mannyng executrix of Thomas Mannyng.
• accounts of Ann Fowlar administratrix of John Fowlar.
• accounts of Elinor Ellt & Rebecca Ellt executrices of Elisabeth Turner.
• accounts of John Brome, Jr. administrator of Henry Brome.
• accounts of James Dodson & Joseph Wooden administrators of John Dodson.
• accounts of Dorothy Cay executrix of Rev. Jonathon Cay.

Mr. Charles Hynson (KE) to examine accounts of:
• Hannah Falconar administratrix of Gilbert Falconar (KE).
• Edward Comegys, executor of William Comegys (KE).
• Katherine Everett executrix of Joseph Everett (KE).

26 October. Mr. Samuel Hanson (CH) to examine accounts of:
• Percival Pherson & his wife Ruth administratrix of Fra. Brown (CH).
• William Clary & his wife Mary administratrix of Robert King (CH).
• Elisabeth Mudd administratrix of

Court Session: 1737

Henry Mudd (CH).
* Thomas Middleton & his wife Susanna
executrix of George Brett (CH).
* Anne Gardiner executrix of Francis
Gardiner (CH). Additional accounts.

Capt. John Pitt (DO) to examine
accounts of:
* Sarah Kirk executrix of John Kirk
(DO). Additional accounts.
* Thomas Woolford & Henry Trippe
administrators of Rev. Thomas
Thompson (DO).

Mr. James Earle (QA) to examine
accounts of:
* Nicholas Broadaway administrator of
William Edwards (QA).
* Mary Kemp administratrix of Richard
Kemp (QA).

30:359 Mr. William Rumsey (CE) to examine
accounts of:
* Mary Carroll administratrix of
Dominick Carroll (CE).
* Peter Bouchelle & Sluyter Bouchelle
executors of Peter Bouchelle (CE).

Mr. Thomas Aisquith (SM) to examine
accounts of:
* George Aisquith surviving
administrator of John Young (SM).
* Edward Oriel & his wife Elenor
administratrix of Jacob Morrice
(SM).
* Dorothy Leigh executrix of John
Leigh

Mr. Peter Dent (PG) to examine accounts
of:
* William Eilbeck executor of John
Edgar (PG).
* Elinor Deveron executrix of William
Deveron (PG).

Mr. Tench Francis (TA) to examine
accounts of:
* William Sharpe & Solomon Sharpe
executors of Peter Sharpe (TA).
* Robert Biglands administrator of
Richard Biglands (TA).
* Lambert Shield administrator of

Court Session: 1737

William Shield (TA).

27 October. Exhibited from AA:
* inventory of Robert Freshwater.

28 October. Exhibited from CE:
* inventory of Joseph Young, Esq., in AA.

Exhibited from AA:
* inventory of Samuel Young, Esq., in AA & BA. Also, additional inventory in BA.

Mr. Humphrey Wells Stokes (BA) to examine accounts of:
* William Hughes & his wife Hannah administratrix of Joseph Bankson (BA).

30:360 Mr. Charles Hynson (KE) to examine additional accounts of:
* George Garnett executor of Thomas Garnett (KE).

Risdon Bozman executor of John Knowles (QA) vs. Elisabeth Millington (QA). Sheriff (QA) to summon defendant to show cause why she conceals estate of dec'd.

29 October. John Mathews & his wife Ann, John Hall & his wife Hannah, & James Maxwell vs. William Savory administrator dbn of Col. James Maxwell (BA) & administrator of James Maxwell (BA). Plaintiff Ann Mathews is a daughter of said Col. Plaintiff Hannah Hall is the widow & residuary legatee of Asael Maxwell (BA) one of sons of said Col. Plaintiff James Maxwell is another son of said Col. Sheriff (BA) to summon defendant to render answer.

Mr. Humphrey Wells Stokes (BA) to examine accounts of:
* John Chinoworth, Sr. & his wife Jane administratrix of William Wood, Sr. (BA).

1 November. Peter Dent (g, PG) exhibited:
* will of Clement Brooke, constituting

Court Session: 1737

Jane Brooke executrix. Said Jane
was granted administration.
Sureties: Clement Sewall (SM),
William Digges, Sr. (PG). Date: 5
October 1737.
* additional accounts of Mary Reiley
executrix of Bryan Reiley.

Mr. Peter Dent (PG) to examine accounts
of:
* John Stoddart administrator of
William Stoddart (PG).
* Thomas Marshall, Sr. executor of
William Marshall (PG). Additional
accounts.

2 November. Exhibited from AA:
* accounts of Dr. Charles Carroll
administrator of Justinian Barwell.

30:361 5 November. Sheriff (AA) to summon Jane
Linthicum wife of Gideon Linthicum
executrix of John Ford (AA) to take LoA.

Court Session: 8 November 1737

Docket:
* sheriff (SO) to summon John Whaley &
his wife widow of John Darby (SO) to
take LoA.
* sheriff (DO) to summon Comfort
Hopkins widow of John Hopkins (DO)
to take LoA.
* W.C. for John Phillips & his wife
Ann (PG) vs. B.Y. for Nicholas
Downing & his wife Elisabeth
executrix of John Clarvo. Libel,
answer, general replication,
rejoynder.
* sheriff (KE) to render attachment to
Mary Rasin executrix of Thomas Rasin
(KE) to take LoA. Said Mary has
taken LoA. Discontinued.
* coroners (SO) to render attachment
to sheriff (SO). Discontinued.
30:362 * Sheriff (AA) to summon (A) Austin
wife of Henry Austin late widow of
William Pearce (AA) to take LoA.
* sheriff (DO) to summon Joseph
Ennalls executor of William Ennalls
(DO) to render additional accounts.
* W.C. for Roger Peele for self & his

Court Session: 8 November 1737

2 brothers Robert & Samuel Peele
(AA) vs. E.J. for William Peele
administrator of Samuel & Robert
Peele. Libel, answer.

- Abigail Ryan executrix of Cornelius
Ryan (KE) vs. Edmund Jenings,
procurator for Henry Truelock (KE).
Sheriff (KE) to summon defendant to
show cause why said will should not
be proved. Defendant exhibited a
subsequent will, constituting
defendant executor. Plaintiff given
notice.

- E.J. for Joseph Allen (CH) vs. W.C.
for Barbara Allen administratrix of
Joseph Allen. Libel, answer,
general replication.

- Robert Gordon, Esq. one of sureties
on estate of John Cromwell (AA) vs.
William Worthington & his wife
Hannah executrix of said Cromwell.
Zach. Maccubbin (sheriff, AA) to
summon defendants to render
accounts.

30:363 • Mr. Edward Fottrell vs. Richard
Young & Samuel Young surviving
executors of Col. Samuel Young
(AA). Sheriff (CV) to summon
defendants to render inventory.
Struck off.

- Mr. Henry Wright (PG) one of
sureties on estate of Richard Moore
(AA) vs. Margaret Moore, Samuel
Preston Moore, & Mordecai Moore
executors of said dec'd. Zach.
Maccubbin (sheriff, AA) to summon
defendants to render accounts.

- William Robison one of sureties on
estate of John Little (BA) vs.
Thomas Farlow & his wife Elisabeth
(late Elisabeth Little)
administratrix of said dec'd.
Sheriff (BA) to summon defendants to
render accounts.

- Risdon Bozman executor of John
Knowles (QA) vs. Elisabeth
Millington (QA). R. N. Wright
(sheriff, QA) to summond defendant
to show cause why she conceals
estate of dec'd.

30:364 NEI. Sheriff (TA) to summon said
Millington as Elisabeth Loockerman

Page 88

Court Session: 8 November 1737

wife of Jacob Loockerman (TA).
- E.J. for James Maxwell et.al. (BA)
  vs. Richard Francis, Esq.
  procurator for William Savory
  administrator dbn of Col. James
  Maxwell & administrator of James
  Maxwell. Libel. W. Hammond
  (sheriff, BA) to summon defendant to
  render answer.
- Zach. Maccubbin (sheriff, AA) to
  summon Jane Linthicum wife of Gideon
  Linthicum executrix of John Ford
  (AA) to take LoA.

Court Session: 1737

30:365 8 November. Exhibited from DO:
- 2nd additional accounts of Jacob
  Loockerman administrator dbn of Col.
  Jacob Loockerman.

10 November. Exhibited from AA:
- accounts of Henry Howard, Ephraim
  Howard, & Cornelius Howard executors
  of Joseph Howard.
- inventory of Mary Richardson.

11 November. Exhibited from AA:
- bond of Mary Hughes executrix of
  Thomas Hughes. Sureties: William
  Hammond (BA), Thomas Hughes (AA).
  Also, renunciation of Thomas Hughes
  (AA) one of executors. Date: 11
  November 1737. Witness: William
  Rogers.

12 November. Mr. James Earle (QA) to
examine accounts of:
- Albert Johnson administrator of
  Henry Johnson (QA).

Exhibited from AA:
- accounts of Edward Nicholls & his
  wife Mary administratrix of Joseph
  White.

14 November. Exhibited from AA:
- bond of John Cockey executor of Col.
  Thomas Cockey. Sureties: Luke
  Stansbury (BA), Mordecai Hammond
  (AA). Date: 14 November 1737.
- additional inventory of Pleasance

Court Session: 1737

Wainwright.
• accounts of James Moore & his wife
  Mary administratrix of Robert
  Freshwater.

30:366 Exhibited from CE:
• additional accounts of William Ward
  executor of John Kimber.

15 November. Capt. John Prichard &
William Wilkins to appraise estate of
Philip Smith in AA.

16 November. Exhibited from AA:
• will of Robert Reynolds,
  constituting John Reynolds & William
  Reynolds executors.

17 November. Exhibited from AA:
• bond of John Reynolds & William
  Reynolds executors of Robert
  Reynolds. Sureties: Patrick Creagh,
  Robert McLeod (Annapolis). Date: 17
  November 1732.

18 November. William Rumsey (g, CE)
exhibited:
• will of John Bass, constituting
  Sarah Bass & Joseph Bass executors.
  Said Sarah & Joseph were granted
  administration. Surety: Edward
  Jackson. Date: 10 November 1737.
• will of Ephraim Hamm, constituting
  Elisabeth Hamm & Robert Veazey
  executors.
• inventory of Henry Register.
• inventory of Peter Numbers.
• additional accounts of Joshua George
  one of administrators of Capt.
  James Moody.
• accounts of Samuel Young executor of
  John Johnson.

21 November. Dr. George Buchanan (BA)
& Mr. John Risteau (BA) to appraise
estate of Col. Thomas Cockey in BA.

24 November. Charles Hynson (g, KE)
exhibited:
• bond of Elisabeth Hebron
  administratrix of John Hebron.
  Sureties: Thomas Hebron, John

30:367 •

Redgrave. Date: 12 November 1737.
bond of David Crane administrator of
Daniel Madden. Sureties: George
Garnett, John Stevenson. Date: 12
November 1737.
• will of Mary West. Also, bond of
George Garnett administrator.
Sureties: Christopher Bateman, David
Crane. Date: 12 November 1737.
• will of Simon Wilmer, constituting
James Moore & Lambert Wilmer
executors.
• will of John Wright, constituting
Mary Wright executrix.
• will of Elias Ringgold, constituting
Mary Ringgold executrix.
• inventory & LoD of John Johnson.
• additional inventory of William
Comegys.
• inventory & LoD of Rebecca Evans.
• additional accounts of Thomas Hynson
& William Hynson executors of
Margaret Murfey.
• 3rd additional accounts of James
Stout & his wife Ann administrators
dbn of St. Leger Codd, Esq.

28 November. Gabriel Parker (g, CV)
exhibited:
• inventory of Henry Cox.

1 December. Michael Macnemara (g, AA)
exhibited:
• bond of George Chocke administrator
of John Chocke. Sureties: David
Weems, John Elliot Browne. Date: 6
May 1736.
• will of Richard Galloway,
constituting Sarah Galloway &
Richard Galloway executors. Said
executors were granted
administration. Sureties: William
Richardson, Sr., John Galloway,
Joseph Galloway. Date: 31 December
1737.
• will of Samuel Chew, Sr. Also,
renunciation of executors. Also,
bond of Samuel Chew & Philip Thomas
administrators. Sureties: Samuel
Chew (chirurgeon), Joseph Cowman.
Date: 31 December 1736.
• bond of Sarah Smith administratrix

Court Session: 1737

of John Smith. Sureties: Charles
Carroll, William Stevenson. Date:
30 March 1737.

30:368
- bond of Nicholas Norman & Augustine
Randall administrators of John Kerr.
Sureties: John Colston, Joseph
Cowman. Date: 10 August 1737.
- bond of Mary Gary administratrix of
Everett Gary. Sureties: Samuel
Whitehead, Robert Tillotson. Date:
24 April 1736.
- will of John Ford, constituting Jane
Ford executrix.
- will of Col. Thomas Cockey,
constituting John Cockey executor.
- inventory of John Rakestraw.
- inventory & LoD of William Ruley.
- inventory of William Williamson.
- inventory of Elisabeth Larkin.
- inventory of Peter Robinson.
- inventory of William Monroe.
- inventory of John Smith.
- inventory of Capt. John Cromwell.
- inventory & Lod of Everard Gary.
- inventory & additional inventory of
Maj. Josias Towgood.
- inventory & LoD of Jane Saunders.

Gabriel Parker (g, CV) exhibited:
- bond of John Conwell & Richard
Conwell administrators of Elisabeth
Conwell. Sureties: Daniel Talbott,
Richard Talbott. Date: 29 October
1737.
- inventory of William Day.

2 December. Michael Macnemara (g, AA)
exhibited:
- inventory of Dr. David Mercer.
- inventory of Lawrence Geary.

30:369 James Earle (g, QA) exhibited:
- bond of Peter Duhamell & Rachel
Duhamell administrators of Ann
Denney. Sureties: Matthew Dockery,
John Tucker. Date: 8 October 1737.
- bond of Esther Williams
administratrix of Christopher
Williams. Sureties: John Scotten,
Richard Scotten, James Cassey.
Date: 21 November 1737.
- bond of Alice Robinson

Court Session: 1737

administratrix of Thomas Robinson.
Sureties: Thomas Walters, William
Emory. Date: 22 November 1737.
- will of Charles Vanderford,
  constituting Vincent Vanderford
  executor.
- will of John Leonard, constituting
  John Leonard executor.
- additional inventory & LoD of Henry
  Johnson.
- additional inventory of James
  McClean.
- inventory & LoD of John Roe.
- inventory & LoD of Thomas Poole.
- accounts of Sarah Chetham executrix
  of Edward Chetham.
- accounts of Ann McClean executrix of
  James McClean.
- accounts of Daniel Griffith
  administrator of Thomas Barber.

3 December. Tench Francis (g, TA)
exhibited:
- bond of Alice Higgins administratrix
  of James Higgins. Sureties: Thomas
  Bruff, John Reynolds. Date: 31
  October 1737.
- will of Francis Sherwood,
  constituting John Sherwood & Francis
  Sherwood executors. Said executors
  were granted administration.
  Sureties: Joseph Hopkins, Robert
  Harrison. Date: 31 October 1737.
- inventory & LoD of John Quinn.
- accounts of Elisabeth Collisson
  executrix of George Collisson.

30:370 6 December. Capt. John Pitt (DO)
exhibited:
- bond of Isaac Richardson
  administrator of Solomon Richardson.
  Surety: Joseph Allford. Date: 24
  October 1737.
- bond of Charles Nutter administrator
  of Charles Nutter. Sureties: John
  Brown 2nd, Phillip Recards. Date:
  11 November 1737.
- will of Richard Willis. Also, bond
  of Mary wife of Hugh Rimmar
  executrix. Sureties: Edward Newton,
  Thomas Canner. Date: 19 November
  1737.

- inventory & LoD of William Laton.
- inventory & LoD of Thomas Courson.
- inventory & LoD of James Paulson.
- 1st additional accounts of Joseph Allford & his wife Margaret executors of Joseph Nicholls.
- accounts of Edward Wright administrator of Edward Wright.
- accounts of John Stewart administrator of Michael Mackormick.

Exhibited from AA:
- additional accounts of Dr. Charles Carroll administrator of Justinian Barwell.

10 December. Samuel Hanson (g, CH) exhibited:
- will of Randolph Morris, constituting Elisabeth Morris & Richard Johns executors. Said executors were granted administration. Sureties: Charles Somersett Smith, John Estep. Date: 25 October 1737.
- inventory of William Whitter.
- inventory of Eleonar Sanders.
- accounts of Eleanor Hunter administratrix of John Glashon.
- accounts of John Craen executor of John Craen.

30:371 13 December. Mr. Samuel Hanson (CH) to examine accounts of:
- Meverill Hulse & his wife Elisabeth & John Moran executors of Gabriel Moran (CH).

Exhibited from AA:
- bond of Samuel Preston Moore administrator of George Delap. Sureties: Margaret Moore, Mordecai Moore. Date: 5 December 1737.

14 December. Exhibited from AA:
- will of Elisabeth Lamb, constituting Nicholas Watkins executor. Said Watkins was granted administration. Sureties: Samuel Smith, John Watkins. Date: 14 December 1737.

29 December. Samuel Hanson (g, CH)
exhibited:
- bond of Michael Hyns Roby
administrator of Peter Roby.
Sureties: Francis Ware, Alexander
McPherson. Date: 21 December 1737.
- bond of Sarah Miller executrix of
Jacob Miller. Sureties: John
Marten, Barton Hungerford. Date: 1
December 1737.
- will of William Thorn, constituting
Isaac Shemwell executor. Said
Shemwell was granted administration.
Sureties: Thomas Birch, James Thorn.
Date: 15 December 1737.
- accounts of William Clary & his wife
Mary administratrix of Robert King.
- accounts of Thomas Middleton & his
wife Susanna executrix of George
Brett.
- additional accounts of Anne Gardiner
executrix of Francis Gardiner.
- accounts of Elisabeth Mudd executrix
of Henry Mudd.

30 December. Mr. William Rumsey (CE)
to examine accounts of:
- Joseph Wood one of securities on
estate of Samuel Lowman (CE), by
Letitia his widow & administratrix
dbn of said Lowman.
- said Letitia Lowman on estate of
Samuel Lowman (CE).
- said Wood on estate of said Lowman
(CE).
30:372 - Joseph Wood administrator of Letitia
Lowman (CE).

Mr. James Earle (QA) to examine
accounts of:
- John Walker executor of Daniel
Walker (QA).
- William Joyner executor of John
Roberts (QA).
- Trustram Thomas 3rd & his wife Jane
administratrix of John Smith (QA).
- Lylly Burroughs administratrix of
William Burroughs, Jr. (QA).
- John Alley, Jr. administrator of
Thomas Richardson (QA).

Mr. Tench Francis (TA) to examine accounts of:
• John Carslake administrator dbn of Solomon Horney who married Jane widow & executrix of John Kersey (TA).

Humphrey Wells Stokes (BA) to examine accounts of:
• Patrick Lynch administrator of Jonas Hewling (BA).

Peter Dent (PG) to examine accounts of:
• Thomas Clarkson surviving executor of William Clarkson (PG).
• Ann Jones executrix of John Jones (PG).

29 November. Risdon Bozman administrator of John Knowles (QA) vs. Elisabeth Loockerman (late Elisabeth Millington) wife of Jacob Loockerman (TA). Sheriff (QA) to summon Sarah Cooper wife of William Cooper & Francis Stevens to testify concerning defendant's concealment of effects of said dec'd.

30 December. Christopher Gardiner (AA) vs. Lloyd Harris administrator dbn of Christopher Gardiner (BA). Sheriff (BA) to summon defendant

30:373 to render accounts.

31 December. Nehemiah King (g, SO) exhibited:
• bond of Elisabeth Dickenson administratrix of James Dickenson. Sureties: James Baker, George Layfield. Date: 16 November 1737.
• will of Godfrey Sprogle. Also, bond of Edmund Crapper administrator. Sureties: Thomas Tull, Sr., Charles Whaley. Date: 17 December 1737.
• will of Joseph Hall, constituting George Howard executor. Said Howard was granted administration. Sureties: Robert Wood, Nehemiah Howard. Date: 12 November 1737.
• will of Gabriel Cooper, constituting Thomas Cooper executor. Said Thomas was granted administration.

Court Session: 1737

Sureties: James Tulley, William
Sherreden. Date: 19 July 1737.
- will of Richard Rycroft. Sarah
Hooper, Col. Thomas Maxwell, & Maj.
Edward Parres were appointed
executors.
- inventory of John Townsend.
- inventory of Richard Hill.
- inventory of Walter Taylor.
- inventory of Joy Hobbs.
- inventory & LoD of Teague Donohoe.
- inventory of John Williams.
- inventory of Thomas Handy.
- 2nd accounts of Stephen Odear, Jr.
administrator of Stephen Odear, Sr.
- additional accounts of James Mumford
executor of Thomas Mumford.
- accounts of John Horsey
administrator of William Horsey.
- accounts of William Bozman
administrator of William Bozman.
- accounts of Stephen Hopkins
administrator of Jane Hopkins.

3 January. Exhibited from AA:
- 2nd additional accounts of Thomas
Harrison & his wife Dorcas executrix
of Francis Hardisty.

4 January. Exhibited from AA:
- inventory of John Laurence.

30:374 Peter Dent (g, PG) exhibited:
- bond of Ann Clegett executrix of
Thomas Clegett. Sureties: Dr.
Patrick Sim, David Crauford. Date:
23 November 1737.
- bond of Philip Marshment & his wife
Mary executrix of Robert Coots.
Sureties: William Clark, Benjamin
Waringford. Date: 23 November 1737.
- will of Thomas Millstead,
constituting Joanna Millstead
executrix. Also widow's election.
Said Joanna was granted
administration. Sureties: William
Eilbeck, William Tyler. Date: 3
December 1737.
- additional accounts of Mary Clegett
executrix of Capt. Thomas Clegett.
- accounts of Elenor Deveron executrix
of William Deveron.

Court Session: 1737

- accounts of John Stoddart administrator of William Stoddart.

5 January. Exhibited:
- declaration & right of dower. Date: 16 November 1737. Mrs. Elisabeth Cockey widow of Col. Thomas Cockey (AA) refused any legacy from his estate in lieu of satisfaction of her thirds.

William Rumsey (g, CE) exhibited:
- will of John Reynolds, constituting Mary Reynolds & Edward Reynolds executors.
- inventory & LoD of Hyland Price.

Court Session: 10 January 1737

30:375 Docket:
- sheriff (SO) to summon John Whaley & his wife widow of John Darby (SO) to take LoA.
- sheriff (DO) to summon Comfort Hopkins widow of John Hopkins (DO) to take LoA.
- W.C. for John Phillips & his wife Ann (PG) vs. B.Y. for Nicholas Downing & his wife Elisabeth executrix of John Clarvo. Libel, answer, general replication, rejoynder.
- sheriff (AA) to summon (N) Austin wife of Henry Austin late widow of William Pearce (AA) to take LoA. Said (N) Austin relinquished administration. Discontinued.
- sheriff (DO) to summon Joseph Ennalls executor of William Ennalls (DO) to render additional accounts.
30:376 - W.C. for Roger Peele for self & his 2 brothers Robert & Samuel Peele (AA) vs. E.J. for William Peele administrator of Samuel & Robert Peele. Libel, answer.
- Abigail Ryan executrix of Cornelius Ryan (KE) vs. Edmund Jenings, procurator for Henry Truelock (KE). Sheriff (KE) to summon said defendant to show cause why said will should not be proved. Defendant exhibited a subsequent will, constituting

Page 98

defendant executor. Plaintiff given notice.

- E.J. for Joseph Allen (CH) vs. W.C. for Barbara Allen administratrix of Joseph Allen. Libel, answer, general replication.
- Robert Gordon, Esq. one of sureties on estate of John Cromwell (AA) vs. William Worthington & his wife Hannah executrix of said Cromwell. Sheriff (A) to render attachment to defendants to render accounts. Accounts exhibited. Discontinued.
- Mr. Henry Wright (PG) one of sureties on estate of Richard Moore (AA) vs. Margaret Moore, Samuel Preston Moore, & Mordecai Moore executors of said dec'd. Sheriff (AA) to summon defendants to render accounts. Accounts exhibited. Discontinued.

30:377
- William Robison one of sureties on estate of John Little (BA) vs. Thomas Farlow & his wife Elisabeth (late Elisabeth Little) administratrix of said dec'd. Sheriff (BA) to summon defendants to render accounts.
- Risdon Bozman administrator of John Knowles (QA) vs. Elisabeth Loockerman wife of Jacob Loockerman (TA). John Goldsborough (sheriff, TA) to summon defendant to show cause why she conceals effects of estate of dec'd. Exhibited deposition of plaintiff. Said Goldsborough exhibited that the defendant declared that she would not come over to appear. Date: 10 January 1737.
- E.J. for James Maxwell et.al. (BA) vs. Richard Francis, Esq. procurator for William Savory administrator dbn of Col. James Maxwell & administrator of James Maxwell. Libel.
- sheriff (AA) to render attachment to Jane Linthicum wife of Gideon Linthicum widow & executrix of John Ford (AA) to take LoA. Said Jane relinquished administration,

30:378 recommending Mr. Richard Snowden.

Court Session: 10 January 1737

> Discontinued.
> - R. N. Wright (sheriff, QA) to summon Sarah Cooper wife of William Cooper (QA) & Francis Stevens (QA) to testify regarding Elisabeth Loockerman (late Elisabeth Millington) wife of Jacob Loockerman (TA) concealment of effects of John Knowles, at request of Risdon Bozman administrator. Said Sarah Cooper & Francis Stevens deposed. Discontinued.
> - William Savory administrator dbn of Col. James Maxwell (BA) vs. Roger Matthews (BA) & Hannah Hall wife of John Hall (BA). Sheriff (BA) to summon defendants to show cause why they conceal effects of dec'd.
> - Risdon Bozman administrator of John Knowles (QA) vs. Elisabeth Loockerman wife of Jacob Loockerman (TA).

Court Session: 1737

30:379 10 January. Mr. Samuel Hanson (CH) to examine accounts of:
- John Wheeler administrator of Thomas Wheeler (CH).

11 January. Risdon Bozman administrator of John Knowles (QA) vs. Elisabeth Loockerman (late Elisabeth Millington) wife of Jacob Loockerman. Sheriff (TA) to summon Margaret Callawhan (TA), Grace Millington wife of Oliver Millington (TA), Frances Camperson (TA), & Jacob Loockerman (TA) to testify regarding defendant's concealment of effects of dec'd. Sheriff (TA) to summon Jannet Moore (QA) to testify regarding defendant's concealment of effects of dec'd.

William Ghiselin (AA) & Richard Tootell (AA) to appraise estate of Sarah Crooke in AA.

14 January. Exhibited from AA:
- bond of Honnor Hugell administratrix of Robert Hugell. Sureties: William Steivenson, Robert Cumming

Court Session: 1737

> (Annapolis). Date: 14 January 1737.
> - inventory of John Carr.

17 January. Joseph Chaplin (PG) on behalf of John Aldred (minor & legatee of Samuel Finley (PG) vs. Henry Enoch (PG) & Joseph Metcalf (PG). Sheriff (PG) to summon defendants, as witnesses to nuncupative will of dec'd, to prove said will.

Mr. Samuel Hanson (CH) to examine accounts of:
- James Keech & his wife Mary administratrix of Joseph Gardiner (CH).
- Mary Haw administratrix of Dr. John Haw (CH).

30:380 19 January. Exhibited from AA:
- bond of Elisabeth Brown administratrix of John Elliot Brown. Sureties: Samuel Smith, George Simmons. Date: 19 January 1737.
- accounts of William Worthington & his wife Hannah executrix of Capt. John Cromwell.

20 January. Mr. Charles Hynson (KE) to examine accounts of:
- Arthur Lee & his wife Phebe executrix of John Gilbert (KE).
- Edward Beck administrator of John Murray (KE).
- Hugh Oneal executor of Dr. William Hume (KE).

Mr. James Earle (QA) to examine accounts of:
- John Leonard, Jr. executor of John Leonard, Sr. (QA).
- Martha Woodall administratrix of John Woodall (QA).

24 January. Mr. William Rumsey (CE) to examine accounts of:
- Mary Price administratrix of Hyland Price (CE).

Exhibited from AA:
- bond of Elisabeth Purdee administratrix of William Purdee.

Surety: John Harding. Date: 24 January 1737.

26 January. Thomas Aisquith (g, SM) exhibited:

- will of Luke Lee, constituting Sarah Lee executrix. Said Sarah was granted administration. Sureties: Thomas Hebb, Patrick Forest. Date: 18 October 1737.
- will of Joseph Hopewell. Also, bond of Charles King, Jr. & William Aisquith on behalf of his wife Susanna Aisquith executors. Sureties: Joseph Cullason, James Talton. Date: 22 October 1737.

30:381
- bond of Elisabeth Salemon administratrix of Robert Salemon. Sureties: George Thompson, Thomas Thompson. Date: 1 November 1737.
- will of Ellen Fenwick, constituting Ignatius Fenwick executor. Said Ignatius was granted administration. Sureties: John Read, James Burne. Date: 1 November 1737.
- bond of Mary Noaks administratrix of George Noaks. Sureties: James Wood, John Murphey. Date: 2 November 1737.
- bond of Monica Elliot administratrix of Robert Elliot. Sureties: Samuel Abell, Stephen Gough. Date: 16 November 1737.
- will of Richard Shirley, constituting Sarah Shirley executrix. Said Sarah was granted administration. Sureties: Francis Hillton, William Aisquith. Date: 19 November 1737.
- bond of William Howell administrator of Lawrence Bateman. Sureties: George Walles, William Alles. Date: 23 November 1737.
- inventory & LoD of William Gibson.
- accounts of George Vaudery & William Bond executors of Thomas Hunt.
- accounts of Theodoras Jordan & his wife Elisabeth administratrix of Charles Mills.
- accounts of George Vaudery & his wife Jane executrix of John Merritt.
- accounts of Ignatius Thompson & his

wife Susanna executrix of William
Medcalfe.

27 January. Tench Francis (g, TA)
exhibited:
- bond of Elisabeth Ward
  administratrix of George Ward.
  Sureties: Hezekiah Mecotter, John
  Shaw. Date: 23 November 1737.
- bond of Katherine Bennett
  administratrix of William Bennett.
  Sureties: Jacob Brumwell, John
  Valliant. Date: 28 November 1737.
- bond of John Studham administrator
  of Thomas Studham. Sureties:
  Lawrence Porter, Francis Porter.
  Date: 2 January 1737.
30:382 - will of Ann Martin. Also, bond of
  William Martin administrator.
  Sureties: Thomas Bowdle, Morris
  Giddens. Date: 19 January 1737.
- inventory of George Hurlock.
- accounts of Robert Biglands
  administrator of Richard Biglands.
- accounts of Lambert Shield
  administrator of William Shield.
- accounts of John Price administrator
  of Edward Eubanks.
- accounts of William Sharp & Solomon
  Sharp executors of Peter Sharp.
- accounts of Rachel Wrightson
  administratrix of John Wrightson.

28 January. Gabriel Parker (g, CV)
exhibited:
- inventory of Elisabeth Conwell.

31 January. Mr. Nehemiah King (SO) to
examine accounts of:
- Mary Gray (alias Mary Anderson)
  executrix of Thomas Gray (SO).
- Ann Haith executrix of William Haith
  (SO).
- John Walters & his wife Mary
  Elisabeth administrators of John
  Denwood (SO).
- Sarah Murray administratrix of John
  Murray (SO).
- William Nelson executor of Hugh
  Nelson (SO). Additional accounts.
- John Sheldon & his wife Mary
  administratrix of Waistcoat Gray

(SO). Additional accounts.

Walter Dallas executor of Robert Ritchie (DO) vs. Walter Campbell (DO) & Elenor Cornish (DO). Sheriff (DO) to summon defendants to show cause why they conceal effects of dec'd.

30:383 2 February. Exhibited from PG:
- bond of Joseph Chaplin administrator of Samuel Finnly (merchant). Sureties: Henry Enoch, Maj. Edward Sprigg. Also, deposition of Henry Enoch (p, PG) & Joseph Metcalf (p, PG), that said Finnley left all to Johny Aldridge. Also, renunciation of Henry Enoch (p, PG), recommending Joseph Chaplin (p, PG). Date: 2 February 1737.

3 February. Exhibited from AA:
- inventory of Lance Todd.
- accounts of Elisabeth Todd administratrix of Lance Todd.
- accounts of John Watkins administrator of Ann Disney executrix of James Disney.

30:384 6 February. Petition of Tench Francis (TA). Dominick Kenslagh (KE, dec'd) was indebted to petitioner. Bond on said estate assigned to petitioner.

7 February. Humphrey Wells Stokes (g, BA) exhibited:
- bond of Thomas Sligh administrator of Edward Cox. Sureties: George Buchanan, George Harryman. Date: 20 December 1737. Also, renunciation of Jane Cox widow, recommending Mr. Thomas Sligh. Date: 12 December 1737. Witness: T. Sheredine.
- will of Sarah Crooke, constituting Charles Crooke executor. Said Charles was granted administration. Sureties: Walter Dallas, Christopher Duke. Date: 30 December 1737.
- will of Joseph Mead, constituting Benjamin Cadle executor. Said Cadle was granted administration. Sureties: James Maxwell, Jacob Jackson. Date: 5 January 1737.

Court Session: 1737

- bond of Winifred Cutchin administratrix of Robert Cutchin. Sureties: Thomas Brereton, John Roberts. Date: 23 January 1737.
- will of Bloys Wright, constituting Thomas Wright executor. Said Thomas was granted administration. Sureties: Charles Rockhould, John League. Date: 31 January 1737.

30:385
- inventory & LoD of Benjamin Hanson.
- inventory of Bryan Taylor.

8 February. James Earle (g, QA) exhibited:
- will of Col. Ernault Hawkins, constituting Elisabeth Hawkins executrix.

Mr. Gabriel Parker (CV) to examine accounts of:
- Alice Bourne executrix of Jesse Jacob Bourne (CV).
- John Prindowell & his wife Elisabeth executrix of Rober Heighe (CV).

11 February. Exhibited from SM:
- accounts of John Dorsey who married Ann Cooper (dec'd) administratrix of Mary Cooper.

Mr. John Cockey executor of Col. Thomas Cockey was granted continuance. "Goods & chattels lie dispersed in so many places".

Mr. Thomas Aisquith (SM) to examine accounts of:
- John Burroughes & Benjamin Burroughes executors of John Burroughes (SM).
- Mary Taylor executrix of Robert Taylor (SM).
- Aaron Hoskins executor of John Redman (SM).
- Mary Taylor executrix of Joseph Taylor (SM). Additional accounts.
- John Dossey who married Ann Cooper administratrix of Mary Cooper (SM). Additional accounts.

30:386 13 February. Exhibited from AA:
- accounts of Elisabeth Merriott

Court Session: 1737

executrix of Samuel Harvey.

14 February. Exhibited from AA:
- accounts of William Richardson &
  Joseph Richardson administrators of
  William Richardson, Jr.

16 February. Exhibited from AA:
- accounts of Margaret Moore, Samuel
  Preston Moore, & Mordecai Moore
  executors of Richard Moore.

17 February. Exhibited from BA:
- additional accounts of Charles
  Ridgely & his wife Elisabeth
  executors of Richard Hewitt.
- additional accounts of Charles
  Ridgely executor of Richard Hewitt.

Exhibited from AA:
- additional accounts of Edward
  Thursby & his wife Ann
  administratrix of Abraham Parkinson.

18 February. Exhibited from AA:
- additional inventory of Peter
  Overard.
- accounts of James Haddock & his wife
  Elisabeth administratrix of Peter
  Overard.

21 February. Exhibited from BA:
- inventory of Philip Smith, in BA &
  AA.

Mr. Charles Hynson (KE) to examine
accounts of:
- James Calder administrator of
  Richard Foulston (KE).
- George Garnett executor of Thomas
  Garnett (KE). Additional accounts.

22 February. Exhibited from AA:
- accounts of John Atwell & Lucas
  Burch (formerly Lucas Bibby)
  administrators of Margaret Attwell.

30:387 24 February. Capt. John Pitt (DO)
exhibited:
- bond of Mary Brown administratrix of
  Benjamin Brown. Sureties: Thomas
  Howell, John Stewart. Date: 3

Court Session: 1737

January 1737.
- will of Elinor Handley, constituting Marmaduke Handley executor. Said Marmaduke was granted administration. Sureties: Thomas Canner, James Brown, Jr. Date: 6 February 1737.
- will of William Green, constituting Elisabeth Green executrix. Said Elisabeth was granted administration. Sureties: John Sumners, Francis Watson. Date: 13 February 1737.
- inventory & LoD of Thomas Wall.
- inventory & LoD of Richard Smith.
- accounts of John Saide & his wife Elisabeth administrators of Nicholas Paul.
- 1st additional accounts of Sarah Kirke executrix of John Kirke.
- accounts of Thomas Mears executor of Robert Mears.
- accounts of Thomas Woolford & Henry Trippe administrators of Rev. Thomas Thompson.

27 February. Mr. Charles Hynson (KE) to examine accounts of:
- Katherine Everett executrix of Joseph Everett (KE).

Mr. James Earle (QA) to examine accounts of:
- Esther Baynard, John Baynard, & George Baynard executors of Thomas Baynard (QA).

Mr. Tench Francis (TA) to examine accounts of:
- Thomas Medcalf & his wife Mary administratrix of Richard Holmes (TA).
- Katherine Bennett administratrix of William Bennett administrator of Thomas Tenant (TA).

30:388 1 March. Nehemiah King (g, SO) exhibited:
- bond of Patience Powson administratrix of William Powson. Sureties: John Houfington, Walter Darby. Date: 14 January 1737.

Page 107

- will of John Tingle, constituting Mary Tingle executrix. Also, widow's election. Said Mary was granted administration. Sureties: Joseph Gray, William Rickards. Date: 18 January 1737.
- nuncupative will of Richard Lockwood. Also, bond of Mary Lockwood administratrix. Sureties: Joseph Gray, John Newbold. Date: 19 January 1737.
- will of George Downes, constituting Margaret Downes executrix. Said Margaret was granted administration. Sureties: Robert Downes, Robert Laws. Date: 23 January 1737.
- will of John Carter, constituting Charles Carter executor. Said Charles was granted administration. Sureties: Aaron Lynn, Jehu Young. Date: 26 January 1737.
- will of Benjamin Aydelott. Also, bond of Thomas Aydelott surviving executor. Sureties: William West, William Beasey. Date: 14 February 1737.
- will of Sarah Aydelott, constituting Benjamin Fooks executor. Said Fooks was granted administration. Sureties: William West, George West. Date: 14 February 1737.
- will of Sturgis Dixon, constituting Joice Dixon executrix.
- inventory of Walter Jacobs.
- inventory of James Dashiell.
- inventory of Gabriel Cooper.

Mr. Nehemiah King (SO) to examine accounts of:
- Daniel Cordary administrator of Ann Evans (SO).
- Roland Hodson & his wife Margarett administratrix of Edward Chapman (SO).
- Capell King administrator of James Dashiell (SO).
- William Turvill administrator of William Turvill, Sr. (SO).

30:389 2 March. Capt. John Pitt (DO) to examine accounts of:
- Mary Money administratrix of Francis

Court Session: 1737

Money (DO).

3 March. Mr. Humphrey Wells Stokes (BA) to examine accounts of:
- William Hughes & his wife Hannah administratrix of Joseph Bankson (BA).

6 March. Humphrey Wells Stokes (g, BA) exhibited:
- bond of John Hall & Parker Hall executors of John Hall, Esq. Sureties: Aquila Paca, Roger Matthews. Date: 9 February 1737. Also, renunciation of Edward Hall son, recommending his brothers John & Parker. Date: 13 October 1737. Before: Thomas White.
- nuncupative will of Henry Millain, exhibited by George Lester & his wife Alice legatees.
- accounts of Patrick Lynch administrator of Jonas Hewling.

10 March. Exhibited from BA:
- inventory of Charles Daniell.

11 March. Gabriel Parker (g, CV) exhibited:
- accounts of Jane Charlton administratrix of Edward Charlton.
- accounts of Thomas Reynolds administrator of James Cooley.

30:390 Thomas Aisquith (g, SM) exhibited:
- bond of Mary Tennison administratrix of Abraham Tennison. Sureties: Gilbert Heart, John Griges. Date: 16 January 1737.
- will of William Veale, constituting Margaret Veale executrix. Said Margaret was granted administration. Sureties: William Harrison, John Guyther. Date: 30 January 1737.
- bond of Margaret Bisco administratrix of Jonathon Bisco. Sureties: John Stiles, John Stevens. Date: 30 January 1737.
- bond of Ann Smith administratrix of Charles Smith. Sureties: Solomon Jones, Joseph Kirk. Date: 30 January 1737.

- will of John Baxter. Also, bond of William Baxter administrator. Sureties: William Sword, William Welsh. Date: 21 February 1737.
- inventory & LoD of Ellen Fenwick.
- inventory & LoD of Luke Lee.
- inventory & LoD of Richard Shirley.
- additional inventory of Robert Wiseman.
- accounts of George Aisquith surviving administrator of John Young.
- accounts of Sarah Broughton administratrix of Daniel Broughton.
- accounts of William Quidly & his wife Mary administratrix of Robert Terring.

13 March. Michael Macnemara (g, AA) exhibited:
- will of David Mackellfresh, constituting Martha Mackellfresh executrix.

Mr. James Earle (QA) to examine additional accounts of:
- James Sudler administrator of Samuel Griffith (QA).

Mr. Edward Fottrell (AA) vs. Richard Young & Samuel Young surviving executors of Col. Samuel Young (AA). Sheriff (AA) to summon defendants to render accounts.

Court Session: 14 March 1737

30:391   Docket:
- sheriff (SO) to summon John Whaley & his wife widow of John Darby (SO) to take LoA.
- Jacob Hindman (sheriff, DO) to summon Comfort Hopkins widow of John Hopkins (DO) to take LoA. NE.
- W.C. for John Phillips & his wife Ann vs. B.Y. for Nicholas Downing & his wife Elisabeth executrix of John Clarvo. Libel, answer, general replication, rejoynder.
- Jacob Hindman (sheriff, DO) to summon Joseph Ennalls executor of William Ennalls (DO) to render

additional accounts.

- W.C. for Roger Peele for self & his 2 brothers Robert & Samuel Peele (AA) vs. E.J. for William Peele administrator of Samuel & Robert Peele. Libel, answer. Witnesses are in New England. Mentions: summons to London to take the answer of John Peele.

- Richard Francis, Esq. procurator for Abigail Ryan widow & executrix of Cornelius Ryan (KE) vs. Edmund Jenings, Esq. procurator for Henry Truelock (KE). Sheriff (KE) to summon defendant to show cause why the will of dec'd, constituting plaintiff executrix, should not be proved. Defendant exhibited a subsequent will, constituting the defendant executor.

30:392
- E.J. for Joseph Allen (CH) vs. W.C. for Barbara Allen administratrix of Joseph Allen. Libel, answer, general replication.

- William Robison one of sureties on estate of James Little (BA) vs. Thomas Farlow & his wife Elisabeth (late Elisabeth Little) administratrix of said James. Sheriff (BA) to summon defendant to render accounts.

- Risdon Bozman administrator of John Knowles (QA) vs. Elisabeth Loockerman wife of Jacob Loockerman (TA). J. Goldsborough (sheriff, TA) to summon defendant to show cause why she conceals estate of dec'd.

- Risdon Bozman administrator of John Knowles (QA) vs. Margaret Callawhan (also Margaret Callahawn, TA), Grace Millington wife of Oliver Millington (TA), Frances Camperson (TA), Jacob Loockerman (TA). J. Goldsborough (sheriff, TA) to summon the defendants concerning Elisabeth Loockerman (late Elisabeth Millington) wife of said Jacob concealing estate of John Knowles (QA). Said Grace & Frances deposed. Discontinued. Process against said Margaret discontinued.

- Risdon Bozman administrator of John

Knowles (QA) vs. Jannet Moore (QA).
Robert Norr. Wright (sheriff, QA) to
summon the defendant concerning
Elisabeth Loockerman (late Elisabeth
Millington) wife of said Jacob
concealing estate of John Knowles
(QA). Said Moore deposed.
Discontinued.

30:393 • E.J. for James Maxwell, et.al. (BA)
vs. R.F. for William Savory
administrator dbn of Col. James
Maxwell & administrator of James
Maxwell. Libel. Nat. Rigbie
(sheriff, BA) to render attachment
to defendant. Answer filed.

• William Savory administrator dbn of
Col. James Maxwell (BA) vs. Roger
Matthews (BA) & Hannah Hall wife of
John Hall (BA). Nat. Rigbie
(sheriff, BA) to summon defendants
to show cause why they conceal
effects of dec'd.

• Christopher (AA) Gardiner vs. Lloyd
Harris administrator dbn of Chris.
Gardiner (BA). Nat. Rigbie
(sheriff, BA) to summon defendant to
render accounts. Said Harris
exhibited accounts. Discontinued.

• Joseph Chaplin (PG) on behalf of
John Aldred minor & legatee of
Samuel Finley (PG) vs. Henry Enoch
& Joseph Metcalf witnesses to
nuncupative will of dec'd. Sheriff
(PG) to summon defendants to prove
said will. Said Enoch & Metcalf
deposed. Discontinued.

• Walter Dallas executor of Robert
Ritchie (DO) vs. Walter Campbell
(DO) & Elenor Cornish (DO). Jacob
Hindman (sheriff, DO) to summon
defendants to show cause why they
conceal effects of dec'd. Said
Cornish is NE.

• Mr. Edward Fottrell (AA) vs.
Richard Young & Samuel Young
surviving executors of Col. Samuel
Young (AA). Zach. Maccubbin
(sheriff, AA) to summon defendants
to render accounts. Samuel Young is
NEI. Said Richard appears &
exhibited that he has been prevented
by sickness & that his brother &

Court Session: 14 March 1737

co-executor is not in town.

Court Session: 1737

30:394 16 March. Samuel Hanson (g, CH)
exhibited:
- will of Joshua Ratcliff,
  constituting Mary Ratcliff
  executrix. Also, widow's election.
  Said Mary was granted
  administration. Sureties: Lodowick
  Adams, William Brooke. Date: 4
  January 1737.
- bond of Elisabeth Wathen
  administratrix of Henry Wathen.
  Sureties: John Wathen, Hudson
  Wathen. Date: 30 January 1737.
- inventory of James Proffiy.
- inventory of Peter Robey.
- inventory of Peter Robey [!].
- additional inventory of Peter Babb.
- additional inventory of Dr. John
  Haw.
- inventory of Jacob Miller.
- accounts of Percival Fearson & his
  wife Ruth administratrix of Francis
  Brown.
- accounts of Stephen Mankin
  administrator of John Macoy.
- accounts of Edmund Devene
  administrator of James Proffee.
- accounts of James Keech & his wife
  Mary administratrix of Joseph
  Gardiner.
- accounts of Mary Ratcliff executrix
  of Joseph Ratcliff administrator of
  Charles MacDaniel.
- accounts of Mary Haw administratrix
  of Dr. John Haw.
- accounts of William Sisson surviving
  executor of Peter Babb.
- accounts of John Parnham
  administrator of John Bowling.
- accounts of Meverel Hulse & his wife
  Elisabeth & John Moran executors of
  Gabriel Moran.

Exhibited from AA:
- inventory & LoD of John Ashman.

17 March. Exhibited from AA:
- accounts of John Watkins

Page 113

Court Session: 1737

administrator of Ann Disney
administratrix of James Disney.

18 March. Mr. John Pitt (DO) to
examine additional accounts of:
• Levin Hicks administrator of
  Elisabeth Lemee (DO).

Mr. Gabriel Parker (CV) to examine
accounts of:
• Thomas Freeman administrator of
  Thomas Freeman (CV).

30:395 20 March. Risdon Bozman administrator
of John Knowles (QA) vs. George
Besswick & his wife Sarah (TA). Sheriff
(TA) to summon defendants to testify
concerning Elisabeth Loockerman (late
Elisabeth Millington) wife of Jacob
Loockerman concealing effects of dec'd.

21 March. Exhibited from KE:
• bond of Charles Hynson, James Smith,
  Roberts Roberts, & Joseph Nicholson
  administrators of Richard
  Normansell. Sureties: Alexander
  Williamson, James Calder. Date: 10
  December 1737.

22 March. Mr. Peter Dent (PG) to
examine additional accounts of:
• Leonard Marbury & Luke Marbury
  executors of Francis Marbury (PG).

Court Session: 1738

25 March. Mr. Samuel Hanson (CH) to
examine accounts of:
• Robert Doyne & his wife Jane
  administratrix of Joseph Sanders
  (CH).
• Francis Meeke administrator of John
  King (CH). Additional accounts.

James Earle (g, QA) exhibited:
• bond of William Prior administrator
  of Edmund Prior. Sureties: Trustram
  Thomas the 3rd, William Emory.
  Date: 16 January 1737. Also,
  renunciation of Catherine Pryor
  widow, recommending her son William
  Pryor. Date 14 January 1737/8.

Page 114

Witness: Will. Emory.

- bond of Thomas Tanner administrator of William Tanner. Sureties: William Joyner, John Legg, Jr. Date: 17 January 1737/8.
- bond of George Sparkes administrator of Cornelia Sparkes. Sureties: Thomas Obryan, William Robinson. Date: 23 January 1737/8.

30:396 • bond of Violet Primrose administrator of Elisabeth Bath. Sureties: Richard Gould, Joseph Whittington. Date: 30 January 1737/8. Also, renunciation of George Primrose (son) & Lilley Manson (daughter), recommending their brother Violet Primrose. Date: 13 January 1737. Witness: E. Comegys.

- will of Dennis Clanning, constituting Thomas Dodd executor. Said Dodd was granted administration. Sureties: Thomas Wilkinson, Alexander King. Date: 3 February 1737.
- bond of John Earle administrator of Ann McClean. Sureties: Edward Brown, John Collins, Jr. Date: 22 February 1737/8. Also, renunciation of Daniell McClean. Date: 21 February 1737/8. Witness: William Bishop.
- nuncupative will of William Barbutt. Also, bond of Thomas Wilkinson administrator. Sureties: George Mattershaw, Thomas Dodd. Date: 6 March 1737/8. Also, renunciation of William Barbutt son, recommending Thomas Wilkinson. Date: 2 March 1737/8.
- inventory of Ann Denney.
- additional inventory & LoD of William Hemsley.
- additional inventory of Ann Marshall.
- additional inventory & LoD of Dr. William Edwards.

30:397 • inventory of James Gould.
- inventory of Christopher Williams.
- additional accounts of William Austin, Jr. administrator of William Austin, Sr.

- accounts of Anna Maria Hemsley administratrix of William Hemsley.
- accounts of Albert Johnson administrator of Henry Johnson.
- accounts of Mary Kemp administratrix of Richard Kemp.
- accounts of Nicholas Broadaway administrator of Richard Clouds.
- accounts of Nicholas Broadaway administrator of Dr. William Edwards.
- accounts of William Parker, Jr. administrator of William Parker, Sr.
- accounts of Trustram Thomas the 3rd & his wife Jane administratrix of John Smith.

Humphrey Wells Stokes (g, BA) exhibited:
- bond of George Lester administrator of Henry Millain. Sureties: Henry Rhodes, Adam Burchfeild. Date: 21 March 1737.
- nuncupative will of Joseph Foulkes, exhibited by Buckler Partridge legatee.
- accounts of Nicholas Day administrator of Sarah Day.

28 March. Exhibited from BA:
- accounts of Thomas Beddeson one of sureties for Cornelius Angling administrator of Robert Gardiner.

31 March. Peter Dent (g, PG) exhibited:
- bond of Elisabeth Allder administratrix of George Allder. Sureties: John Hawkins, Sr., John Hawkins, Jr. Date: 24 January 1737.
- will of Charles Williams, constituting Charles Williams executor. Said executor was granted administration. Sureties: David Williams, Marren Duvall. Date: 8 February 1737/8.
- will of William Ray, constituting Joseph Ray executor.

30:398
- accounts of William Eilbeck executor of John Edgar.
- accounts of Ann Jones executrix of John Jones.

Court Session: 1738

1 April. Exhibited from BA:
* accounts of Lloyd Harris administrator dbn of Christopher Gardiner.

3 April. William Rumsey (g, CE) exhibited:
* bond of John McCollough administrator of Tole McCollough. Sureties: William Hood, Thomas Ebtharpe, Nicholas Vandergrift. Date: 16 January 1737. Also, renunciation of Mary McCollough sister, recommending John McCollough son of John McCollough the elder (brother, dec'd). Date: 19 December 1737. Witnesses: Will. Hood, Alice Hood.
* will of Mr. Robert Thompson. Also, bond of John Thompson acting executor. Sureties: John Baldwin, Hugh Matthews. Date: 23 January 1737. Also, renunciation of Aug. Thompson executor (QA), recommending Mr. John Thompson. Date: 18 January 1737. Witnesses: John Carpenter, Hercules Carter. Also, renunciation of Richard Thompson executor, recommending Mr. John Thompson. Date: 13 January 1737. Witnesses: John Baldwin, William Rumsey.
* 30:399 will of William Freeman. Also bond of Ann Freeman executrix. Sureties: Henry Pennington, Sr., John Cooper. Date: 13 February 1737. Also, renunciation of Isaac Freeman (son) executor, recommending Ann Freeman widow. Date: 3 February 1737. Witnesses: William Lovelin, Peter Willson.
* will of John McManus. Also, bond of Elisabeth McManus executrix. Sureties: John Campbell, John Baldwin. Also, renunciation of John Campbell executor, recommending Elisabeth McManus widow. Date: 16 February 1737. Sureties: John Baldwin, William Rumsey.
* will of Sarah Bass, constituting Joseph Bass executor.
* will of John McManus, concerning his

Page 117

estates in IRE, constituting
Elisabeth McManus & Brian Eagleson
executors.
- inventory of John Bass.
- inventory of James Foster.
- inventory of Tole McCollough.
- accounts of Mary Carroll
  administratrix of Dominick Carroll.
- accounts of Peter Bouchelle &
  Sluyter Bouchelle executors of Peter
  Bouchelle.
- accounts of Thomas Boulding
  administrator of Jane Clark.
- accounts of Joshua Campbell & his
  wife Esther administratrix of
  Richard Warner.

30:400 5 April. Mr. William Rumsey (CE) to
examine accounts of:
- Aaron Latham executor of James
  Forster (CE).
- Joseph Bass surviving executor of
  John Bass (CE).

7 April. Mr. Charles Hynson (KE) to
examine accounts of:
- Thomas Williams & his wife Mary
  administratrix of Benjamin Hopkins
  (KE).
- John Cleaver & his wife Elisabeth
  executrix of John Spencer (KE).
  Additional accounts.

11 April. Capt. John Pitt (DO) to
examine additional accounts of:
- Ann Cox executrix of Daniel Cox
  (DO).

12 April. Samuel Hanson (g, CH)
exhibited:
- inventory of William Thorn.
- inventory & LoD of Randolph Morris.
- accounts of Robert Doyne & his wife
  Jane administrators of Joseph
  Sanders.
- accounts of Benoni Harrison
  administrator of Charles Montoe.

Petition of Jacob Giles & his wife
Johanah (BA). James Philips (BA)
devised to said Johanah. Bond on said
Philips' estate assigned to said Giles.

Mr. Samuel Hanson (CH) to examine accounts of:
- Sarah Bruce administratrix of John Bruce (CH).
- Priscilla Newman administratrix of John Newman (CH).
- William Penn executor of William Penn (CH).

30:401
- John Thomas & his wife Ann executrix of William Atchison (CH).
- Robert Hanson & Ann Eburnethy executors of John Eburnethy (CH). Additional accounts.
- Hugh Stone & his wife Mary administratrix of Charles Jones (CH). 2nd additional accounts.

Mr. Gabriel Parker (CV) to examine accounts of:
- John Dorrumple & his wife Elinor executrix of Charles Allen (CV).
- Thomas Preston executor of Dr. William Hodgshon (CV). Additional accounts.
- Jannett Kent administratrix of John Kent (CV). Additional accounts.
- Margaret Hickman executrix of William Hickman (CV).

13 April. Capt. John Pitt (DO) to examine additional accounts of:
- James Phillips administrator of John Mahaun (DO).
- Archibald Adams executor of Thomas Coulson (DO).

Mr. James Earle (QA) to examine accounts of:
- John Ruth & Jane Ruth executors of Ann Marshall (QA).
- Abigail Fisher administratrix of John Fisher (QA).
- Matthew Griffith & John Griffith executors of Ann Price (QA).
- Margaret Pinder executrix of William Pinder (QA). Additional accounts.

Capt. John Pitt (DO) exhibited:
- bond of Huett Nutter administrator dbn of Capt. Charles Nutter. Sureties: Christopher Nutter, Matthew Kemp. Date: 7 March 1737.

30:402

Also, renunciation of Charles Brown, Mager Brown, Roger Addams, Betty Addams, Thomas Winder, Alice, & Allender Winde on estate of Mr. Charles Nutter, Sr., recommending Huett Nutter (SO). Witness: Joshua Jackson. Also, renunciation of Mary Hooper on estate of Mr. Charles Nutter & Mrs. Sarah Nutter, recommending Huett Nutter (SO). Date: 3 March 1737. Witness: Thomas Hicks.

- bond of Jacob Low administrator of William Dorington. Sureties: Joseph Alford, Francis Watson. Date: 16 March 1737.

- bond of Huett Nutter administrator of Sarah Nutter. Surety: Thomas Winder (SO). Also, renunciation of Charles Brown, Mager Brown, Roger Addams, Betty Addams, Thomas Winder, Alice, & Allender Winder. Date: 11 February 1737/8. Witness: Joshua Jackson. Also, renunciation of Mary Hooper on estate of Mr. Charles Nutter & Mrs. Sarah Nutter, recommending Huett Nutter (SO). Date: 3 March 1737. Witness: Thomas Hicks.

- bond of John Scott administrator of Richard Smart. Sureties: charles Hodson, Levin Hicks. Date: 30 March 1738. Also, renunciation of

30:403

Thomas Ennalls & Elisabeth Ennalls on estate of Richard Smart, Jr. Date: 7 March 1737. Witnesses: Charles Hodson, Frances Langfitt.

- will of Elisabeth Smart. Also, bond of John Scott administrator. Sureties: Charles Hodson, Levin Hicks. Date: 30 March 1738. Also, renunciation of Thomas Hayward cousin to said Elisabeth. Date: 11 March 1737.

- bond of John Stewart administrator of Benjamin Brown. Sureties: Thomas Howell, William Cullen. Also, renunciation of John Mackgraw, recommending John Stewart. Date: 31 March 1738. Witness: James Mackgraw.

- bond of Sarah Jones administratrix

of John Jones. Sureties: William
Cullen, John Vickers, Jr. Date: 5
April 1738.
- bond of Hannah Brahawn
administratrix of Patrick Brahawn.
Sureties: Absalom Thompson, William
Murfy. Date: 5 April 1738.
- inventory of Richard Willis.
- inventory of Thomas Ramsey.
- 2nd additional accounts of John
Cannon administrator of Andrew
Major.

Mr. Thomas Aisquith (SM) to examine
accounts of:
- Robert Gordon administrator of
Arthur Hambleton (SM).
- Ignatius Fenwick executor of Ellen
Fenwick (SM).
- Dorothy Leigh executrix of John
Leigh (SM).

30:404 17 April. Exhibited from AA:
- accounts of Dr. Samuel Chew
surviving executor of Mary Chew
executrix of Nathaniel Chew.
- accounts of Dr. Samuel Chew
surviving executor of Mary Chew.

Exhibited from BA:
- bond of John Robinson who married
Mary Robinson administratrix of
Philip Jarvis. Sureties: Thomas
Porter, Thomas Floyd. Date: 17
April 1738.

18 April. MM John Bullen (AA) & John
Lomas (AA) to appraise estate of William
Merriott (AA).

19 April. Gabriel Parker (g, CV)
exhibited:
- bond of James Heighe & John
Prindowell administrators of Arthur
Jones. Sureties: Sabrett Sollars,
Samuel Young. Date: 14 April 1738.
- nuncupative will of Arthur Jones.
- accounts of Thomas Freeman
administrator of Thomas Freeman.
- accounts of John Prindowell & his
wife Elisabeth administratrix of
Robert Heighe.

Court Session: 1738

• accounts of Alice Bourne executrix of Jesse Jacob Bourne.

21 April. Richard Carter son of Valentine Carter (QA, dec'd) vs. John Collins & his wife Rebecca administratrix of said Valentine. Sheriff (QA) to summon defendants to render 2nd additional accounts.

30:405 22 April. Exhibited from AA:
• Abraham Child, constituting Richard Hampton executor.

25 April. Tench Francis (g, TA) exhibited:
• will of Richard Harrington, constituting Jane Harrington, Joseph Harrington, & William Harrington executors. Said executors were granted administration. Sureties: Joseph Hicks, Thomas Smith. Date: 8 February 1737.
• will of Kenelm Skillington, constituting Elijah Skillington executor. Said Elijah was granted administration. Sureties: John Lurtey, Matthew Kirby. Date: 14 February 1737. Also, Lidia Skillington made the widow's election. Date: 28 February 1737. Witnesses: William Berry, Joseph Denny.
• bond of Sarah Brown administratrix of Nicholas Brown. Sureties: Thomas Turner, James Morgan. Date: 27 February 1737.
• will of Caleb Clark, constituting Rebecca Clark executrix. Said Rebecca was granted administration. Sureties: Aaron Parratt, William Scott. Date: 2 March 1737.
• bond of Katherine Kinnimont administratrix of Ambrose Kinnimont. Sureties: William Edmondson, Solomon Warner. Date: 3 March 1737.
• will of William Michael, constituting Elisabeth Michael executrix. Said Elisabeth was granted administration. Sureties: David Kirby, John Herrington. Date: 13 March 1737.

Court Session: 1738

- will of Jeffery Horney, constituting Jeffery Horney executor. Said executor was granted administration. Sureties: William Thomas, Jr., Robert Harwood. Date: 27 March 1738.

30:406
- inventory of Jacob Cole.
- inventory of James Higgins.
- additional inventory of Mary Wiles.
- inventory of Thomas Studham.
- accounts of John Carslake administrator dbn of Solomon Horney who married Jane Kersey executrix of John Kersey.

27 April. Exhibited from AA:
- bond of Richard Hampton executor of Abraham Child. Surety: Mordecai Hammond. Date: 26 April 1738.

3 May. Thomas Aisquith (g, SM) exhibited:
- will of Thomas Knott, constituting Ann Knott executrix. Also, widow's election. Said Ann was granted administration. Sureties: George Knott, Thomas Mattingley. Date: 7 March 1737.
- bond of Matthew Cannaday administrator of John Russell. Sureties: John Temple, John Tuttle. Date: 8 March 1737.
- will of Thomas King, constituting Elisabeth King executrix. Also, widow's election. Said Elisabeth was granted administration. Sureties: John Abell, Samuel Abell. Date: 9 March 1737.
- bond of James Egerton administrator of Charles Egerton. Sureties: William Jones, John Dossey. Date: 21 March 1737/8.
- bond of Dryden Forbes administratrix of John Forbes. Sureties: John Read, Kenelm Jowles. Date: 24 March 1737.
- bond of James Taylor administrator of George Chambers. Sureties: Henry Taylor, John Price. Date: 17 April 1738.
- bond of Ellenor Foster administratrix of James Foster.

Sureties: James Compton, John Tipet.
Date: 19 April 1738.
- will of Patrick Burn, constituting
  Dennis Burn executor. Said Dennis
  was granted administration.
  Sureties: Ignatius Fenwick, James
  Burne. Date: 24 April 1738.

30:407 • bond of James Burn administrator of
  Catherine Waughop. Sureties:
  Ignatius Fenwick, Dennis Burne.
  Date: 24 April 1738.
- bond of Frances Cole administratrix
  of Mary Cole. Sureties: James
  Farthing, James Tarlton. Date: 29
  April 1738.
- inventory & LoD of John McGraw.
- inventory of Robert Salmond.
- inventory of George Noakes.
- inventory of Lawrence Bateman.
- accounts of William David & his wife
  Sarah administratrix of John
  Patchall.
- accounts of Luke Bayley & his wife
  Esther administratrix of John
  Wattson.
- accounts of Mary Taylor executrix of
  Robert Taylor.
- accounts of Mary Taylor executrix of
  Joseph Taylor.
- accounts of Mary Asbeston executrix
  of William Asbeston.
- accounts of Aaron Hoskins executor
  of John Redman.

3 May. Exhibited from CV:
- accounts of Thomas Wilson, Joseph
  Wilson, James Wilson, & John Wilson
  executors of Frances Wilson.

5 May. William Rumsey (g, CE)
exhibited:
- bond of Ann Cox administratrix of
  Abraham Cox. Sureties: Albert Cox,
  James Morgan. Date: 10 April 1738.
- bond of Elisabeth Frisby
  administratrix of Peregrine Frisby.
  Sureties: John Baldwin, William
  Knight. Date: 26 April 1738.
- inventory of Robert Thompson.
- accounts of Joseph Wood one of
  sureties for Letitia Lowman
  administratrix of Samuel Lowman.

Court Session: 1738

30:408
- accounts of Joseph Wood administrator dbn of Samuel Lowman.
- accounts of Joseph Wood administrator of Letitia Lowman.
- accounts of Mary Price administratrix of Hyland Price.

6 May. Charles Hynson (g, KE) exhibited:
- bond of John Gresham administrator of Dominick Kenslagh. Sureties: Jacob Jones, Charles Hynson. Date: 8 December 1736.
- bond of Katherine Hankin administratrix of John Hankin. Sureties: Edward Mitchell, George Wilson, Daniel Bryann. Date: 26 November 1737.
- bond of Thomas Johnson administrator of Patrick Fitzgerald. Sureties: George Wilson, Samuel Tovey, Simon Wilmer. Date: 23 December 1737. Also, renunciation of James Deoran, recommending Mr. Thomas Johnson (CE). Date: 25 November 1737. Witnesses: Lew. Williams, Alexander Lane.
- bond of Samuel Wickes administrator of Simon Wickes. Sureties: Thomas Smith, James Ringgold.
- will of James Keare, constituting John Rasin executor. Said Rasin was granted administration. Sureties: John Gale, William Wilmer. Date: 21 January 1737.
- will of Thomas Rasin, constituting John Rasin executor. Said John was granted administration. Sureties: John Gale, William Wilmer. Date: 21 January 1737.
- bond of John Gale administrator of James Gale. Sureties: Griffith Jones, John Rasin. Date: 1 April 1738.

38:409
- bond of Sarah Wilson administratrix of William Wilson. Sureties: Benjamin Ricaud, John Wilson. Date: 8 April 1738.
- bond of Barbara Corse administratrix of William Corse. Sureties: James Corse, John Corse. Date: 21 April 1737.

Court Session: 1738

- bond of Charles Smith administrator of Edward Patten. Sureties: James Ringgold, George Garnett. Date: 22 April 1738.
- bond of Jane Frisby administratrix of William Frisby. Sureties: Augustine Thompson (QA), Thomas Smith (KE). Date: 28 April 1738.
- bond of Mary Farmer administratrix of John Farmer. Sureties: Edward Lamb, William Bootes. Date: 29 April 1738.
- will of Philip Spearman, constituting Ann Spearman & Richard Peacock executors. Said executors were granted administration. Sureties: Robert Meeks, Aaron Alford. Date: 29 APril 1738.
- will of John Mills, constituting Mary Mills executrix.
- will of Simon Wickes, exhibited by Joseph Wickes legatee.
- will of Edmund Coy, constituting Philip Kennard executor.
- will of Darby Sulivant, constituting John Sulivant executor.
- LoD of John Chipley.
- inventory of John Reading.
- inventory & LoD of John Hebron.
- inventory & LoD of Dr. William Hume.
- inventory of John Hankin.
- inventory & LoD of Patrick Fitzgerald.
- inventory & LoD of Simon Wickes.
- inventory of Mary West.
- accounts of Edward Comegys executor of William Comegys.
- accounts of Elenor & John Chipley administrators of William Chipley.
- accounts of James Price & his wife Sarah administratrix of John Reading.
- accounts of Edward Beck administrator of John Murray.
- accounts of Hugh Oneal executor of William Hume.
- accounts of Arthur Lee & his wife Phebe executrix of John Gilbert.

30:410 8 May. Capt. John Pitt (DO) exhibited:
- will of Walter Campbell,

Court Session: 1738

constituting Elisabeth Campbell,
Adam Muire, & Thomas Muire
executors. Said executors were
granted administration. Sureties:
Thomas Woolford, Thomas Hicks.
Date: 14 April 1738.
- bond of Rachell Smith administratrix
of Andrew Smith. Sureties: Henry
Hooper, Jr., Isaac Patridge. Date:
18 April 1738.
- bond of Elisabeth Cole
administratrix of John Cole.
Sureties: Benjamin Wheyland, John
Nuner. Date: 19 April 1738.
- will of John Bacon, constituting
William Stevens executor.
- inventory of Solomon Richardson,
exhibited by Isaac Richardson
administrator.

Court Session: 9 May 1738

Docket:
- Sheriff (SO) to summon John Whaley &
his wife widow of John Darby (SO) to
take LoA.
- Sheriff (DO) to summon Comfort
Hopkins widow of John Hopkins (DO)
to take LoA.
30:411 • W.C. for John Phillips & his wife
Ann (PG) vs. B.Y. for Nicholas
Downing & his wife Elisabeth
executrix of John Clarvo. Libel,
answer, general replication,
rejoynder.
- Jacob Hindman (sheriff, DO) to
render attachment to Joseph Ennalls
executor of William Ennalls (DO) to
render additional accounts.
- W.C. for Roger Peele for self & his
2 brothers Robert & Samuel Peele
(AA) vs. E.J. for William Peele
administrator of Samuel Peele &
Robert Peele. Libel, answer.
Depositions from NE returned.
Awaiting deposition of John Peele
from London.
- Richard Francis, Esq. procurator for
Abigail Ryan widow of Cornelius Ryan
(KE) vs. Edmund Jenings, Esq.
procurator for Henry Truelock (KE).
Sheriff (KE) to summon defendant to

show cause why will of dec'd,
constituting plaintiff executrix,
should not be proved. Defendant
exhibited a subsequent will,
constituting defendant executor.

30:412 • E.J. for Joseph Allen (CH) vs. W.C.
for Barbara Allen administratrix of
Joseph Allen. Libel, answer,
general replication.

• William Robison one of sureties on
estate of James Little (BA) vs.
Thomas Farlow & his wife Elisabeth
(late Little Farlow) administratrix
of said James. Sheriff (BA) to
summon defendants to render
accounts. Discontinued.

• Risdon Bozman administrator of John
Knowles (QA) vs. Elisabeth
Loockerman (late Elisabeth
Millington) wife of Jacob Loockerman
(TA). Sheriff (TA) to render
attachment to defendant to show
cause why she conceals estate of
dec'd. J. Goldsborough (sheriff,
TA) to summon said Jacob Loockerman
concerning the effects of said
dec'd. Said Jacob deposed.
Discontinued.

30:413 • E.J. for James Maxwell, et. al. (BA)
vs. R.F. for William Savory
administrator dbn of Col. James
Maxwell & administrator of James
Maxwell. Libel, answer.

• William Savory administrator dbn of
Col. James Maxwell (BA) vs. Hannah
Hall wife of John Hall (BA).
Sheriff (BA) to summon defendant to
show cause why she conceals effects
of dec'd. Said Hannah deposed,
before Humphrey Wells Stokes (g).
She is former wife of Asael Maxwell
(dec'd) son of said Col. James
Maxwell (dec'd), now wife of John
Hall (son of John Hall, Esq.), age
27. Said Savory is also
administrator of James Maxwell son
of said Col. Discontinued.

• William Savory administrator dbn of
Col. James Maxwell (BA) vs. Roger
Matthews (BA). Nat. Rigbie
(sheriff, BA) to render attachment
to defendant to show cause why he

conceals effects of dec'd. NEI.
Said Roger deposed, but not before
Commissary General.

- Walter Dallas executor of Robert
Ritchie (DO) vs. Walter Campbell
(DO) & Elinor Cornish (DO). Sheriff
(DO) to summon defendants to show
cause why they conceal effects of
dec'd. Said Campbell is dec'd.

30:414 Discontinued.

- Mr. Edward Fottrell (AA) vs.
Richard Young & Samuel Young
surviving executors of Col. Samuel
Young (AA). Sheriff (AA) to summon
defendants to render accounts.
Summons directed to sheriff (CV).
- Risdon Bozman administrator of John
Knowles (QA) vs. Elisabeth
Loockerman (late Elisabeth
Millington) wife of Jacob
Loockerman. J. Goldsborough
(sheriff, TA) to summon George
Besswick & his wife Sarah (TA) to
testify concerning defendant's
concealment of effects of dec'd.
Said George & Sarah testified.
Discontinued.
- Richard Carter son of Valentine
Carter (QA, dec'd) vs. John Collins
& his wife Rebecca administratrix of
said Valentine. Robert Norr. Wright
(sheriff, QA) to summon defendants
to render 2nd additional accounts on
estate of dec'd. Said Collins
exhibited said accounts.
Discontinued.

Court Session: 1738

30:415 9 May. Nehemiah King (g, SO) exhibited:
- bond of Rebecca Beard administratrix
of Lewis Beard. Sureties: Robert
Henderson, John Wolter. Date: 4
March 1737.
- bond of William Kennett
administrator of Andrew Roberson.
Sureties: Thomas Coffin, John
Marsey. Date: 22 March 1737/8.
- will of Mathew Nutter, constituting
Christopher Nutter executor. Said
Christopher was granted
administration. Sureties: Abraham

Cordary, Daniel Cordary. Date: 22 March 1737/8.

- bond of Isaac Costin administrator of Amy Costin. Sureties: Henry Miles, Richard Knight. Date: 23 March 1737/8.
- bond of James Stephen Bredell administrator of Isaiah Bredell. Sureties: John Dale, Jr., John Dale, Sr. Date: 23 March 1737/8.
- bond of Elisabeth Nutter administratrix of William Nutter. Sureties: Benjamin Townsend, Joseph Dashiels. Date: 29 March 1728.
- will of Timothy Atkinson, constituting Levin Gale executor. Said Gale was granted administration. Sureties: Christopher Piper, Robert Collier. Date: 29 March 1738.
- inventory of Godfrey Sprogle.
- inventory of Jonathon Stanton.
- inventory of Robert Carney.
- inventory & LoD of Joseph Hall.
- inventory of Barkley Fisher.
- inventory of John Carter.
- inventory of Joseph Wails.
- inventory & LoD of William Powson.
- inventory of George Downes.
- accounts of John Water & his wife Mary Elisabeth executors of John Denwood.
- accounts of John Fleming administrator of Robert Carney.
- accounts of Duncan Murray administrator of John Williams.
- accounts of Charles Rackliffe executor of Richard Hill.
- accounts of John Dale administrator of William Stevenson.
- accounts of Mary Anderson executrix of Thomas Gray.
- 30:416 • accounts of Francis Harper administrator of Thomas Scott.
- additional accounts of John Sheldon & his wife Mary administratrix of Westcoat Gray Gray.
- accounts of Sarah Dashiels administratrix of John Murray.
- accounts of William Turvill administrator of William Turvill, Sr.

- accounts of William Nelson executor of Hugh Nelson.
- accounts of Capell King administrator of James Dashiel.
- accounts of Roland Hodson & his wife Margarett administratrix of Edward Chapman.

10 May. Exhibited from QA:
- 2nd additional accounts of John Collins & his wife Rebecca administratrix of Valentine Carter.
- accounts of John Alley, Jr. administrator of Thomas Richardson.

11 May. Mr. James Earle (QA) to examine accounts of:
- John Leonard, Jr. executor of John Leonard (QA).

Mr. Tench Francis (TA) to examine accounts of:
- Edward Shropshire & his wife Alice administratrix of James Higgins (TA).
- Robert Harwood administrator of Isaac Dixon (TA).
- Lambert Shield administrator of William Shield (TA). Additional accounts.
- Elisabeth Collisson executrix of George Collisson (TA). Additional accounts.
- Frances Ungle administratrix of Robert Ungle (TA). 2nd additional accounts.

Exhibited from CV:
- will of Col. John Smith, constituting Joseph Hall executor. Also, widow's election. Said Hall was granted administration. Sureties: Richard Young, Samuel Young. Date: 11 May 1738.

30:417 MM John Risteau (BA), George Baily (BA), Thomas Mathews (BA), & Henry Satur (BA) to appraise estate of Col. John Smith in BA.

12 May. Mr. Gabriel Parker (CV) to examine accounts of:

Court Session: 1738

- Samuel Stallings & Joseph Stallings executors of John Betenson (CV).

Capt. John Pitt (DO) to examine accounts of:
- Garey Warner administrator of William Thomas (DO).
- Ann Cox executrix of Daniel Cox (DO).

Exhibited from AA:
- additional accounts of Thomas Stockett administrator of Rev. Joseph Colbatch.

13 May. Exhibited from AA:
- bond of Charles Brown administrator of John Goff. Sureties: Joshua George (CE), Michael Courts (CE). Date: 13 May 1738.
- inventory of Col. Thomas Cockey, in AA & BA.

15 May. Exhibited from DO:
- accounts of Mary Grainger administratrix of John Grainger

16 May. Exhibited from AA:
- inventory of Robert Hugell.

17 May. Exhibited from AA:
- bond of Martha Mackellfresh executrix of David Mackelfresh. Sureties: Samuel Chambers, John Selman. Date: 17 May 1738.

30:418 Tench Francis (g, TA) exhibited:
- bond of Jane Garey administratrix of George Garey. Sureties: John Carslake, Joseph Kinnimont. Date: 8 May 1738.
- bond of Elisabeth Beezley administratrix of Thomas Beezley. Sureties: Solomon Warner, Vincent Jones. Date: 17 April 1738.
- will of Roger Clayland, constituting Harris Clayland & William Harper executors. Said executors were granted administration. Sureties: Richard Besswicke, William Edmondson. Date: 17 April 1738.
- inventory of Thomas Tenant.

- inventory & LoD of Ann Martin.
- inventory of Richard Harrington.
- additional inventory of John Quinn.
- accounts of Thomas Metcalfe & his wife Mary administratrix of Richard Holmes.

18 May. Petition of Theop. Swift attorney for Richard Smith (AA). John Davie (SM) died in 1733, indebted to petitioner. Petitioner initiated action against Ann Davie widow & executrix. Sheriff has exhibited that said Ann is not to be found. Bond on said estate assigned to petitioner.

19 May. Mr. Nehemiah King (SO) to examine accounts of:
- Woney McClammey & his wife Elenor executrix of Jonathon Stanton (SO).
- Thomas Seon & his wife Jane administratrix of Thomas Handy (SO).
- Sarah Donahoe executrix of Teague Donahoe (SO).
- Tabitha Holland & William Holland executors of John Holland (SO).

30:419 Hump. Wells Stokes (g, BA) exhibited:
- bond of Buckler Partridge administrator of Joseph Foulks. Sureties: Samuel Maccubbin, Jr., Joseph Thomas. Date: 5 April 1738.
- bond of Thomas Biddeson administrator of Cornelius Anglin. Sureties: Thomas Sheredine, Edward Stevenson. Date: 5 April 1738. Also, renunciation of Barbara Anglin, recommending Thomas Biddison. Date: 30 March 1738. Witness: Christopher Duke.
- bond of Rebecca Boreing administratrix of James Boreing. Sureties: Charles Green, John Green. Date: 15 April 1738.
- bond of Edmund Hernley administrator of Joseph Cox. Sureties: John Fuller, Jr., Darby Hernley. Also, renunciation of Elisabeth Cox widow, recommending Edmond Hernley. Date: 1 May 1738. Witness: Jos. Allen.
- will of Charles Simmans, constituting Hannah Simmans, George

Simmans, & Charles Simmans
executors. Said executors were
granted administration. Sureties:
John Taylor, Richard Robinson.
Date: 8 May 1738.
- will of Henry Wetherall,
constituting William Bradford
executor. Said Bradford was granted
administration. Sureties: John
Paca, George Presbury. Date: 8 May
1738.
- inventory of Robert Robertson.

30:420
- inventory & LoD of Edward Painter.
- inventory of Edward Cox.
- accounts of William Hughs & his wife
Hannah administratrix of Joseph
Bankson.

Exhibited from AA:
- will of William Ijams, constituting
Thomas Ijams & John Ijams executors.

20 May. Edward Hall (BA) vs. estate of
John Hall (BA). Said John (dec'd) is
father of petitioner. Caveat against
recording inventory.

23 May. Exhibited from SM:
- additional accounts of Charles
Digges administrator of Nicholas
Lowe.

Exhibited from AA:
- accounts of George Presbury & his
wife Mary administratrix of John
Nicholson.

Mr. Nehemiah King (SO) to examine
accounts of:
- Mary Benson executrix of Thomas
Benson (SO).
- Helena Wailes executrix of Joseph
Wailes (SO).

Mr. Charles Hynson (KE) to examine
accounts of:
- Edward Dicas administrator of
William Dicas (KE).
- James Calder administrator of
Richard Foulston (KE).

30:421 Capt. John Pitt (DO) to examine accounts of:
- Joseph Ennalls & his wife Mary executrix of Thomas Haskins (DO).
- Mary Uscears administratrix of John Uscears (DO).
- Elisabeth Green executrix of William Green (DO).

Mr. Thomas Aisquith (SM) to examine accounts of:
- Sarah Lee executrix of Luke Lee (SM).
- Mary Jones & William Jones executors of William Jones (SM).
- Elisabeth Wiseman administratrix of Robert Wiseman (SM).
- Jane Smith executrix of John Smith (SM).
- John Angel executor of James Angel (SM).
- Matthew Wise & his wife Barbara administratrix of John Frasher (SM).

Mr. Francis Tench (TA) to examine accounts of:
- Elisabeth Quinn administratrix of John Quinn (TA).

Mr. William Rumsey (CE) to examine accounts of:
- Catherine Numbers executrix of Peter Numbers (CE).

24 May. Exhibited from SM:
- accounts of Charles Sewall acting executor of Maj. Nicholas Sewall.

29 May. Mr. Humphrey Wells Stokes (BA) to examine additional accounts of:
- Christopher Shepard administrator of Rowland Shepard (BA).

30 May. Exhibited from AA:
- bond of Elisabeth Roberts administratrix of Samuel Roberts. Sureties: joseph Barrett, John Conner, Charles Drury. Date: 30 May 1738.

30:422 31 May. William Chapman one of administrators of Philip Smith

(merchant, London) was granted
continuance.

2 June. Exhibited from AA:
* bond of John Ijams one of executors
of William Ijams. Sureties:
Elisabeth Ijams, Richard Williams,
Jr. Date: 18 May 1738.

3 June. Exhibited from CE:
* inventory of Joseph Young, Esq. in
CE, KE, & BA.
* additional accounts of Araminta
Young administratrix of Col.
Ephraim Herman.
* accounts of Araminta Young executrix
of Joseph Young.

6 June. Exhibited from PG:
* inventory of Clement Brooke.

13 June. Exhibited from AA:
* will of Thomas Cheney, constituting
Susanna Cheney executrix. Said
Susanna was granted administration.
Sureties: Walter Phelpes, William
Phelpes. Date: 13 June 1738.
* 2nd additional accounts of Thomas
Higgins & his wife Dorothy assignees
of Samuel Cottrell administrator of
John Hobbs.

Gabriel Parker (g, CV) exhibited:
* will of Francis Hutchins,
constituting Elisabeth Hutchins
executrix. Said Elisabeth was
granted administration. Sureties:
Richard Young, Samuel Young,
Littleton Waters, John Yoe. Date: 6
May 1738.
* accounts of Margaret Hickman
executrix of William Hickman.
* additional accounts of Jannet Kent
administratrix of John Kent.

30:423 14 June. Josias Towgood son of Col.
Josias Towgood (AA, dec'd) vs. Mary
Towgood & Richard Lane executors of said
Towgood (dec'd). Sheriff (AA) to summon
defendants to render accounts.

Court Session: 1738

Exhibited from AA:
- 2nd additional accounts of Edward Thursby & his wife Ann administratrix of Abraham Parkinson.
- additional accounts of Samuel Chew (Maidstone) surviving executor of Mary Chew executrix of Nathaniel Chew.
- accounts of Samuel Chew (Maidstone) surviving executor of Mary Chew.

15 June. Exhibited from AA:
- additional accounts of Rachel Welsh executrix of Capt. John Welsh.

17 June. Appointment of Mr. Thomas Bullen as Deputy Commissary (TA), in room of Mr. Tench Francis (TA).

21 June. Mr. Samuel Hanson (CH) to examine additional accounts of:
- Robert Gladen & his wife Mary administratrix of Abraham Parker (CH).

22 June. Mr. William Rumsey (CE) to examine accounts of:
- Rachel Penington administratrix of Robert Penington (CE).

Mr. Peter Dent (PG) to examine accounts of:
- Susanna Ray administratrix of George Ray (PG).

30:423a Gabriel Parker (g, CV) exhibited:
- bond of Elisabeth Lewis administratrix of Charles Lewis. Sureties: Philip Dowell, John Dowell. Date: 21 June 1738.
- additional accounts of Thomas Preston executor of Dr. William Hodgshon.
- additional accounts of John Wenman & John Ramsey administrators of Bryan Macdaniel.
- accounts of Sarah Stallings & Joseph Stallings executors of John Betenson.

24 June. Capt. John Pitt (DO) exhibited:

Court Session: 1738

- will of Charles Nutter, constituting
William Nutter executor. Said
William was granted administration.
Sureties: William Owens (DO),
Francis Parsons (SO). Date: 10 May
1738.
- will of John Hollock, constituting
Martha Hollock executrix. Said
Martha was granted administration.
Sureties: Patrick Mccalister, Robert
Dines. Date: 27 May 1738.
- bond of Thomas Ross administrator of
Elisabeth Robson. Sureties: Joseph
Mills, John Medkin. Date: 14 June
1738. Also, renunciation of Noah
Pearson & his wife Justine. Date:
10 June 1738.
- will of Richard Manning. Also, bond
of Nathaniel Manning executor.
Sureties: John Stewart, Daniel
Bruffitt. Also, renunciation of
Margrett Manning & John Stewart
executors. Date: 15 June 1738.
Witness: Daniel Bruffitt.
- inventory & LoD of Elinor Handly.
- inventory of William Green.
- inventory of Capt. Charles Nutter.
- inventory of Sarah Nutter.
- inventory of Patrick Brahawn.
- inventory of John Jones.
- additional inventory of David
Robson.
- accounts of William Guy executor of
George Drew.
- accounts of Isaac Richardson
administrator of Solomon Richardson.
- 1st additional accounts of Levin
Hicks administrator of Elisabeth
Lemee.
- additional accounts of Summar Addams
administrator of Rachel Coles.
- 1st additional accounts of James
Phillips administrator of John
Mahaun.
- 1st additional accounts of Archibald
Addams executor of Thomas Coulson.

30:424

26 June. Capt. John Pitt (DO) to
examine accounts of:
- Rebecca Wall administratrix of
Thomas Wall (DO).

Court Session: 1738

Exhibited from AA:
* bond of Elisabeth Anderson
  administratrix of William Anderson.
  Sureties: Hezekiah Clarke, John
  Jones. Date: 26 June 1738.

3 July. Samuel Hanson (g, CH)
exhibited:
* bond of Joseph Douglass
  administrator of Thomas Hamilton.
  Sureties: Richard Marshall, John
  Brown. Date: 17 April 1738.
* will of John Parnham, constituting
  John Parnham & Francis Parnham
  executors. Said executors were
  granted administration. Sureties:
  Charles Neale, William Neale. Date:
  4 May 1738.
30:425 * bond of Mary Hanna administratrix of
  Alexander Hanna. Sureties: Barton
  Waring, George Scroggen. Date: 11
  May 1738.
* bond of Joseph Allen administrator
  of Elisabeth Allen. Sureties:
  Samuel Love, Thomas Dyson. Date: 7
  June 1738.
* inventory of Isaac Bennett.
* inventory of Alexander Lisay.
* inventory of Henry Wathen.
* accounts of Joseph Douglass
  administrator of James Ronald.
* accounts of William Cage
  administrator of Richard Lloyd.
* accounts of Priscilla Newman
  administratrix of John Newman.
* accounts of Robert Hanson & Ann
  Eburnethy executors of John
  Eburnethy.
* accounts of Susanna Bennett
  administratrix of Isaac Bennett.
* accounts of Sarah Bruce
  administratrix of John Bruce.
* accounts of William Penn executor of
  William Penn.

Peter Dent (g, PG) exhibited:
* bond of Joseph Ray executor of
  William Ray, Sr. Sureties: Robert
  Pottinger, Thomas Mullikin. Date:
  28 March 1738.
* bond of Barbara Wood administratrix
  of John Wood Sureties: John Hawkins,

Page 139

Sr., Thomas Middleton, Jr. Date: 15 April 1738.

- bond of Clement Craycroft administrator of Jane Craycroft. Sureties: Dr. Patrick Sim, Henry Hill. Date: 18 May 1738.
- bond of Dr. Charles Stewart administrator of Nicholas Brumley. Sureties: Dr. James Boswell, Hugh Taylor. Date: 26 May 1738.
- will of Robert Pottinger, constituting Anne Pottinger executrix. Also, widow's election. Said Anne was granted administration. Sureties: Francis Hall, John Bowie, Jr. Date: 5 June 1738.

30:426
- will of Charles Willett, constituting Mary Willett executrix. Said Mary was granted administration. Sureties: Thomas Middleton, Sr., Thomas Middleton, Jr. Date: 9 June 1738.
- inventory of Robert Coots.
- inventory of Abraham Boyd.
- inventory of Thomas Clagett.
- additional inventory of George Noble.
- inventory of Charles Willett.
- accounts of Susanna Ray administratrix of George Ray.
- additional accounts of Thomas Marshall executor of William Marshall.
- accounts of Thomas Clarkson surviving executor of William Clarkson.

4 July. Mr. Pent (PG) to examine 2nd additional accounts of:
- Mary Reyley executrix of Bryan Reyley (PG).

6 July. Exhibited from AA:
- 2nd additional accounts of Samuel Chew (Maidstone) surviving executor of Mary Chew executrix of Nathaniel Chew.
- 2nd additional accounts of Samuel Chew (Maidstone) surviving executor of Mary Chew.

Court Session: 1738

7 July. Mr. James Earle (QA) to examine accounts of:
- Mary Wright administratrix of Robert Jones (QA).
- said Mary Wright executrix of Solomon Wright (QA).
- Albert Johnson administrator of Henry Johnson (QA). Additional accounts.

Court Session: 11 July 1738

30:427 Docket:
- sheriff (SO) to summon John Whaley & his wife widow of John Darby (SO) to take LoA. Struck off.
- Jacob Hindman (sheriff, DO) to summon Comfort Hopkins widow of John Hopkins (DO) to take LoA. NE. Struck off.
- William Cumming, Esq. procurator for John Phillips (p) & his wife Ann (PG) vs. Benjamin Young, Esq. procurator for Nathaniel Downing & his wife Elisabeth executrix of John Clarvo.
Text of libel. Plaintiff Ann Phillips is formerly Ann Jenkins one of the children of Francis Clarvo (PG, dec'd). Said Francis died in 1721, leaving a wife, 1 son, & 3 daughters: Frances Dickison, Ann Jenkins wife of Enoch Jenkins & her son Francis (under age), John Clarvo, wife Bridgett Clarvo. Said Bridgett renounced administration in favor of her son John Clarvo.

30:428 Said John made his will, constituting his wife Elisabeth & John Howell executors. Said Howell died soon after said John Clarvo. Mentions: Richard Lee (sheriff, PG). Text of answer.

30:429 Mentions: Negro Moll (girl).
30:430 Ruling: struck off.
30:431 • Jacob Hindman (sheriff, DO) to render attachment to Joseph Ennalls executor of William Ennalls (DO) to render additional accounts. Said accounts exhibited. Discontinued.
- W.C. for Roger Peele for self & his 2 brothers Robert & Samuel Peele

Page 141

Court Session: 11 July 1738

(AA) vs. E.J. for William Peele administrator of Samuel & Robert Peele. Libel, answer, depositions from NE. Deposition from John Peele (London) has not yet returned.

- Abigail Ryan widow & executrix of Cornelius Ryan (KE) vs. Edmund Jenings, Esq. for Henry Truelock (KE). Sheriff (KE) to summon defendant to show cause why will of dec'd constituting plaintiff should not be proved. Defendant exhibited subsequent will, constituting defendant executor.
- E.J. for Joseph Allen (CH) vs. W.C. for Barbara Allen administratrix of Joseph Allen. Libel, answer, general replication.
- Richard Francis, Esq. procurator for Risdon Bozman administrator of John Knowles (QA) vs. Edmund Jenings, Esq. procurator for Elisabeth Loockerman wife of Jacob Loockerman (TA). Sheriff (TA) to render attachment to defendant to show cause why she conceals effects of dec'd.

30:432
- E.J. for James Maxwell, et.al. (BA) vs. R.F. for William Savory administrator dbn of Col. James Maxwell & administrator of James Maxwell. Libel, answer.
- William Savory administrator dbn of Col. James Maxwell (BA) vs. Roger Matthews (BA). Sheriff (BA) to render attachment to defendant to show cause why he conceals effects of dec'd.
  - Roger Matthews, age 54, deposed. Mentions: Asael Maxwell (son of dec'd), James Maxwell (son of dec'd, dec'd), Hannah Hall (daughter of deponent & widow of said Asael). Before: H. Wells Stokes.

Discontinued.
- Edward Fottrell vs. Richard Young & Samuel Young surviving executors of Col. Samuel Young (AA). Posth. Thornton (sheriff, CV) to render attachment to defendants to render accounts.

Page 142

Court Session: 11 July 1738

30:433   Accounts exhibited. Discontinued.
- Josias Towgood son of Col. Josias
Towgood (AA, dec'd) vs. Mary
Towgood & Richard Lane executors of
dec'd. Zach. Maccubbin (sheriff,
AA) to summon defendants to render
accounts. Accounts exhibited.
Discontinued.

Court Session: 1738

11 July. Mr. Gabriel Parker (CV) to
examine accounts of:
- Aaron Williams administrator dbn of
William Ladyman (CV).
- Roger Boyce executor of Roger Boyce
(CV). Additional accounts.

12 July. Exhibited from BA:
- additional accounts of William
Savory administrator of James
Maxwell.

Exhibited from AA:
- accounts of Mary Towgood & Richard
Lane executors of Col. Josias
Towgood.

William Rumsey (g, CE) exhibited:
- bond of John Husband administrator
of William Husband. Sureties:
Robert Veazey, Thomas Beaston.
Date: 29 May 1738.
- bond of Thomas Davis administrator
of Fouch Davis. Sureties: John Cox,
David Ricketts. Date: 5 June 1738.
- will of John Currer, constituting
John Currer executor. Said executor
was granted administration.
Sureties: William Currer, George
Simco. Date: 13 June 1738.
30:434 - will of John Piggott. Also, bond of
John Piggott & Samuel Piggott
administrators. Sureties: Elihu
Hall, Thomas Kelley. Date: 14 June
1738.
- additional probate of will of Edward
Cooper.
- inventory of William Freeman.
- additional inventory & LoD of Peter
Numbers.
- accounts of Aaron Latham executor of

James Foster.
- accounts of John Ford & his wife Ann administratrix of John Hukill.
- accounts of Catherine Numbers executrix of Peter Numbers.
- accounts of William Brown & his wife Martha administratrix of John Crow.

13 July. Exhibited from DO:
- accounts of Roger Adams & his wife Betty administratrix of John Mackmory.

Capt. John Pitt (DO) to examine accounts of:
- Jacob Loockerman administrator dbn of Govert Loockerman (DO). Additional accounts.

14 July. Exhibited from DO:
- additional accounts of Joseph Ennalls executor of Col. William Ennalls.

17 July. Peter Dent (g, PG) exhibited:
- bond of William Beall & John Beall administrators of Dr. Thomas Creagie. Sureties: John Magruder, Thomas Wilson. Date: 28 June 1738.
- bond of Elisabeth Beckwith administratrix of William Beckwith. Sureties: Col. Joseph Belt, Henry Watson. Date: 28 June 1738.
- bond of Margaret Hook administratrix of James Hook. Sureties: James Lee, James Hook. Date: 3 July 1738.
- will of Henry Odall, constituting Ann Odall executrix.
- inventory of William Ray.
- inventory of Charles Williams.
- inventory & additional inventory of Samuel Finley.

30:435
- inventory of John Wood.

18 July. Mr. Gabriel Parker (CV) to examine accounts of:
- Mary Cox executrix of Henry Cox (CV).

Mr. Nehemiah King (SO) to examine accounts of:
- Elisabeth Nutter administratrix of

Court Session: 1738

William Nutter (SO).

19 July. Mr. Samuel Hanson (CH) to examine additional accounts of:
- Thomas Mitchell executor of Richard Wheeler (CH).
- Jane Luckett executrix of Ignatius Luckett (CH).

Exhibited from AA:
- inventory of John Elliot Brown.

Michael Macnemara (g, AA) exhibited:
- bond of Elisabeth Merriott administratrix of George Merriott. Sureties: William Cumming, William Steivenson. Date: 8 February 1737/8.
- bond of Francis Day & Stephen Higgins administrators of John Ford. Sureties: Thomas Baldwin, Samuel Burgess. Date: 3 March 1737.
- will of John Donaldson, constituting Bridgett Donaldson executrix. Said Bridgett was granted administration. Sureties: William Alexander (CE), William Stievenson (AA). Date: 15 March 1737.
- bond of Catherine Howard administratrix of Benjamin Howard. Sureties: John Howard, John Dorsey, Jr. Date: 17 March 1737.
- bond of Jane Sutton administratrix of John Sutton. Sureties: Robert McLeod, William Roberts. Date: 25 March 1738.
- inventory of William Merriott.

30:436 20 July. Exhibited from AA:
- accounts of Richard Shipley executor of Peter Shipley.

21 July. Mr. Charles Hynson (KE) to examine accounts of:
- Robert Mansfield & Samuel Mansfield executors of Robert Mansfield (KE).
- Susanna Johnson executrix of John Johnson (KE). Additional accounts.

Mr. Thomas Aisquith (SM) to examine 3rd additional accounts of:
- William Deacon, Esq. & his wife Mary

Court Session: 1738

administratrix of Joseph
Vansweringen (SM).

Exhibited from AA:
* accounts of Richard Young & Samuel
  Young surviving executors of Col.
  Samuel Young.

Samuel Young one of executors of Col.
Samuel Young vs. Samuel White, Jr.
overseer to said dec'd. Sheriff (BA) to
summon defendant to show cause why he
conceals effects of dec'd.

1 August. Mr. Peter Dent (PG) to
examine accounts of:
* Gabriel Parker, Esq. & his wife
  Elisabeth executrix of William Pile
  (PG).

2 August. Exhibited from AA:
    ;li. inventory of David
    Mackelfresh.

4 August. Exhibited from AA:
* additional accounts of Henry Howard,
  Ephraim Howard, & Cornelius Howard
  executors of Joseph Howard.

Court Session: 7 August 1738

30:437 Docket:
* R.F. for Risdon Bozman administrator
  of John Knowles (QA) vs. E.J. for
  Jacob Loockerman & his wife
  Elisabeth (late Elisabeth
  Millington). Caveat concerning the
  defendant's concealing effects of
  dec'd.

Court Session: 1738

7 August. Thomas Aisquith (g, SM)
exhibited:
* will of William Hardy, constituting
  Edmond Bowlen executor. Said Bowlen
  was granted administration.
  Sureties: John Williams, Joseph
  Owens. Date: 8 June 1738.
* bond of Susanna Feilder
  administratrix of John Feilder.
  Sureties: Stephen Chilton, Ralph

Court Session: 1738

Stocking. Date: 6 June 1738.
- bond of Mary Hartley administratrix of Joshua Hartley. Sureties: Thomas Hall, Roger Copley. Date: 7 June 1738.
- inventory of Patrick Burn.
- inventory of Thomas King.
- inventory & LoD of George Chambers.
- inventory of John Russell.
- inventory & LoD of William Veale.
- inventory & LoD of Arthur Hamilton.
- inventory & LoD of Charles Smith.
- inventory & LoD of Abraham Tennison.
- inventory & LoD of Jonathon Bisco.
- inventory & LoD of Charles Egerton.
- inventory & LoD of William Knott.

30:438
- inventory & LoD of John Forbes.
- inventory & LoD of James Foster.
- accounts of Dorothy Leigh executrix of Capt. John Leigh.
- accounts of Robert Gordon administrator of Arthur Hamilton.
- accounts of Ignatius Fenwick executor of Ellen Fenwick.

Exhibited from AA:
- inventory of Elisabeth Lamb.
- inventory of John Ford.
- inventory of William Ijams.

8 August. Exhibited from TA:
- bond of Thomas Bullen as Deputy Commissary (TA). Sureties: John Edmondson, William Thomas, Jr. Date: 13 July 1738.
- bond of Martha Vickars administratrix of John Vickars. Sureties: Richard Beswicke, Robert Stonestreet. Date: 21 July 1738.
- bond of Elisabeth Seeny administratrix of Joshua Seeny. Sureties: James Merrick, Edmund Fish, Jr. Date: 28 July 1738.

Exhibited from QA:
- bond of Henrietta Maria Chew administratrix of Philemon Lloyd, Esq. Sureties: Thomas Lane, Thomas Randolph. Date: 24 July 1738.

Risdon Bozman administrator of John Knowles (QA) vs. Elisabeth Loockerman (late Elisabeth Millington) wife of Jacob Loockerman. Sheriff (TA) to summon Michael Fletcher to testify regarding the defendant's concealing effects of dec'd.

Exhibited from QA:
- accounts of Joseph Wickes administrator dbn of John Rowles

30:439 Mr. Gabriel Parker (CV) to examine accounts of:
- John Dorrumple & his wife Elinor administratrix dbn of James Maldin (CV).

9 August. Exhibited from AA:
- additional accounts of James Sweeny administrator of James Sweeny.

10 August. Exhibited from AA:
- inventory of Samuel Chew, Sr., in AA, CE, & BA.

11 August. Exhibited from AA:
- additional accounts of Adam Shipley administrator of John Whips.
- accounts of Nicholas Norman & Augustine Randall administrators of John Carr.

12 August. Mr. Thomas Aisquith (SM) to examine accounts of:
- Edward Oriel & his wife Elinor administratrix of Jacob Morrice (SM).

14 August. Penelope Dye guardian of Thomas Cockey Dye (infant) vs. John Cockey (BA) executor of Col. Thomas Cockey (AA). Sheriff (BA) to summon defendant to show cause why he doesn't deliver legacy to plaintiff.

Mr. Samuel Hanson (CH) to examine additional accounts of:
- Francis Meeke administrator of John King (CH).

17 August. Notly Maddox (CH) guardian to Charles Bruce one of children of John Bruce (CH, dec'd) vs. Sarah Bruce

Court Session: 1738

administratrix of said dec'd. Sheriff
(CH) to summon defendant to render
accounts.

Exhibited from AA:
* inventory of James Donaldson.

30:440 19 August. Samuel Hanson (g, CH)
exhibited:
* bond of Benjamin Adams administrator
  of John Macoy. Sureties: Thomas
  Mudd, Alexander McPherson. Date: 18
  July 1738.
* additional inventory of Col. John
  Fendall.
* accounts of William Robinson
  executor of Eleanor Sanders.
* accounts of John Thomas & his wife
  Ann executrix of William Atchison.

Gabriel Parker (g, CV) exhibited:
* will of William Skinner,
  constituting John Skinner executor.
  Said John was granted
  administration. Sureties: Benjamin
  Sedwick, William Miller. Date: 17
  August 1738.
* bond of Richard Gibson administrator
  of Peter Sewell. Sureties: Philip
  Dowell,
* John Dowell. Date: 22 July 1738.
* inventory of Francis Hutchins.
* inventory of Col. John Smith, in CV
  & BA.
* accounts of John Dorrumple & his
  wife Elinor executrix of Charles
  Allen.
* accounts of Aaron Williams
  administrator dbn of William
  Ladyman.

21 August. Exhibited from CE:
* additional accounts of Mary Carroll
  executrix of William Frisby.
* additional accounts of Robert Blunt
  & his wife Mary executrix of Samuel
  Wright.

Mr. Thomas Bullen (TA) to examine
accounts of:
* Sarah Mullican & William Mullican
  executors of John Mullican (TA).

Court Session: 1738

22 August. Mr. Gabriel Parker (CV) to examine additional accounts of:
- Joshan Mannyng executrix of Thomas Mannyng (CV).
- John Ivey & his wife Elinor executrix of Daniel Day (CV).

Exhibited from AA:
- additional inventory & LoD of Col. Thomas Cockey.

30:441 23 August. Peter Dent (g, PG) exhibited:
- bond of George Frazer administrator of John Frazer. Sureties: Thomas Owen, James Edelen. Date: 21 August 1738.
- additional accounts of Leonard Marbury & Luke Marbury executors of Francis Marbury.

Capt. John Pitt (DO) exhibited:
- bond of Mary Hooper administratrix of Thomas Hooper. Sureties: Thomas Hicks, Henry Cannon. Date: 10 July 1738.
- bond of Benjamin Granger administrator of Mary Granger. Sureties: Matthew Driver, Philip Tall. Date: 9 August 1738.
- inventory of John Cole.
- inventory of Andrew Smith.
- inventory & LoD of Richard Smith.
- inventory & LoD of Elisabeth Smith.
- inventory of Benjamin Brown.
- inventory & LoD of Charles Nutter.
- accounts of Garey Warner administrator of William Thomas.
- accounts of Elisabeth Green executrix of William Green.
- accounts of Mary Uscears administratrix of John Uscears.
- accounts of Rebecca Wall administratrix of Thomas Wall.
- accounts of Joseph Ennalls & his wife Mary executrix of Thomas Haskins.
- 1st additional accounts of Ann Cox executrix of Daniel Cox.
- accounts of Mary Summers administratrix of John Summers.

24 August. Humphrey Wells Stokes (g, BA) exhibited:

30:442

- bond of William Dallam administrator of WIlliam Monk. Sureties: Samuel Webster, John Taylor. Date: 27 May 1738.
- will of Josias Hendon, constituting Hannah Hendon executrix. Said Hannah was granted administration. Sureties: John Elliott, Thomas Hutchins. Date: 26 June 1738.
- will of William Wheeler, constituting Martha Wheeler executrix. Said Martha was granted administration. Sureties: Richard Gott, Edward Stevenson. Date: 7 June 1738.
- will of Philip Sindall, constituting Elisabeth Sindall executrix. Said Elisabeth was granted administration. Sureties: Thomas Green, John Gregory. Date: 13 June 1738.
- inventory & LoD of Joseph Mead.
- inventory of Henry Millain.
- inventory & LoD of Robert Cutchin.
- inventory & LoD of Joseph Foulks.
- inventory of Henry Wetherall.
- additional accounts of Christopher Shepherd executor of Rowland Shepherd.

28 August. Nehemiah King (g, SO) exhibited:

- will of Fisher Walton, constituting Elisabeth Walton & William Walton executors. Also, widow's election. Said Elisabeth & William were granted administration. Sureties: John Scarborough, Stephen Walton. Date: 7 July 1738.
- will of Listian Alexander, constituting Agnes Alexander executrix.
- inventory of Lewis Beard.
- inventory & LoD of Benjamin Aydelott.
- inventory of Francis Ellit.
- inventory & LoD of Isaiah Bredell.
- inventory of Richard Lockwood.
- inventory of John Singleton.
- inventory of William Nutter.

- accounts of William Creagh & his wife Neomy executrix of Nicholas Readey.
- accounts of Ann Haith executrix of William Haith.
- 2nd accounts of Joseph Houston executrix of Benjamin Houston.
- accounts of Alexander Buncle administrator of Francis Ellit.
- accounts of Sarah Donahoe executrix of Teague Donahoe.
- accounts of Helena Wailes executrix of Joseph Wailes.
- accounts of Mary Benson executrix of Thomas Benson.
- accounts of Tabitha Holland & William Holland executors of John Holland.
- accounts of William Holland administrator of John Singleton.

30:443 4 September. Mr. Humphrey Wells Stokes (BA) to examine accounts of:
- John Chinoworth, Sr. & his wife Jane administratrix of William Wood (BA).
- Josias Middlemore executor of Richard Jenkins (BA). Additional accounts.

6 September. Mr. Charles Hynson (KE) to examine accounts of:
- Bastin Tyschow & his wife Elisabeth administratrix of John Hebron (KE).
- Edward Comegys & Thomas Wilkins executors of Rebecca Evans (KE).
- Thomas Richardson & his wife Ann administratrix of David Thomas (KE).

9 September. Exhibited from AA:
- 2nd additional accounts of Edmund Jenings, Esq. & his wife Ariana executrix of Thomas Bordley, Esq.

11 September. Mr. Samuel Hanson (CH) to examine accounts of:
- John Wheeler administrator of Thomas Wheeler (CH).
- Solomon Nicholls executor of James Boyce (CH).
- Mary Ratcliffe executrix of Joshua Ratcliffe (CH).

Court Session: 1738

James Earle (g, QA) exhibited:
- bond of Elisabeth Hawkins executrix of Col. Ernault Hawkins. Sureties: William Turbutt, John Emory, Jr. Date: 16 March 1737/8.
- will of Joseph Shaw, constituting John Sayer Blake executor. Said Blake was granted administration. Sureties: William Tilghman, James Earle. Date: 4 May 1738.
- will of Martha Rowles, constituting Joseph Wickes executor. Said Wickes was granted administration. Sureties: Samuel Blunt, John Elliott. Date: 25 May 1738.
- will of Mary Johnson, constituting Peter Lawrence & James Willson executors. Said executors were granted administration. Sureties: Thomas Vanderford, Walter Nevill, Jr. Date: 29 May 1738.
- will of George Lambden, constituting Ann Lambden executrix. Said Ann was granted administration. Sureties: Jacob Boone, James Knotts. Date: 26 July 1738.
- will of John Wells, constituting Ruth Wells executrix. Also, widow's election. Said Ruth was granted administration. Sureties: Joseph Wickes, John Elliott. Date: 28 July 1738.

30:444
- bond of Rachel Mason administratrix of Matthew Mason. Sureties: Joseph Mason, Ambrose Wright. Date: 20 March 1737/8.
- bond of Mary Devonish administratrix of Ishmael Devonish. Sureties: William Carman, Thomas Shoebrook. Date: 20 March 1737/8.
- bond of Joan Tillotson & John Tillotson administrators of Christopher Tillotson. Sureties: Robert Certain, Edward Lloyd. Date: 1 April 1738.
- bond of Margaret Burn administratrix of Arthur Burn. Sureties: Henry Covington, John Miller. Date: 10 April 1738.
- bond of George Sparkes administrator dbn of John Sparkes. Sureties: John Earle, Richard Collins. Date: 13

April 1738.

- bond of Margaret Bell administratrix of William Bell. Sureties: Jacob Boon, William Purnall. Date: 1 May 1738.
- bond of Mary Finnicum administratrix of Christopher Bateman, Sr. Sureties: John Scotton, Richard Powell. Date: 8 May 1738. Also, renunciation of Chris. Bateman (son). Date: 4 May 1738. Witnesses: Oliver Hastings, Edward John Wight. Also, renunciation of Michael Bateman (son). Date: 8 May 1738. Witnesses: John Perry, T. Powell.
- bond of Joseph Wickes administrator dbn of John Rowles. Sureties: Joseph Elliott, Jacob Winchester. Date: 25 May 1738.
- bond of Elenor Johnson administratrix of Francis Johnson. Sureties: Walter Nevill, Jr., Peter Lawrence. Date: 29 May 1738.
- bond of Hannah Killiow administratrix of William Killiow. Sureties: Edward Killiow, Thomas Parsons, Peter Duhamell. Date: 31 July 1738.
- bond of William Elbert administrator of William Doyle. Sureties: Thomas Chairs, Thomas Price. Date: 4 August 1738. Also, renunciation of Sarah Doyle widow. Date: 26 June 1738. Witnesses: James Earle, John Alley, Jr.

30:445 • bond of Margaret Berry administratrix of James Berry. Sureties: Joseph Tryall, James Everett. Date: 28 August 1738.

- will of Ann Green, constituting Solomon Clayton executor. Also, renunciation of said Clayton.
- will of Mary Ann Sudler, constituting her husband James Sudler, Jr. executor. Also, his approbation.
- will of Christopher Bateman, Sr., constituting no executor.
- inventory & LoD of Ann Denney.
- additional inventory & LoD of John Fisher.

- inventory & LoD of William Barbutt.
- inventory of Cornelia Sparkes.
- inventory of Edmond Pryor.
- inventory & LoD of William Tanner.
- inventory of Elisabeth Bath.
- inventory & LoD of Dennis Clanning.
- additional inventory & LoD of Ann Price.
- additional inventory & LoD of Thomas Baynard.
- additional inventory & LoD of William Swift.
- inventory & LoD of Ishmael Devenish.
- inventory of Ann McClean.
- inventory of Matthew Mason.
- inventory of John Sparkes, Sr.
- inventory of Arthur Burn.
- inventory of William Bell.
- inventory of Mary Johnson.
- additional inventory & LoD of Henry Johnson.
- inventory of Christopher Bateman, Sr.
- accounts of John Walker executor of Daniel Walker.
- accounts of Martha Woodall administratrix of John Woodall.
- accounts of John Welsh administrator of James Towers.
- accounts of John Ruth & Jane Ruth executors of Ann Marshall.
- accounts of Abigail McClean (alias Abigail Fisher) administratrix of John Fisher.
- accounts of Esther Baynard, John Baynard, & George Baynard executors of Thomas Baynard.
- additional accounts of James Sudler, Jr. administrator of Samuel Griffith.
- additional accounts of Margaret Pinder executrix of William Pinder.
- accounts of Margaret Pinder administratrix of Richard Wise.
- accounts of William Wrath & Mary Wrath administrators of Thomas Day.
- 30:446 • accounts of John Leonard, Jr. executor of John Leonard, Sr.
- further additional accounts of Albert Johnson administrator of Henry Johnson.

Court Session: 1738

Tench Francis (g, TA) exhibited:
- will of William Dudley, constituting Mary Dudley executrix. Said Mary was granted administration. Sureties: Samuel Dudley, Thomas Dudley. Date: 30 May 1738.
- bond of John Weymouth administrator of John Halsey. Sureties: John Lenard, George Dewlin. Date: 12 June 1738.
- inventory of Nicholas Brown.
- inventory of William Michael.
- inventory of Jefferey Horney.
- accounts of Elisabeth Quin administratrix of John Quin.
- accounts of Edward Shropshire & his wife Alice administratrix of James Higgins.
- additional accounts of Lambert Shield administrator of William Shield.
- accounts of Robert Harwood administrator of Isaac Dixon.

Thomas Bullen (g, TA) exhibited:
- bond of Margaret Connolly administratrix of Christopher Connolly. Sureties: William Carey, John Alexander. Date: 24 August 1738.
- inventory of Thomas Beesley.
- inventory of Ambrose Kinnimont.
- inventory & LoD of William Elbert.
- inventory of George Garey.
- inventory & LoD of Roger Clayland.
- inventory & LoD of William Dudley.
- inventory & LoD of Caleb Clark.
- inventory of George Ward.

Court Session: 12 September 1738

30:447 Docket:
- W.C. for Roger Peele for self & his 2 brothers Robert & Samuel Peele (AA) vs. E.J. for William Peele administrator of Samuel & Robert Peele. Libel, answer, depositions from NE. Awaiting deposition of John Peele (London).
- Richard Francis, Esq. procurator for Abigail Ryan executrix of Cornelius Ryan (KE) vs. Edmund Jenings, Esq.

procurator for Henry Truelock (KE).
Sheriff (KE) to summon defendant to
show cause why the will of dec'd,
constituting plaintiff executrix,
should not be proved. Defendant
exhibited a subsequent will,
constituting defendant executor.

- Edmund Jenings, Esq. procurator for
Joseph Allen (CH) vs. William
Cumming, Esq. procurator for Barbara
Allen administratrix of Joseph
Allen.
Text of libel. Plaintiff is son of
dec'd.

30:448 Mentions: George Dent (sheriff, CH).
Text of answer. Defendant is the
widow of dec'd.

30:449 Summons to Thomas Burch, Sr. (CH),
Thomas Dyson, Sr. (CH), John Poston,
Sr. (CH), John Allen (CH), & William
Gill (CH) to testify.
Ruling: agreed.

- R.F. for Risdon Bozman administrator
of John Knowles (TA) vs. E.J. for
Jacob Loockerman & his wife
Elisabeth. Attachment rendered to
defendant.

- E.J. for James Maxwell, et.al. (BA)
vs. R.F. for William Savory
administrator dbn of Col. James
Maxwell & administrator of James
Maxwell. Libel, answer. Summons to
John Moale, William Fell, John Paca,
& Charles Worthington.

30:450 - Richard Young & Samuel Young
executors of Samuel Young, Esq. (AA)
vs. Samuel White, Jr. (BA).
Sheriff (BA) to summon defendant to
show cause why he has disposed of &
concealed some of effects of dec'd.

- Risdon Bozman administrator of John
Knowles (QA) vs. Michael Fletcher
(TA). J. Goldsborough (sheriff, TA)
to summon defendant concerning
concealment of effects of dec'd by
Elisabeth Loockerman (late Elisabeth
Millington) wife of Jacob Loockerman
(TA). Said Fletcher deposed.
Discontinued.

- Richard Francis, Esq. procurator for
Penelope Deye guardian of Thomas
Cockey Deye (infant) vs. John

Court Session: 12 September 1738

Cockey (BA) executor of Col. Thomas
Cockey (AA). Sheriff (BA) to summon
defendant to show cause why he
doesn't deliver legacy.
- Notley Maddox (CH) guardian of
Charles Bruce one of children of
John Bruce (CH, dec'd) vs. Sarah
Bruce administratrix of said John.
Sheriff (CH) to summon defendant to
render accounts.
- Margaret Harris widow of William
Harris (AA) vs. George Lawson (CE)
executor of said William Sheriff
(CE) to summon defendant to render
final accounts.
- Christopher Gardiner son of
Christopher Gardiner (BA, dec'd) vs.
Lloyd Harris (BA) administrator dbn
of said dec'd. Sheriff (BA) to
summon defendant to show cause why
he conceals effects of dec'd.

30:451
- William Savory administrator
of James Maxwell (BA) was granted
continuance.

Court Session: 1738

12 September. Exhibited from AA:
- accounts of Richard Warfield &
Thomas Worthington executor of John
Rawlings.
- inventory of Samuel Roberts.

Mr. William Rumsey (CE) to examine
additional accounts of:
- Thomas Henny & his wife Sarah
administratrix of Henry Touchstone
(CE).

Exhibited from TA:
- 2nd additional accounts of Frances
Ungle administratrix of Robert
Ungle, Esq.

Exhibited from QA:
- inventory of Samuel Chew, Jr., in
QA, TA, & AA. Also, accounts of
Henrietta Maria Chew executrix of
Samuel Chew, Jr.

13 September. Exhibited from AA:
- inventory of Thomas Cheney.

Court Session: 1738

Mr. Thomas Bullen (TA) to examine
accounts of:
- Jacob Loockerman administrator of
  John Hendrick (TA).
- Mary Dudley executrix of William
  Dudley (TA).
- Harris Clayland & William Harper
  executors of Roger Clayland (TA).
- Jane Garey administratrix of George
  Garey (TA).
- James Melton & his wife Elisabeth
  administratrix of George Ward (TA).

30:452 14 September. Exhibited from BA:
- will of Joshua Howard, constituting
  Cornelius Howard executor. Said
  Cornelius was granted
  administration. Sureties: Josephus
  Murray, Edmund Howard. Date: 14
  September 1738.

Mr. Gabriel Parker (CV) to examine
additional accounts of:
- Mary Wilkinson executrix of Capt.
  Joseph Wilkinson (CV).

19 September. Mr. Nehemiah King (SO)
to examine accounts of:
- Mary Lockwood administratrix of
  Richard Lockwood (SO).
- Isaac Addams administrator of David
  Addams (SO).
- Abraham Smith executor of Price
  Collins (SO). Additional accounts.

Capt. John Pitt (DO) to examine
accounts of:
- John Scott (SO) administrator dbn of
  Richard Smart (DO).
- John Scott (SO) administrator of
  Elisabeth Smart (DO).

28 September. Thomas Aisquith (g, SM)
exhibited:
- will of Thomas Plummer, constituting
  Margaret Plummer executrix. Also,
  widow's election. Said Margaret was
  granted administration. Sureties:
  John Bisco, William Cutler. Date:
  14 September 1738.
- will of Richard Edelen, Jr.,
  constituting Margaret Edelen &

Page 159

Court Session: 1738

Philip Edelen executors. Said
Margaret & Philip were granted
administration. Sureties: William
Neale, Henry Neale. Date: 15 August
1738.
- bond of Elisabeth Harrison & William
  Harrison administrators of John
  Harrison. Sureties: Benjamin
  Burroughs, Thomas Sont. Date: 1
  August 1738.
- bond of Philip Merrell administrator
  of Catherine Merrell. Sureties:
  Mark Cooper, James Johnson. Date:
  28 August 1738.
- inventory & LoD of John Fielder.
- inventory of William Hardy.
- inventory & LoD of Mary Cole.
- inventory & LoD of John Baxter.
- accounts of Mary Jones & William
  Jones executors of William Jones.

30:453 - accounts of Sarah Lee executrix of
  Luke Lee.
- accounts of Elisabeth Wiseman
  administratrix of Robert Wiseman.
- accounts of Matthew Wise & his wife
  Barbara administratrix of John
  Frasier.
- accounts of Jane Smith executrix of
  William Smith.

30 September. Mr. James Earle (QA) to
examine accounts of:
- Margaret Bell administratrix of
  William Bell (QA).
- Joan Tillotson & John Tillotson
  administrators of Christopher
  Tillotson (QA).

3 October. Samuel Hanson (g, CH)
exhibited:
- bond of Thomas Brittain
  administrator of John Terrill.
  Sureties: Daniel McDaniel, Benjamin
  Reeder. Date: 7 September 1738.
- inventory & additional inventory of
  John Watts.
- inventory of John Parnham.
- inventory of Alexander Hanna.
- inventory of John Macoy.
- accounts of Eleanor Tanner
  administratrix of Henry Tanner.
- additional accounts of Jane Lucket

Court Session: 1738

executrix of Ignatius Lucket.
- additional accounts of Thomas Mitchell & Richard Wheeler.

Gabriel Parker (g, CV) exhibited:
- will of James Dixon, constituting James Dixon executor. Said executor was granted administration. Sureties: Benjamin Dixon, Obed Dixon. Date: 23 September 1738.
- inventory of Charles Lewis.
- accounts of Mary Cox executrix of Henry Cox.
- additional accounts of Roger Boyce executor of Roger Boyce.
- additional accounts of Joshan Mannyng executrix of Thomas Mannyng.
- additional accounts of John Ivey & his wife Elinor executrix of Daniel Day.

30:454 6 October. Exhibited from CV:
- accounts of John Conwill & Richard Conwill administrators of Elisabeth Conwill.

7 October. Exhibited from AA:
- inventory of John Sutton.

9 October. Peter Dent (g, PG) exhibited:
- will of Robert Tyler, constituting Mary Tyler executrix. Said Mary was granted administration. Sureties: Nathaniel Wickham, Jr., John Lamar. Date: 24 August 1738.
- will of Samuel Williams, constituting Thomas Middleton, Jr. executor. Said Middleton was granted administration. Sureties: John Hawkins, Jr., John Goddard. Date: 26 September 1738.
- will of John Docwra, constituting Salome Docwra executrix.
- nuncupative will of Alexander Brodey.
- inventory of Robert Skinner.
- additional inventory of Bryan Reily.
- inventory of George Alder.

11 October. Exhibited from BA:
- accounts of Christopher Sheapard

executor of Rowland Sheapard.

Petition of William Cumming attorney for William Peele administrator of Samuel Peele. Unless Susannah Holland widow of Francis Holland (BA) takes LoA, preference on administration should be granted to said Peele.

12 October. William Peele administrator of Samuel Peele vs. Susannah Holland widow of Francis Holland (BA). Sheriff (BA) to summon defendant to show cause why administration on said estate should not be granted to plaintiff.

Exhibited from AA:
• inventory of John Buck.
• inventory of Benjamin Howard.
• 13 October. accounts of Capt. John Cockey executor of Col. Thomas Cockey.

30:455   14 October. Exhibited from AA:
• bond of Helena Uriell administratrix of Capt. George Uriell. Sureties: James Jackson (AA), James Welsh (BA). Date: 14 October 1738.

17 October. Mr. Thomas Aisquith (SM) to examine accounts of:
• John Burroughes & Benjamin Burroughes executor of John Burroughes (SM).
• John Dossey who married Ann Cooper administratrix of Mary Cooper (SM). Additional accounts.
• Aaron Hoskins executor of John Redmon (SM). Additional accounts.

18 October. Nehemiah King (g, SO) exhibited:
• will of John Gilliland. Also, widow's election. Also, renunciation of one of executors. Also, bond of Jane Gilliland acting executrix. Sureties: Dennis Hudson, Edward Maglammery. Date: 29 September 1738.
• bond of Francis Allen, Sr. administrator of John Allen. Sureties: Charles Townsend, Francis

Allen, Jr. Date: 30 September 1738.
- bond of Rebecca Taylor administratrix of Thomas Taylor. Sureties: William Stevens, Lewis Disharoon. Date: 7 October 1738.
- accounts of Woney McClemey & his wife Elinor acting executrix of Jonathon Stanton.

Mr. Peter Dent (PG) to examine accounts of:
- James Bolton & his wife Elisabeth executrix of Robert Cloyd (PG).
- Mary Willitt executrix of Charles Willitt (PG).
- William Deoreger & his wife Ann executrix of John Jones (PG). Additional accounts.

19 October. Mr. Samuel Hanson (CH) to examine accounts of:
- Samuel Adams & his wife Charity administratrix of Zachariah Wade (CH).
- Isaac Shemwell executor of William Thorn (CH).
- Sarah Bruce administratrix of John Bruce (CH).

30:456 Mr. Charles Hynson (KE) to examine accounts of:
- Mary Rasin executrix of Thomas Rasin (KE).
- Robert Green administrator of Richard Davis (KE). 2nd additional accounts.

Mr. Nehemiah King (SO) to examine accounts of:
- Littleton Townsend executor of John Townsend (SO).
- Absolam Hobbs executor of Joy Hobbs (SO).
- Joseph Nicholson & his wife Hannah executrix of Edward Scott acting executor of Col. Edward Scott (KE). Additional accounts.
- Joseph Nicholson & his wife Hannah executrix of Edward Scott (KE). 2nd additional accounts.

Capt. John Pitt (DO) exhibited:
- will of Andrew Willis, constituting Rebecca Willis executrix.
- will of Mary Peterkin, constituting James Peterkin executor.
- inventory of Elisabeth Robson.
- inventory of John Hollock.
- inventory of William Dorington.
- inventory of Thomas Hooper.
- accounts of Thomas Ross administrator of Elisabeth Robson.

20 October. Exhibited from QA:
- additional probate of will of Solomon Wright, at request of Thomas Hynson Wright.

Capt. John Pitt (DO) to examine accounts of:
- Hugh Rimer & his wife Mary executrix of Richard Willis (DO).

23 October. William Rumsey (g, CE) exhibited:
- bond of Martha Wood administratrix of Joseph Wood. Sureties: Peter Bayard, James Bayard. Date: 31 July 1728.
- bond of Elisabeth Cosden administratrix of Alfonso Cosden. Sureties: Hugh Jones, John Ryland, Sr. Date: 7 AUgust 1738.

30:457
- bond of Sarah Pearce administratrix of William Pearce. Sureties: Thomas Pearce, John Poilloun. Date: 5 September 1738.
- bond of Edward Rumsey administrator of John Caspar Hoodt. Surety: Abraham Alman. Date: 14 October 1738.
- will of William Taylor, constituting Mary Taylor executrix.
- nuncupative will of Mary Taylor.
- inventory of Abraham Cox.
- inventory & LoD of John Currey.
- inventory of Fouch Davis.
- inventory of William Husband.
- inventory of John McManus.
- accounts of Rachel Pennington administratrix of Robert Pennington.

Court Session: 1738

8 November. Charles Hynson (g, KE) exhibited:

- bond of John Gleaves administrator of Sarah Gleaves. Sureties: Robert Meeks, Daniel Shawhun. Date: 7 January 1736.
- bond of Alexander McClain administrator of John Gray. Sureties: John James, Joseph Read. Date: 24 June 1738.
- will of Frederick Hanson, constituting Mary Hanson & Hanse Hanson executors. Also, widow's election. Said executors were granted administration. Sureties: John Gresham, Philip Kennard. Date: 14 July 1738.
- bond of John Sullivant executor of Darby Sullivant. Sureties: James Ringgold, Robert Green. Date: 29 July 1738.
- will of Mary Dunn. Also, bond of Mary Blackiston administratrix. Sureties: Ebenezar Blakiston, Vincent Blakiston. Date: 1 August 1738.
- bond of William Wilmer administrator of Hugh Mattison. Sureties: James Moore, Lambert Wilmer. Date: 8 August 1738.
- will of Thomas Hynson. Also, bond of Charles Hynson, Jr. acting executor. Sureties: William Hynson, Morgan Hurt. Also, renunciation of W. Hynson (brother), recommending Charles Hynson, Jr. Date: 8 September 1738.

30:458
- bond of Edward Rogers administrator of Elisabeth Rogers. Sureties: Nathaniel Hynson, Nathaniel Cooley. Date: 7 October 1738.
- bond of John Gleaves & Joseph Gleaves administrators dbn of George Gleaves. Sureties: Robert Meeks, William Walls. Date: 14 October 1738.
- will of Margaret Falconar, constituting Hannah Falconar (mother) executrix.
- will of Solomon Parsons, constituting Mary Parsons executrix. Also, widow's election.

- will of James Lloyd, constituting Richard Lloyd & Rebecca Lloyd executors.
- will of John Grant, constituting no executor.
- inventory of Sarah Gleaves.
- additional inventory of Robert Mansfield.
- inventory of Gilbert Falconar.
- additional inventory of Rebecca Evans.
- inventory of John Farmer.
- inventory of Elliott Patten.
- inventory of William Corse.
- inventory of Thomas Rasin.
- inventory & LoD of William Frisby.
- inventory of William Spearman.
- inventory of John Gray.
- inventory of Frederick Hanson.
- inventory of James Gale.
- accounts of Katherine Everett executrix of Joseph Everett.
- accounts of John Cleaver & his wife Elisabeth executrix of John Spencer.
- accounts of Robert & Samuel Mansfield executors of Robert Mansfield.
- accounts of William Trew administrator of James Norman.

13 November. Thomas Aisquith (g, SM) exhibited:
- inventory of Joshua Hartley.
- accounts of Edward Oriel & his wife Elenor administratrix of Jacob Morris.
- accounts of Edmond Bowling executor of William Hardy.
- 3rd additional accounts of William Deacon, Esq. & his wife Mary administratrix of Joseph Vansweringen.

Court Session: 14 November 1738

30:459 Docket:
- W.C. for Roger Peele for self & his 2 brothers Robert & Samuel Peele (AA) vs. E.J. for William Peele administrator of Samuel & Robert Peele. Libel, answer, depositions from NE. Awaiting an answer from

John Peele (London).
- Richard Francis, Esq. procurator for Abigail Ryan executrix of Cornelius Ryan (KE) vs. Edmund Jenings, Esq. procurator for Henry Truelock. Sheriff (KE) to summon defendant to show cause why will of dec'd, constituting plaintiff executrix, should not be proved. Defendant exhibited a subsequent will, constituting defendant executor.
- Richard Francis, Esq. procurator for Risdon Bozman administrator of John Knowles (TA) vs. Edmund Jenings, Esq. procurator for Jacob Loockerman & his wife Elisabeth. Sheriff (TA) to summon defendant to show cause why she conceals estate of dec'd (QA).
  - Sarah Cooper wife of William Cooper (QA) deposed on 11 January 1737 that Mary Knowles lay sick at the house of Elisabeth Millington then a widow, now wife of Jacob Loockerman.

30:460
  Mentions: servant Peggy.
  - Francis Stevens (schoolmaster, QA) deposed on 11 January 1737. Mentions: children of Mrs. Knowles.
  - Elisabeth Loockerman wife of Jacob Loockerman deposed on 14 March 1737/8. Mentions: Francis Stevens, Isaac Tunney (prisoner), Risdon Bozman & his wife, Francis Stevens (priest).

30:461-2 ...
30:463
  - Grace Millington wife of Oliver Millington (p, TA) deposed on 14 March 1737/8. Mentions: children of Mary Knowles, Mr. Bozman, Mr. Bullen.
  - Frances Camperson (widow, TA) deposed on 14 March 1737/8. Mentions: Margaret Callaghan, Mr. Thomas Bullen, Mr. Risdon Bozman, children of said Elisabeth.

30:464
  - Jennett Moore wife of Josias Moore (shipwright, QA) deposed on 14 March 1737/8.

Court Session: 14 November 1738

30:465
- Jacob Loockerman (TA) deposed on 12 May 1738. Mentions: November last he married Elisabeth Millington, her former husband Alembey Millington, Sarah Besswick wife of George Besswick (TA).
- George Besswick (p, TA) deposed on 12 May 1738. Mentions: John Knowles, 2 children of Mrs. Knowles, Francis Stevens (QA). Signed: George Besswicke.

30:466
- Sarah Besswick wife of George Besswick (TA) deposed on 12 May 1738. Mentions: deponent is sister to Elisabeth Millington now wife of Jacob Loockerman, Michael Fletcher father of Mary Knowles, Josias Moore (QA).
- Margaret Callahane (QA) deposed on 12 May 1738. Mentions: Negro Great James of Mrs. Knowles.

30:467
Signed: Margaret Callahaune.
- Joshua Clarke (p, TA), age 41, deposed on 8 September 1738.
- Thomas Kelld (p, TA), age 30, deposed on 25 September 1738. Mentions: Mr. John Robins (justice), Negro Jemmey (slave of John Knowles).
Ruling: plaintiff.

30:468
- E.J. for James Maxwell, et.al. (BA) vs. R.F. for William Savory administrator dbn of Col. James Maxwell & administrator of James Maxwell. Libel, answer
- Richard Young & Samuel Young surviving executors of Samuel Young, Esq. (AA) vs. Samuel White, Jr. (BA). Sheriff (BA) to summon defendant to show cause why he disposed of & concealed effects of dec'd.
- Notley Maddox (CH) guardian to Charles Bruce one of children of John Bruce (CH) vs. Sarah Bruce administratrix of said John. Sheriff (CH) to summon defendant to render accounts. Deputy Commissary (CH) to examine accounts of said Sarah. Discontinued.
- William Peele administrator of

Page 168

Court Session: 14 November 1738

    Samuel Peele vs. Susannah Holland
    widow of Francis Holland (BA). Nat.
    Rigbie (sheriff, BA) to summon
    defendant to show cause why LoA
    should not be granted to plaintiff.
- Chris. Gardiner son of Christopher
    Gardiner (BA, dec'd) vs. William
    Cumming, Esq. procurator for Lloyd
    Harris (BA) administrator dbn of
    said dec'd. Nat. Rigbie (sheriff,
    BA) to summon defendant to show
    cause why he conceals effects of
    dec'd.
- Margaret Harris widow of William
    Harris (AA) vs. George Lawson (CE)
    executor of dec'd. John Baldwin
    (sheriff, CE) to summon defendant to
    render final accounts & pay the
    widow.
30:469 • William Savory administrator of
    James Maxwell (BA) was granted
    continuance.

                Court Session: 1738

14 November. Exhibited from AA:
- 2nd additional accounts of Jerome
    Plummer & his wife Margaret
    administratrix of Henry Childs, Jr.

15 November. Exhibited from BA:
- accounts of William Ghiselin &
    Robert Lusby executors of George
    Drew.

17 November. Exhibited from AA:
- 2nd additional accounts of Thomas
    Hall & his wife Catherine executrix
    of John Conaway.
- 18 November. inventory of Elinor
    Rawlings.

Exhibited from TA:
- accounts of John Studham
    administrator of Thomas Studham.

20 November. Mr. Thomas Aisquith (SM)
to examine accounts of:
- Mary Clark administratrix of Robert
    Clark (SM).
- Mary Tennison administratrix of
    Abraham Tennison (SM).

- Isaac Pavett & his wife Margaret administratrix of Jonathon Bisco (SM).

Exhibited from SM:
- accounts of Philip Key administrator of Charles Slye.

22 November. Exhibited from AA:
- additional inventory of John Cromwell.
- additional accounts of William Worthington & his wife Hannah executrix of John Cromwell.

23 November. Exhibited from AA:
- 2nd additional accounts of William Worthington & his wife Hannah executrix of John Cromwell.

24 November. Gabriel Parker (g, CV) exhibited:
- additional accounts of Hyde Hoxton & his wife Susannah executrix of Walter Smith.
- **30:470** will of Capt. Posthumus Thornton, constituting Elinor Thornton executrix. Said Elinor was granted administration. Sureties: Patrick Sim, William Murdock. Date: 10 October 1738.
- bond of John Brome, Jr. administrator of Winefred Wood. Sureties: Richard Young, James Duke. Date: 12 October 1738.
- will of George Harris, constituting William Harris executor. Said William was granted administration. Sureties: John Wilkinson, Joseph Harris. Date: 30 October 1738.
- inventory of Peter Sawell.
- accounts of John Dorrumple & his wife Elinor administratrix dbn of James Malden.
- accounts of John Brome, Jr. administrator dbn of Winifred Wood.
- accounts of Mary Wilkinson executrix of Capt. Joseph Wilkinson.
- additional accounts of James Dodson & Joseph Wooden administrators of John Dodson.

Court Session: 1738

28 November. Exhibited from AA:
- accounts of Jane Sutton administratrix of John Sutton.

Charles Hynson (g, KE) exhibited:
- bond of Francis Holliday administrator of Edward Holliday. Sureties: Thomas Hepburn, Samuel Milbourne. Date: 28 October 1738.
- bond of John David administrator of John Phillips. Sureties: David Hall, Hugh Wallis, Francis Bellus. Date: 30 October 1738.
- will of John Devenish, constituting Mary Devenish
- inventory of Mary Dunn.
- additional accounts of Joseph Nicholson & his wife Hannah executrix of Edward Scott.
- additional accounts of Joseph Nicholson & his wife Hannah executrix of Edward Scott acting executor of Col. Edward Scott.
- accounts of Edward Comegys & Thomas Wilkins executor of Richard Evans.

1 December. Peter Dent (g, PG) exhibited:
- inventory of Thomas Millstead.
- inventory of Samuel Williams.
- inventory of William Offutt, Jr.
- additional inventory of William Offutt, Jr.
- 2nd additional accounts of Mary Reiley executrix of Bryan Reily.

30:471 Exhibited from AA:
- inventory of Alexander Rind.

4 December. Gabriel Parker (g, CV) exhibited:
- bond of Mary Cotten administratrix of John Braban. Sureties: Benjamin Dixon, William Sharples. Date: 30 November 1738.
- inventory of James Dixon.

Mr. Gabriel Parker (CV) to examine accounts of:
- William Matthews & his wife Alice executrix of Jesse Jacob Bourne (CV).

7 December. Capt. John Pitt (DO)
exhibited:
- inventory of Richard Manning.
- inventory & LoD of Mary Granger.
- inventory of Walter Campbell.
- accounts of Hugh Rimmer & his wife Mary executrix of Richard Willis.

Exhibited:
- William Worthington, Jr. (p, BA) deposed on 22 November 1738, regarding William Robinson (AA, died April last), who was indebted to deponent's father. Dec'd left no wife, but 1 son Peter (age 17). Said Worthington petitioned for LoA on said estate, as greatest creditor. Said Peter renounced administration on estate of his father William Robins, recommending William Worthington, Jr. Date: 5 December 1738. Witness: William Daviss.
- bond of said William. Sureties: Vachel Denton, James Jackson. Date: 7 December 1738.

30:472 8 December. Peter Dent (g, PG)
exhibited:
- inventory of David Jones.
- inventory of Robert Pottenger.
- inventory of Jane Craycroft.

Exhibited from AA:
- accounts of Nicholas Watkins executor of Elisabeth Lamb.

11 December. Humphrey Wells Stokes (g, BA) exhibited:
- bond of Ann Higginson administratrix of John Higginson. Sureties: Samuel Hughes, Nicholas Baucum. Date: 28 November 1738.
- inventory of William Wheeler.
- inventory & LoD of Philip Sindall.
- inventory & LoD of James Boreing.
- inventory of Blois Wright.
- inventory of Charles Simmans.
- inventory of Cornelius Anglin.
- inventory of Joseph Cox.
- additional accounts of Josias Middlemore executor of Richard

Court Session: 1738

Jenkins.
• accounts of Thomas Biddison administrator of Cornelius Anglin.
• accounts of Thomas Farlow & his wife Elisabeth administratrix of James Little.

Exhibited from AA:
• bond of Deborah Syng administratrix of John Syng. Sureties: Humphrey Meredith, Jonas Green. Date: 11 December 1738.

Exhibited from BA:
• LoD of Bryan Taylor. Mentions: partnership with Philip Smith.
• accounts of Richard Caswell administrator of Bryan Taylor.

13 December. Samuel Hanson (g, CH) exhibited:
• bond of Ann Ramsey administratrix of John Ramsey. Sureties: John Wilson, Richard Adams. Date: 3 October 1738.
• inventory of John Terrill.
• inventory of Henry Coody.
• accounts of Solomon Nicholls executor of James Boyce.
• accounts of John Theobalds administrator of Henry Coody.
• additional accounts of Francis Meek administrator of John King.
• additional accounts of Sarah Bruce administratrix of John Bruce.
• accounts of Isaac Shemwell executor of William Thorn.

30:473 Mr. Samuel Hanson (CH) to examine accounts of:
• Sarah Miller administratrix of Jacob Miller (CH).

14 December. Mr. Humphrey Wells Stokes (BA) to examine accounts of:
• Sarah Hanson administratrix of Benjamin Hanson (BA).

Exhibited from AA:
• bond of Rebecca Denune administratrix of James Denune. Sureties: William Steivenson, John

Page 173

Court Session: 1738

Samuel Minskie. Date: 14 December
1738.

15 December. Exhibited from QA:
* additional accounts of Joseph Wickes
  administrator dbn of John Rowles.

20 December. Mr. Charles Hynson (KE)
to examine accounts of:
* Hannah Falconar administratrix of
  Gilbert Falconar (KE).
* Jackson Griffith surviving executor
  of Benjamin Griffith (KE).
* Edward Dicas administrator of
  William Dicas (KE).
* John Young & his wife Elisabeth &
  Hans Hanson administrators of Hannah
  Hanson (KE). Additional accounts.
* Wedge Crouch & his wife Mary
  administratrix of William Taylor
  (KE). Additional accounts.
* Thomas Johnson, Jr. administrator of
  Patrick Fitzgerald (KE).
* Thomas Richardson & his wife Ann
  administratrix of David Thomas (KE).
  Additional accounts.

Peter Dent (g, PG) exhibited:
* bond of Hugh Taylor administrator of
  Solomon Phipps. Sureties: Dr.
  Charles Stewart, Walter Brooke.
  Date: 5 September 1738.
* will of John Turner, constituting
  Elisabeth Turner executrix. Said
  Elisabeth was granted
  administration. Sureties: Samuel
  Bresshear, Sr., Samuel Bresshear,
  Jr. Date: 28 November 1738.
* bond of Charles Beall administrator
  of Alexander Brawdee. Sureties:
  John Bell, Edward Dawson. Date: 29
  November 1738.
* bond of Francis Piles administrator
  of Roger Matthews. Surety: John
  Magruder. Date: 30 November 1738.
* will of Humphrey Sawyer,
  constituting John Oliver executor.
  Said Oliver was granted
  administration. Surety: George
  Scott. Date: 30 November 1738.
* inventory of Solomon Phipps.

30:474 * accounts of George Parker & his wife

Page 174

Court Session: 1738

Elisabeth executrix of William Pile.
- accounts of Philip Marshment & his wife Mary executrix of Robert Coots.

23 December. James Earle (g, QA) exhibited:
- bond of William Bishop administrator dbn of William Bishop. Sureties: William Hopper, Thomas Price. Date: 4 September 1738.
- bond of Elisabeth Holding administratrix of Richard Holding, Sr. Sureties: Richard Holding, John Gwin. Date: 19 September 1738.
- bond of Hannah Melogue administratrix of Samuel Melogue. Sureties: Matthew Griffith, Thomas Harvey. Date: 20 September 1738.
- will of Stephen Rich, constituting Mary Rich executrix. Said Mary was granted administration. Sureties: John Tucker, Thomas Alliband. Date: 13 November 1738.
- bond of Mary Hinsley administratrix of Nathaniel Hinsley. Sureties: Peter Hinsley, Thomas Lee. Date: 20 November 1738.
- bond of Elinor Grey administratrix of Leon Grey. Sureties: John Gwin, Matthew Dockery. Date: 26 November 1738.
- will of John Egon, constituting Esther Williams executrix. Said Williams was granted administration. Sureties: Francis Rochester, Daniel Smith. Date: 29 November 1738.
- bond of Ernault Hawkins administrator of Collan Andrew. Sureties: John Hawkins, Jr., James Salsbury. Date: 4 December 1738.
- bond of John Moffett administrator of Gregory Roch. Sureties: Ernault Hawkins, Daniel McClean. Date: 4 December 1738.
- renunciation of Ernault Hawkins & John Hawkins on estate of Mary Cole, as next of kin. Date: 26 November 1738. Witnesses: James Earle, John Moffett.
- additional inventory & LoD of James Gould.
- inventory & LoD of Francis Johnson.

Court Session: 1738

- inventory & LoD of Christopher Tillotson.
- inventory & LoD of John Wells.
30:475
- additional inventory of Edmund Prior.
- inventory of James Berry.
- inventory of William Doyle.
- inventory & LoD of William Killiow.
- additional inventory & LoD of Christopher Williams.
- accounts of Margaret Bell administratrix of William Bell.

25 December. Nehemiah King (g, SO) exhibited:
- will of William Elgate, constituting Thomas Hall executor. Said Hall was granted administration. Sureties: John Prise, Purnall Johnson. Date: 14 October 1738.
- bond of David Wilson executor of Planner King. Sureties: Samuel Wilson, Edward Waters. Date: 29 October 1738.
- bond of Mary Bosman administratrix of George Bosman. Sureties: William Jones, William McClemmey. Date: 13 November 1738.
- will of John Gillett. Also, bond of Samuel Gillett acting executor. Sureties: John Peden, Moses Mills. Also, renunciation of John Gillett, recommending his brother Samuel Gillett. Date 22 November 1738. Witness: Moses Mills.
- bond of Isabella Onorton administratrix of John Onorton. Sureties: William Beavans, Jonathon Mills. Date: 22 November 1738.
- bond of Mary Sharp administratrix of George Sharp. Sureties: Michell Disheroon, Joshua Porter. Date: 30 November 1738.
- inventory & LoD of Andrew Roberson.
- inventory & LoD of John Tingle.
- inventory & LoD of Fisher Walton.
- inventory & LoD of John Gilliland.
- accounts of Thomas Seon & his wife Jane administratrix of Thomas Handy.
- accounts of Thomas Lindsey & his wife Sarah administrators of Francis Lane.

Page 176

Court Session: 1738

- accounts of George Howard executor of Joseph Hall.
- accounts of William Kennett administrator of Andrew Robison.
- accounts of Isaac Addams administrator of David Addams.

30:476 Mr. Nehemiah King (SO) to examine accounts of:
- Katherine Steward administratrix of William Steward (SO).
- James Stephen Bredell administrator of Isaiah Bredell (SO).
- Elisabeth Walton & William Walton executors of Fisher Walton (SO).
- James Train & his wife Sarah administratrix of Barkley Fisher (SO).
- Edmund Cropper administrator of Godfrey Sprogle (SO).
- Rebecca Beard administratrix of Lewis Beard (SO).

29 December. Exhibited from PG:
- will of Allen Farquhar, constituting William Farquhar executor.

30 December. Exhibited from AA:
- additional accounts of Margaret Moore, Samuel Preston Moore, & Mordecai Moore executors of Richard Moore.

8 January. Exhibited from AA:
- will of Joseph Jones, constituting Isaac Jones executor.

Court Session: 9 January 1738

Docket:
- W.C. for Roger Peele for self & his 2 brothers Robert & Samuel Peele (AA) vs. E.J. for William Peele administrator of Samuel & Robert Peele. Libel, answer, depositions from NE. Answer from John Peele (London) has not been returned.
30:477 - Richard Francis, Esq. procurator for Abigail Ryan widow & executrix of Cornelius Ryan (KE) vs. Edmund Jenings, Esq. procurator for Henry Truelock (KE). Sheriff (KE) to

Court Session: 9 January 1738

summon defendant to show cause why
will of dec'd, constituting
plaintiff executrix, should not be
proved. Defendant exhibited a
subsequent will, constituting
defendant executor. Notice given to
plaintiff.
- E.J. for James Maxwell, et.al. (BA)
vs. R.F. for William Savory
administrator dbn of Col. James
Maxwell & administrator of James
Maxwell. Libel, answer.
- Richard Young & Samuel Young
surviving executors of Samuel Young,
Esq. (AA) vs. Samuel White, Jr.
(BA). Sheriff (BA) to summon
defendant to show cause why he has
disposed of & concealed effects of
dec'd. Struck off.
- William Peele administrator of
Samuel Peele vs. Susannah Holland
widow of Francis Holland (BA).
Sheriff (BA) to summon defendant to
show cause why LoA should not be
granted to defendant. Said
defendant was granted LoA.
Discontinued.

30:478
- Christopher Gardner son of
Christopher Gardner (BA, dec'd) vs.
William Cumming, Esq. procurator for
Lloyd Harris (BA) administrator dbn
of said dec'd. Summons to defendant
to show cause why he conceals
effects of dec'd.
- Margaret Harris widow of William
Harris (AA) vs. George Lawson (CE)
executor of dec'd. Summons to
defendant to render accounts & pay
plaintiff.

Court Session: 1738

20 January. Mr. James Earle (QA) to
examine accounts of:
- Mary Wright widow & executrix of
Solomon Wright (QA).
- Mary Wright administratrix of Robert
Jones (QA).
- Richard Gold executor of James Gold
(QA).
- Peter & Rachel Duhamell
administrators of Ann Denny (QA).

Court Session: 1738

- John Swift executor of William Swift (QA).
- Ruth Wells executrix of John Wells (QA).

22 January. Exhibited from AA:
- additional inventory of Richard Moore.

Exhibited from BA:
- inventory & LoD of Joshua Howard.

Exhibited from AA:
- 2nd additional accounts of Thomas Stockett administrator of Joseph Colbatch.

30:479 23 January. Exhibited from AA:
- accounts of Edward Gaither & his wife Margarett executrix of Benjamin Williams.

Mr. Gabriel Parker (CV) to examine accounts of:
- Samuel Young & his wife Rebecca executrix of Thomas Cockshutt (CV).

24 January. Mr. Thomas Aisquith (SM) to examine accounts of:
- Mary McWilliams administratrix of Thomas McWilliams (SM).

26 January. Mr. James Earle (QA) to examine accounts of:
- Elisabeth Holding administratrix of Richard Holding (QA).

30 January. Gabriel Parker (g, CV) exhibited:
- inventory of William Skinner.

Exhibited from AA:
- LoD of William Merriott.

31 January. Mr. Peter Dent (PG) to examine accounts of:
- Henry Acton & his wife Johanna executrix of Thomas Millstead (PG).
- Eleanor Greenfield administratrix of Capt. James Greenfield (PG). 2nd additional accounts.
- John Boyd administrator of Isaac

Hyde (PG).

30 January. Gabriel Parker (g, CV)
exhibited:
- will of William Gray, constituting
  Everard Taylor & Charles Clagett
  executors. Said executors were
  granted administration. Sureties:
  James Somervell, James Dawkins.
  Date: 5 December 1738.
- will of Peter Davis, constituting
  John Debron executor. Said Debron
  was granted administration.
  Sureties: Samuel Young, Joseph
  Smith. Date: 15 January 1738.
- will of John Brome, constituting Ann
  Brome executrix. Said Ann was
  granted administration. Sureties:
  John Brome, Thomas Brome. Date: 24
  January 1738.

1 February. Charles Digges for self,
et.al. vs. William Digges acting
executor of Edward Digges (PG). Sheriff
(PG) to summon defendant to render
answer.

30:480 3 February. Mr. Peter Dent (PG) to
examine accounts of:
- Elisabeth Alder administratrix of
  George Alder (PG).
- Jane Offutt administratrix of
  William Offutt (PG).

Exhibited from AA:
- additional inventory of William
  Merriott.

8 February. Thomas Bullen (g, TA)
exhibited:
- will of James Dickinson. Also, bond
  of Hannah Dickinson executrix.
  Sureties: Howell Powell, Samuel
  Abbott, Solomon Sharp, David Jones.
  Date: 1 January 1738. Also,
  renunciation of Antho. Richardson,
  recommending Mrs. Hannah Dickinson.
  Date: 30 December 1738.
- will of Daniel Sherwood. Also,
  renunciation of one of executors.
  Also, bond of Daniel Sherwood
  executor. Sureties: Robert

Harrison, Peter Colk, Joseph
Harrison. Date: 9 December 1738.

- inventory of Solomon Horney.
- inventory of John Vickars.
- inventory of William Seeney &
  depositions regarding the signing
  thereof.
- inventory of Francis Sherwood.
- additional inventory of John
  Loveday.
- inventory of Christopher Connolly.
- inventory of Joshua Greason.
- accounts of Mary Dudley executrix of
  William Dudley.
- accounts of Jane Gray executrix of
  George Geary.
- accounts of Harris Clayland &
  William Harper executors of Roger
  Clayland.
- accounts of James Melton & his wife
  Elisabeth administratrix of George
  Ward.

Petition of Mr. Vachel Denton for LoA
on estate of Zachariah Lusby (BA), as
greatest creditor. Mentions: widow of
dec'd.

9 February. Exhibited from BA:
- LoD of Charles Daniel.

Mr. Thomas Bullen (TA) to examine
accounts of:
- John Pritchard & his wife Jane
  administratrix of Patrick Mullican
  (TA).
- Sarah Mullican & William Mullican
  executors of John Mullican (TA).
- Sarah Brown administratrix of
  Nicholas Brown (TA).
- Elisabeth Seeney administratrix of
  William Seeney (TA).
- John Sherwood & Francis Sherwood
  executors of Francis Sherwood (TA).

30:481 12 February. Thomas Aisquith (g, SM)
exhibited:
- will of Michael Raley, constituting
  Grace Raley executrix. Said Grace
  was granted administration.
  Sureties: John Heard, John
  Greenwell. Date: 8 November 1738.

- will of Thomas Shierclieffe,
  constituting Moma Shierclieffe
  executrix. Said Moma was granted
  administration. Sureties: William
  Snowden, George Knott. Date: 20
  November 1738.
- will of William Wilkinson,
  constituting Rebecca Wilkinson &
  John Wilkinson executors. Said
  Rebecca & John were granted
  administration. Sureties: William
  Holland, Jeremiah Pickring. Date:
  18 December 1738.
- bond of William Taite administrator
  of Peter Coutanceau. Sureties: John
  Hicks (SM), William Cumming (AA).
  Date: 9 November 1738.
- bond of John Litherland
  administrator of Charles James.
  Sureties: hugh Hopewell, William
  Litherland. Date: 10 January 1738.
- bond of Priscilla Baker
  administratrix of James Baker.
  Sureties: Francis Hopewell, William
  Hebb. Date: 18 January 1738.
- bond of Ann Blackman administratrix
  of Thomas Blackman. Sureties:
  Jedidah Hening, John Brewer. Date:
  23 January 1738.
- inventory & LoD of Robert Elliott.
- inventory of Catherine Merrill.
- accounts of Aaron Hoskins executor
  of John Redman.
- accounts of John Dossey & Ann Cooper
  administrators of Mary Cooper.

John Hall executor of Johanna Hall (BA)
vs. James Phillips (BA) son of said
dec'd. Sheriff (BA) to summon defendant
to show cause why he conceals effects of
dec'd.

14 February. John Pitt (DO) exhibited:
- nuncupative will of James Miller.
  Also, bond of Samuel Melson
  executor. Sureties: Joseph Ennalls
  (merchant), Francis Carr. Date: 11
  January 1738.
- accounts of John Scott administrator
  dbn of Richard Smart.
- accounts of John Scott administrator
  of Elisabeth Smart.

Court Session: 1738

- accounts of Huett Nutter administrator dbn of Capt. Charles Nutter.

30:482 <u>19 February.</u> Charles Hynson (g, KE) exhibited:

- will of James Doran, constituting Jane Doran & James Doran executors. Said executors were granted administration. Sureties: Ebenezar Perkins, Arthur Lee. Date: 22 January 1738.
- will of Michael Miller, constituting Robert Dunn, Michael Miller, & Martha Miller executors. Said executors were granted administration. Sureties: Morgan Hurt, Benjamin Ricaud. Date: 10 February 1738.
- will of William Pell. Also, bond of George Read administrator. Sureties: Griffith Jones, John Watts. Also, renunciation of Mary Pell widow, recommending her father George Read. Date: 5 December 1738. Witness: Griffith Jones.
- will of Daniel Flynn, constituting his wife Ann & his eldest son Daniel Flynn executors.
- will of James Cruckshanks, constituting his wife Mary Cruckshanks executrix.
- will of William Meglenin, exhibited by Mary Huitts legatee.
- will of William Thornton, constituting Catherine Thornton executrix.
- bond of George Coppen administrator of Elisabeth Coppen. Sureties: James Calder, Bod. Hands. Date: 27 January 1738.
- inventory of James Kear.
- inventory of Elisabeth Rogers (widow).
- inventory of Thomas Hynson, Sr.
- inventory of Darby Sullivan.
- accounts of Mary Rasin executrix of Thomas Rasin.
- additional accounts of Thomas Richardson & his wife Ann administratrix of David Thomas.
- 2nd additional accounts of Robert

Green administrator of Richard Davis.

Mr. Charles Hynson (KE) to examine accounts of:
* Samuel Weeks administrator of Simon Weeks (KE).
* John Gleaves & Joseph Gleaves administrators dbn of George Geaves (KE).
* Martha Burton administratrix of Francis Lewis (KE). Additional accounts.
* George Garnett executor of Thomas Garnett (KE). Additional accounts.

30:483　22 February. Nehemiah King (g, SO) exhibited:
* bond of Sarah Lamberson administratrix of Abraham Lamberson. Sureties: Smith Mills, Robert Stevenson. Date: 19 December 1738.
* inventory of Thomas Taylor.
* inventory of Madam Betty Gale.
* inventory of William Elgate.
* additional accounts of Abraham Smith executor of Price Collins.
* accounts of Absolom Hobbs executor of Joy Hobbs.
* accounts of Littleton Townsend acting executor of John Townsend.

24 February. Mr. Nehemiah King (SO) to examine accounts of:
* William Hicks & his wife Patience administratrix of William Powson (SO).
* Mary Lockwood administratrix of Richard Lockwood (SO).

Exhibited from SM:
* 2nd additional accounts of George Plater & his wife Rebecca executors of James Bowles, Esq.

Exhibited from CH:
* additional accounts of George Plater administrator of William Brogden.

Exhibited from AA:
* will of Margarett Maccnemara, constituting Dr. Charles Carroll

Court Session: 1738

executor.

John Levett (g, PG) son & one of
representatives of Robert Levett (g, PG,
dec'd) vs. George Buchanan & his wife
Margarett & Edward Sprigg administrators
dbn of said Robert. Sheriff (PG) to
summon defendants to render answer.

26 February. Mr. John Pitt (DO) to
examine accounts of:
• William Stokes & his wife Mary
  administratrix of David Robson (DO).

27 February. Exhibited from AA:
• bond of Dr. Charles Carroll
  executor of Margarett Maccnemara.
  Sureties: Thomas John Hammond,
  William Reynolds. Date: 27 February
  1738.

Peter Dent (PG) to examine accounts of:
• Mary Offutt administratrix of
  William Offutt (PG).

30:484 Exhibited from AA:
• additional inventory of Thomas
  Cheney.

28 February. Exhibited from AA:
• additional inventory of John Ashman.

Samuel Hanson (g, CH) exhibited:
• will of Marmaduke Simms,
  constituting Mary Simms executrix.
  Said Mary was granted
  administration. Sureties: Justinian
  Cooksey, Samuel Chunn. Date: 17
  January 1738.
• will of George Thomas. Also, bond
  of George Thomas administrator.
  Sureties: John Farr, James Waters.
  Date: 8 January 1738.
• will of Mark Penn, constituting Jane
  Penn executrix. Said Jane was
  granted administration. Sureties:
  Major Robert Yates, John Courts.
  Date: 17 January 1738.
• will of Charles Som. Smith,
  constituting Margaret Smith
  executrix. Said Margaret was
  granted administration. Sureties:

Elias Smith (CH), John Estep (CH), Samuel Perrie (PG). Date: 20 February 1738.

- will of John Glaze, constituting Sarah Glaze executrix. Said Sarah was granted administration. Sureties: Richard Willson, Henry Hill. Date: 8 February 1738.
- inventory of John Ramsey.
- inventory of Thomas Hamilton.
- accounts of Michael Hinds Robey administrator of Peter Robey.
- accounts of Sarah Miller administratrix of Jacob Miller.
- accounts of Ann Whiller executrix of William Whiller.
- accounts of John Phillpot executor of John Fairfax.

William Rumsey (g, CE) exhibited:
- will of Christopher Mounts, constituting Sarah Smithson executrix.
- will of Martha Mounts, constituting John Beedle & Robert Mercer executors. Said Beedle & Mercer were granted administration. Sureties: William Mercer, Bartholomew Etherington. Date: 18 December 1738.
- will of Joseph Zelefro, constituting his wife Jane & his son Andrew Zelefro executors.
- bond of John Copson administrator of Robert Brown. Surety: Thomas Colvill. Date: 24 November 1738. Also, renunciation of Ann Brown due to great sickness, recommending Maj. John Copson (greatest creditor). She also certifies that Margarett Brown is older than her husband by 3 years & her husband has a brother & sister younger than him in IRE & the brother has 2 sons living. Date: 16 November 1738. Witnesses: Rachel Kelley, William Currer.
- bond of William Hutchinson administrator of Robert Rippon. Sureties: John Baldwin, William Knight. Date: 24 November 1738.
- bond of Alice Husband administratrix

30:485

Court Session: 1738

of James Husband. Sureties: Thomas
Davis, William Freeman. Date: 31
January 1738.
- inventory of John Piggott.
- inventory of Joseph Wood.
- inventory of John Casper Hoodt.
- inventory of William Pearce.
- inventory of Alphonso Cosden.
- accounts of Joseph Bass surviving
  executor of John Bass.
- additional accounts of Thomas Henny
  & his wife Sarah administratrix of
  Henry Touchstone.

2 March. William Rumsey (CE) to examine
accounts of:
- John McCollough administrator of
  Tole McCollough (CE).

Exhibited from AA:
- bond of Edward Fottrell
  administrator of Sarah Fottrell.
  Surety: William Brogden (clerk, PG).
  Date: 28 February 1738.

Mr. Samuel Hanson (CH) to examine
accounts of:
- Mary Ratcliff executrix of Joshua
  Ratcliff (CH).
- Samuel Adams & his wife Charity
  administrators of Zachariah Wade
  (CH).
- Thomas Hardman & his wife Elisabeth
  administratrix of Henry Wathen (CH).
- Mary Hanna administratrix of
  Alexander Hanna (CH).

Thomas Aisquith (SM) to examine accounts
of:
- John Dial & his wife Sarah executrix
  of Richard Shirly (SM).
- Ann Farthing administratrix of
  William Mariea Farthing (SM).

5 March. Edward Fottrell administrator
of his late wife Sarah Fottrell vs.
Richard Young & Samuel Young surviving
executors of Samuel Young, Esq. (AA) &
William Alexander & his wife Araminta
(late Araminta Young) executrix of
Joseph Young. Sheriff (BA) & sheriff
(CV) to summon said Richard Young &

Court Session: 1738

Samuel Young, & sheriff (CE) to summon
said Alexander
30:486 to render answer.

7 March. Charles Hynson (KE) to examine
accounts of:
• Ann Spearman & Richard Peacock
  executors of Philip Spearman (KE).

John Pitt (DO) to examine accounts of:
• John Stewart administrator dbn of
  Benjamin Brown (DO).

9 March. Exhibited from QA:
• additional inventory of John
  Willson.

10 March. Exhibited from QA:
• additional accounts of Mary Willson
  executrix of John Willson.

Exhibited from AA:
• inventory & LoD of John Syng.

Court Session: 13 March 1738

31:1 Docket:
• William Cumming, Esq. procurator for
  Roger Peele for self & his 2
  brothers Samuel & Robert Peele (AA)
  vs. Edmund Jennings, Esq.
  procurator for William Peele
  (merchant) administrator of Samuel
  (merchant) & Robert Peele (taylor).
  Plaintiffs are from Salem, Province
  of Massachusetts Bay, New England.
  Text of libel. Said Roger
  (shipwright) is eldest son of Roger
  Peele (mariner, Salem, dec'd), one
  of the brethren of said Samuel Peele
  & Robert Peele. Said Samuel died in
  May 1733, without wife or children,
  having 3 brothers living: William
  (defendant), John, & Robert & the
  plaintiffs. Said Roger (father)
  died in 1723 at Salem, NE. Said
  Robert also died without wife or
  children.
31:2 Plaintiffs' father had been absent
  from GB for many years.
  Mentions: Zach. Maccubbin (sheriff,
  AA).

Page 188

31:3   Text of answer. Said Roger (dec'd) was the 3rd son of Samuel Peele (father of defendant). Defendant was eldest son; Samuel, the 2nd; John, the 4th; Robert, the 5th. After his father's death, said Roger was bound out as an apprentice to Capt. Gourney, captain of the ship Defyance. Said Gourney died on the Island of Barbadoes. Said Roger was said to have gone to Newfoundland & that in 1700 was in NE. Also, Samuel (father) was Church of England & his wife (mother) was a Dissenter.

31:4   Attestation: Roger Peele married Margarett Kempton on 15 November 1709, by Mr. Nicholas Noyes (minister of Salem).
- son Roger b. 5 August 1710.
- son Robert b. 29 August 1712.
- son Samuel b. 23 March 1716/7.

Signed: John Higginson (clerk). Before: Mitchel Sewall (notary public). Affirmed by Capt. Thomas Dean & Capt. Paul Mansfield of Salem. Before: William Deacon (SM). Date: 20 March 1736.
Affirmed by Malachi Coming & John Webb, Jr. of Salem. Before: William Rogers (AA). Date: 12 April 1737.

31:5   Came Ebenezar Peele (mariner, Salem).
Text of interrogatories.

31:6   Depositions taken at Salem, County of Essex, Massachusetts Bay.
- Perez Webb, age 57, deposed that he heard Roger (dec'd) say that he was born in London on Bishopgate Street.
- Margaret Stone, age 55, deposed that Roger (father) died 8 June 1723, & that his father was Samuel Peele & was in partnership with his wife's brother. There were 4 brothers & 1 sister.

31:7
- Margaret Cook, age 41, deposed that Roger's sister is named Anne.
- Sarah Peard, age 52, deposed.
- Daniel Webb, age 48, deposed

that said Margarett Kempton was a widow.

31:8   Witnesses: Thomas Barton, Ichabod Plaisted, John Higginson, Samuel Barnard.

31:9   Ruling: plaintiffs.

• Richard Francis, Esq. procurator for Abigail Ryan widow & executrix of Cornelius Ryan (KE) vs. Edmund Jenings, Esq. procurator for Henry Truelock (KE). Sheriff (KE) to summon defendant to show cause why will of dec'd, constituting plaintiff executrix, should not be proved.

31:10   Defendant exhibited a subsequent will, constituting defendant executor. Notice given to plaintiff.

• E.J. for James Maxwell, et.al. (BA) vs. R.F. for William Savory administrator dbn of Col. James Maxwell & administrator of James Maxwell. Libel, answer.

• Christopher Gardner son of Christopher Gardner (BA, dec'd) vs. William Cumming, Esq. procurator for Lloyd Harris (BA) administrator dbn of said dec'd. Summons to defendant to show cause why he conceals effects of dec'd.

• Margaret Harris widow of William Harris (AA) vs. George Lawson (CE) executor of dec'd. Sheriff (CE) to Summon defendant to render final accounts & pay plaintiff.

• Benjamin Young, Esq. procurator for Charles Digges, et.al. (PG) vs. Edmund Jenings, Esq. procurator for William Digges acting executor of Edward Digges. William Murdock (sheriff, PG) to summon defendant. Exhibited petition of plaintiff that Charles Neale (CH) & John Darnall & his wife Mary (AA) be parties to suit. William Murdock (PG), John Hepburn (PG), & George Scott (PG) to take testimony of John Digges "de bone esse".

• John Hall executor of Johanna Hall (BA) vs. James Philips (BA) son of said Johanna.

Court Session: 13 March 1738

31:11   Nat. Rigbie (sheriff, BA) to summon
         defendant to show cause why he
         conceals effects of dec'd.
- B.Y. for John Levett (PG) vs.
  Edmund Jenings, Esq. procurator for
  George Buchanan & his wife Margarett
  & Edward Sprigg administrators dbn
  of Robert Levett. William Murdock
  (sheriff, PG) summoned Maj. Edward
  Sprigg & Mrs. Margarett Buchanan.
  George Buchanan is "non est".
- Edward Fottrell (AA) vs. William
  Cumming, Esq. procurator for
  surviving executors of Samuel Young,
  Esq. & William Alexander & his wife
  Araminta executrix of Joseph Young,
  Esq. Nat. Rigbie (sheriff, BA)
  summoned Samuel Young, Esq.

Court Session: 1738

13 March. Thomas Aisquith (g, SM)
exhibited:
- bond of Ann Realey administratrix of
  Robert Realey. Sureties: John Dial,
  William Richardson. Date: 19
  February 1738.
- inventory of John Harrison.
- inventory & LoD of Thomas Plummer.
- inventory & LoD of Joseph Hopewell.
- accounts of Martha Brocklehouse
  administratrix of Anthony
  Brocklehouse.
- accounts of Isaac Pavett & his wife
  Margarett administratrix of Jonathon
  Bisco.
- accounts of Mary Teneson
  administratrix of Abraham Teneson.
- accounts of Mary Clark
  administratrix of Robert Clark.

14 March. H. Wells Stokes (g, BA)
exhibited:
- bond of Elisabeth Grant executrix of
  Alexander Grant. Sureties: Richard
  Gott, John Merryman. Date: 31
  January 1738.
- will of Elisabeth Finshaw,
  constituting Thomas Matthews
  executors. Said Matthews was
  granted administration. Sureties:
  Charles Robinson, William Harvey.

Court Session: 1738

Date: 5 February 1738.
- will of Joseph Beasman, constituting Elisabeth Beasman executrix. Said Elisabeth was granted administration. Sureties: John Hawkins (Patapsco), George Brown (weaver). Date: 20 February 1738.

31:12
- will of William Hitchcock, constituting Ann Hitchcock executrix. Said Ann was granted administration. Sureties: Joseph Harris, William Hitchcock. Date: 8 March 1738.
- will of William Smith, constituting Mary Smith executrix.
- bond of Hester Bond administratrix of Peter Bond. Sureties: Isaac Butterworth, Henry Garrott, Abraham Boyd. Date: 23 December 1737.
- bond of Christiana Gadd executrix of Thomas Gadd. Sureties: William Gadd, William Ditto. Date: 19 February 1738.
- bond of Charles Wells administrator of John Giles. Sureties: Ulrick Burk, William Hughs. Date: 9 March 1738.
- additional inventory & LoD of Benjamin Hanson.
- accounts of Sarah Hanson administratrix of Benjamin Hanson.

15 March. Gabriel Parker (g, CV) exhibited:
- will of Charles Bowen, constituting Ann Bowen executrix. Said Ann was granted administration. Sureties: James Bowen, John Young. Date: 9 March 1738.
- bond of John Prindowell & Ellis Slater administrators of Althea Corkett. Sureties: Benjamin Johns, James Heighe. Date: 30 January 1738.
- bond of Benjamin Sedwick administrator of Elisabeth Sedgwick. Sureties: Samuel Young (attorney), Ellis Slater. Date: 17 February 1738.
- bond of Vachel Denton administrator of Zachariah Lusby. Surety: Edward Fottrell (g, Annapolis, AA). Date:

Court Session: 1738

26 March 1738.
- inventory of George Harris.
- inventory of Capt. Posth. Thornton.
- inventory of William Gray.
- inventory of John Braban.
- accounts of William Matthews & his wife Alice executrix of Jesse Jacob Bourne.

Exhibited from PG:
- bond of William Farqua executor of Allen Farqua. Sureties: Thomas Beatty, James Beatty.

16 March. Mayberry Helm who married Ann one of daughters of Edward Parish (AA, dec'd) vs. Mary Warman wife of Stephen Warman & Edward Parish acting executors of said dec'd. Sheriff (BA) to summon defendants to render final accounts.

17 March. Mr. Gabriel Parker (CV) to examine accounts of:
- Richard Gibson administrator of Peter Sewall (CV).

Mr. Thomas Aisquith (SM) to examine accounts of:
- Thomas Boult & his wife Eliza administrators of Robert Salmon (SM).
- James Egerton administrator of Charles Egerton (SM).

Risdon Bozman administrator of John Knowles vs. Jacob Lockerman & his wife Elisabeth. Bill of costs filed.

31:13   Mr. John Pitt (DO) to examine accounts of:
- Martha Hollock executrix of John Hollock (DO).

Mr. Joseph Earle (QA) vs. John Sutton (TA) one of witnesses to will of Christopher St. Tee (TA). Sheriff (TA) to summon defendant to prove said will.

Exhibited from AA:
- will of Dr. William Stevenson, constituting his wife Francina Augustina Stevenson executrix.

Exhibited petition of Hugh Matthews, Jr.
(CE). Petitioner married Mary Cooper
daughter of Edward Cooper (CE, dec'd).
Said Mary is now dec'd, without issue.
Mentions: Mary Peiree widow & mother to
said Mary. Petitioner was granted LoA
on estate of his wife.

Court Session: 1739

27 March. Exhibited from CE:
• bond of Hugh Matthews, Jr.
  administrator of Mary Matthews.
  Surety: Edward Fottrell (g,
  Annapolis, AA). Date: 26 March
  1739.

Thomas Fisher (QA) vs. estate of Richard
Fisher (QA). Caveat against a pretended
will being probated.

Exhibited from AA:
• bond of Francina Augustina Stevenson
  executrix of Dr. William Stevenson.
  Sureties: Edmond Jenings, Esq.
  (Annapolis, AA), John Brice (g,
  Annapolis, AA). Date: 26 March
  1739.

29 March. Mr. Charles Hynson (KE) to
examine accounts of:
• Richard Ridgeway & Sarah England
  executors of Daniel Greenwood (KE).

31:14   Exhibited from PG:
• LoD of estate of Allen Farquar.

30 March. Peter Dent (g, PG) exhibited:
• inventory of Allen Farquar.
• bond of Elisabeth Walker
  administratrix of John Walker.
  Sureties: James Lee, Sr., James Lee,
  Jr. Date: 26 February 1738.
• inventory of John Frazer, Jr.
• accounts of Mary Willett executrix
  of Charles Willett.
• accounts of Joseph Green Simson &
  his wife Eliza administratrix of
  George Alder.

Thomas Fisher heir at law to Richard
Fisher (QA, dec'd) vs. John Barnard

(QA). Sheriff (QA) to summon defendant to show cause why he does not exhibit pretended will of dec'd.

Exhibited from AA:
- Mary Covell administratrix of Jonathon Covell. Sureties: Nehemiah Mellor, Jeremiah Covell. Date: 30 March 1739.

31 March. Nehemiah King (SO) exhibited:
- will of James Round, Sr., constituting Catherine Round executrix. Said Catherine was granted administration. Sureties: John Henry, Thomas Simpson. Date: 21 March 1738.
- will of William Simpson, constituting Thomas Simpson executor. Said Thomas was granted administration. Sureties: John White (seaside), Hugh Stevenson. Date: 21 March 1738.
- bond of John Handy administrator of George Lank. Surety: Henry Ballard. Date: 5 March 1738. Also, renunciation of Mary Lank widow, recommending John Handy. Date: 27 February 1738/9.
- bond of Elisabeth Beasey administratrix of Richard Simpson. Sureties: Peter Giltrap, William Pepper. Date: 21 March 1738.
- bond of Elisabeth Beasey administratrix of William Beasey. Sureties: George Howard, William Pepper. Date: 21 March 1738.
- bond of Presgrave Turvile administrator of Thomas Howard. Sureties: Thomas Riley, Alexander Linch. Date: 21 March 1738.
- bond of Ann Short administratrix of Edward Short. Sureties: Edward Short, John Short. Date: 24 March 1738.

31:15
- inventory of John Gillett.
- inventory of George Sharp.
- inventory of George Bozman.
- inventory of John Onorton.
- inventory of Abraham Lamberson.
- accounts of Catherine Steward administratrix of Rev. William

Steward.
- accounts of Hannah Hull executrix of
  Daniel Hull.
- accounts of Rebbecca Beard
  administratrix of Lewis Beard.
- accounts of Stephen Bredell
  administrator of Isaiah Bredell.
- accounts of James Train & his wife
  Sarah administratrix of Barkley
  Fisher.

James Earle (g, QA) exhibited:
- will of Samuel Cook (taylor),
  constituting Solomon Clayton
  executor. Said Clayton was granted
  administration. Sureties: Nathaniel
  Cleaves, George Smith. Date: 11
  December 1738.
- bond of John Burk & John Pratt
  executors of Thomas Burk. Sureties:
  John Walker, John Croneen. Also,
  widow's election. Date: 22 January
  1738.
- will of Col. Richard Tilghman,
  constituting Anna Maria Tilghman &
  Richard Tilghman executors. Said
  executors were granted
  administration. Also, widow's
  election. Sureties: Matthew
  Tilghman Ward, Esq., George Robins
  (g). Date: 14 February 1738.
- will of William Whitaker. Also,
  renunciation of widow & executor.
  Also, bond of Richard Houlden
  administrator. Sureties: William
  Murphey, Daniel Griffith. Date: 5
  February 1738.
- bond of Sarah Hammond executrix of
  John Hammond. Sureties: John Welsh,
  Thomas Moody. Date: 19 March 1738.
- bond of John Rawles administrator of
  John Rawles, Sr. Sureties: Joseph
  Deroachburn, Andrew Belgrave. Date:
  16 January 1738.
- bond of Grace Cooper administratrix
  of Rev. Thomas Phillips. Sureties:
  Joseph Wickes, Matthew Brown. Date:
  16 January 1738.
- bond of Elisabeth administratrix of
  John Bolton. Sureties: John Green,
  John Clemans. Date: 4 February
  1738.

Court Session: 1739

- bond of James Williams administrator of John Barncclough. Sureties: John Williams, John Walker. Date: 16 February 1738.
- bond of James Bower administrator of James Bower, Sr. (p). Sureties: John Nabb, Thomas Macclannahan. Date: 28 February 1738. Also, renunciation of Barbara Bower widow. Date: 26 February 1738.
- bond of Tabitha Gwin administratrix of James Gwin. Sureties: Richard Holding, Thomas Smith. Date: 19 March 1738.

31:16
- inventory of Charles Seth.
- additional inventory of Cornelia Sparkes.
- inventory of Samuel Melegue.
- inventory of Richard Holding.
- inventory of Nathaniel Hinsley.
- additional inventory of Mathew Mason.
- inventory of Leon Gray.
- inventory & LoD of Gregory Rock.
- inventory of Cullen Andrew.
- accounts of John Tillottson & John Akinson & his wife Joan administrators of Christopher Tillottson.
- accounts of Richard Gould executor of James Gould.
- additional accounts of John Welsh administrator of James Towers.

2 April. Exhibited from BA:
- will of Thomas Todd, constituting Elenor Todd, Bazil Dorsey, & Caleb Dorsey executors. Said executors were granted administration. Sureties: Richard Dorsey, Samuel Dorsey. Date: 2 April 1739.

7 April. Mr. Michael Macnemara (g, AA) exhibited:
- inventory of James Donaldson.

9 April. Mr. Peter Dent (PG) to examine accounts of:
- Catherine Plafay administratrix of Philip Plafay (PG).
- Barbara Wood administratrix of John Wood (PG).

Court Session: 1739

<u>10 April</u>. Mr. Nehemiah King (SO) to examine accounts of:
- Jane Gilliland acting executrix of John Gilliland (SO).
- Rebecca Taylor administratrix of Thomas Taylor (SO).
- Samuel Gellett acting executor of John Gellett (SO).
- Mary Tingle executrix of John Tingle (SO).
- Mary Sharp administratrix of George Sharp (SO).
- George Gale administrator of John Follows (SO).

Thomas Bullen (g, TA) exhibited:
- will of Edmund Fish, Jr., constituting Sarah Greason executrix. Said Greason was granted administration. Sureties: Park Webb, Ralph Elston. Date: 2 February 1738.
- will of Philip Banan. Also, bond of Mary Banan administratrix. Sureties: Henry Beuges, Dennis Larey, John Porter. Date: 2 February 1738.
- bond of Robert Morris agent for Foster Cunliff, Esq. administrator of Henry Bowdle. Sureties: William White, Risdon Bozman. Date: 27 January 1738.
- bond of Elisabeth Gasken administratrix of John Gasken. Sureties: John Hickson, Andrew Baning. Date: 27 February 1738.
- inventory of William Bennett.
- inventory of Kenelm Skillington.
- inventory of James Horney.
- inventory of Daniel Sherwood.
- additional inventory & LoD of Caleb Clarke.

31:17

Mr. James Earle (QA) to examine accounts of:
- Violet Primrose administrator of Elisabeth Bath (QA).
- Edward Young & Thomas Barnett executors of David Young (QA). Additional accounts.

Court Session: 1739

Mr. Thomas Bullen (TA) to examine
accounts of:
• Margaret Connolly administratrix of
  Christopher Connolly (TA).

16 April. Gabriel Parker (g, CV)
exhibited:
• inventory of Peter Davis.
• inventory of Arthur Jones.
• additional inventory of Peter
  Sawell.
• accounts of Richard Gibson
  administrator of Peter Sawell.

17 April. Mr. Charles Hynson (KE) to
examine accounts of:
• John Rasin executor of John Keare
  (KE).
• John Rasin executor of Thomas Rasin
  (KE).

H. Wells Stokes (BA) to examine accounts
of:
• Benjamin Cadle executor of Joseph
  Mead (BA).

19 April. Mr. Charles Hynson (KE) to
examine accounts of:
• James Moore & Lambert Wilmer
  executors of Simon Wilmer (KE).

25 April. Samuel Hanson (g, CH)
exhibited:
• inventory of George Thomas.
• accounts of Mary Hanna
  administratrix of Alexander Hanna.
• accounts of Bathea Higton
  administratrix of John Higton.
• accounts of Thomas Hardman & his
  wife Elisabeth administratrix of
  Henry Wathen.
• additional accounts of Bathea Higton
  administratrix of John Higton.

26 April. H. Wells Stokes (g, BA)
exhibited:
• will of Thomas Dulany, constituting
  Sarah Dulany executrix. Said Sarah
  was granted administration.
  Sureties: Stephen Boddy, Nicholas
  Haile. Date: 4 April 1739.
• will of John Simkin, constituting

Priscilla Simkin executrix. Said Priscilla was granted administration. Sureties: Edward Roberts, Charles Motherby. Date: 23 April 1739.

31:18 • bond of Elisabeth Garrettson & George Garrettson administrators of Garrett Garrettson. Sureties: John Garrettson, James Garrettson. Date: 23 March 1738.

• bond of Isabella Bond administratrix of John Bond. Sureties: Benjamin Bond, Charles Baker. Date: 4 April 1739.

• bond of John Chamberlaine administrator of Thomas Chamberlaine. Sureties: William Standiford, Samuel Standiford. Date: 5 April 1739.

• inventory of Elisabeth Fisham.
• inventory & LoD of Peter Bond.
• inventory of Joseph Beasman.
• accounts of Elisabeth Miles administratrix of Evan Miles.

28 April. Mr. James Earle (QA) to examine accounts of:
• Thomas Tanner administrator of William Tanner (QA).
• William Joyner executor of John Roberts (QA).
• George Sparks administrator dbn of John Sparks (QA).

1 May. Thomas Aisquith (g, SM) exhibited:
• will of Ubgate Reeves, constituting Thomas Reeves executor. Said Thomas was granted administration. Sureties: Justinian Jordan, John Tipett. Date: 6 March 1738.
• will of John Stewart, constituting Monaca Stewart executrix. Said Monaca was granted administration. Sureties: Jonathon Leate, James Brown. Date: 6 March 1738.
• will of William Alburt, constituting Elisabeth Alburt executrix. Said Elisabeth was granted administration. Also, widow's election. Sureties: John Urquhart, Samuel Wood. Date: 7 March 1738.

- will of William Anderson, constituting Mary Anderson executrix. Said Mary was granted administration. Also, widow's election. Sureties: John Welch, Barnaby Angell. Date: 19 March 1738.
- will of Charles King, constituting Charles King executor. Said executor was granted administration. Sureties: Hugh Hopewell, Stephen Milburn. Date: 9 April 1739.
- will of Elisabeth Albert, constituting George Bowles executor. Said Bowles was granted administration. Sureties: James Keech, Samuel Keech. Date: 27 April 1739.
- will of John Millman, constituting Mary Millman executrix. Also, widow's election.
- inventory of Richard Edelen.
- inventory & LoD of Michael Raley.
- inventory & LoD of Thomas Blackman.
- inventory & LoD of William Wilkinson.
- inventory & LoD of James Baker.
- accounts of Elenor Foster administratrix of James Foster.
- accounts of Mary MacWilliams administratrix of Thomas MacWilliams.
- accounts of Thomas Chamberlaine & his wife Catherine executrix of John Bullock.
- accounts of Christopher Shener administrator of John Sweatman.
- accounts of Elisabeth Haseler administratrix of Richard Haseler.

31:19
- accounts of Ann Farthing administratrix of William Meriea Farthing.
- accounts of Justinian Teneson administrator of William Gibson.
- accounts of John Dial & his wife Sarah executrix of Richard Shirley.

5 May. Michael Macnemara (g, AA) exhibited:
- inventory of Dr. William Stevenson.

Court Session: 1739

7 May. Exhibited from TA:
* will of Christopher Santee,
  constituting his wife Ann & his son
  Christopher executors.

Edward Hall (g, BA) vs. estate of his
father John Hall (BA). Caveat against
recording inventory.

Court Session: 8 May 1739

Docket:
* Richard Francis, Esq. procurator for
  Abigail Ryan executrix of Cornelius
  Ryan (KE) vs. Edmund Jennings, Esq.
  procurator for Henry Truelock (KE).
  Sheriff (KE) to summon defendant to
  show cause why dec'd's will,
  constituting plaintiff executrix,
  should not be proved. Defendant
  exhibited a subsequent will,
  constituting defendant executor.
  Said Francis has removed to VA.
  Dismissed.
* E.J. for James Maxwell, et.al. (BA)
  vs. B.Y. & W.C. for William Savory
  administrator dbn of Col. James
  Maxwell & administrator of James
  Maxwell. Libel, answer.
* Christopher Gardner son of
  Christopher Gardner (BA, dec'd) vs.
  William Cumming, Esq. procurator for
  Lloyd Harris administrator dbn of
  dec'd. Summons to defendant to show
  cause why he conceals effects of
  dec'd.
* Margaret Harris widow of William
  Harris (AA) vs. George Lawson (CE)
  executor of said William. Sheriff
  (CE) to summon defendant to render
  final accounts & render payment to
  plaintiff. Agree. Struck off.
* B.Y. for Charles Digges for self,
  et.al. (PG) vs. E.J. for William
  Digges acting executor of Edward
  Digges. Petition. Summons to take
  testimony from John Digges "de bene
  esse".
* William Cumming, Esq. procurator for
  John Hall executor of Johanna Hall
  (BA) vs. James Phillips (BA) son of
  said Johanna. Nat. Rigbie (sheriff,

31:20

Court Session: 8 May 1739

BA) to summon defendant to show
cause why he conceals estate of
dec'd.

- B.Y. for John Levett (PG) vs.
George Buchanan & his wife Margaret
& Edward Sprigg administrators dbn
of Robert Levett. Petition. Edmund
Jenings, Esq. procurator for said
Edward.

- Edward Fottrell (AA) vs. W.C. for
surviving executors of Samuel Young,
Esq. & William Alexander & his wife
Araminta executrix of Joseph Young,
Esq. Libel. William Cumming, Esq.
procurator for Samuel Young.

31:21 • Mr. Joseph Earle (QA) vs. John
Sutton (TA) one of witnesses to will
of Christopher St. Tee (TA). J.
Goldsborough (sheriff, TA) to summon
defendant to prove said will. Said
Sutton proved said will.
Discontinued.

- Maybery Helm who married Ann one of
daughters of Edward Parish (AA,
dec'd) vs. Mary Warman wife of
Stephen Warman & Edward Parish
acting executors of dec'd. Zach.
Maccubbin (sheriff, AA) to summon
defendants to render final accounts.
Said Edward Parish deposed that said
Mary Warman is so very ill that he
is thereby rendered incapable of
attending this Court.

- Thomas Fisher heir at law to Richard
Fisher (QA) vs. John Barnard (QA).
Robert Norr. Wright (sheriff, QA) to
summon defendant to produce
pretended will of dec'd.

- W.C. for Roger Peele for self & his
2 brothers Robert & Samuel Peele vs.
William Peele administrator of
Samuel & Robert Peele.

Court Session: 1739

31:22   8 May. John Pitt (g, DO) exhibited:
- will of Archibald Simpson,
constituting Elioner Simpson
executrix. Said Elioner was granted
administration. Sureties: John
McKeel, William Grantham. Date: 14
March 1738.

Court Session: 1739

- will of James Mosley. Also, bond of Thomas Nevett administrator. Sureties: William Cullen, Charles Powell. Also, renunciation of William Treeg & Henry Hooper. Date: 15 March 1738.
- will of James Treeg, constituting Capt. Henry Tripp executor.
- bond of James Peterkin executor of Mary Peterkin. Sureties: John McKeele, William Byus. Date: 10 April 1739.
- bond of Mary Branklin administratrix of Henry Branklin. Sureties: Thomas Vickars, John Vickars. Date: 14 March 1738.
- bond of John Sumners administrator of Isaac Sumners. Sureties: Benjamin Nicholls, Francis Watson. Date: 14 March 1738.
- bond of William Cullen administrator of James Cullen. Sureties: Thomas Nevett, Charles Powell. Date: 15 March 1738.
- bond of Anarah Coxon administratrix of Edward Coxon. Sureties: Abraham Clarke, Stephen Fleearty. Date: 31 March 1739.
- accounts of William Stokes & his wife Mary administrators of David Robson.

9 May. Charles Hynson (g, KE) exhibited:
- will of Mary Smithers, constituting John Carvill executor. Said Carvill was granted administration. Sureties: Samuel Groome, William Hynson. Date: 10 March 1738.
- will of William Thomas, constituting Henry Thomas & William Thomas executors. Said executors were granted administration. Sureties: William Trew, Edward Beck. Date: 20 April 1739.
- will of Sarah Evans, constituting Abraham Corwardine executor.
- bond of Mary Cruckshanks executrix of James Cruckshanks. Sureties: William Harris, John Carvill. Date: 1 March 1738.
- bond of Daniel Flinn & Ann Flinn

executors of Daniel Flinn.
Sureties: Bowles Green, Joseph
Mason. Date: 10 March 1738.
- bond of Mary Bellos administratrix
of Francis Bellos. Sureties:
Francis Lamb, Daniel Perkins. Date:
17 March 1738.
- bond of William Savory administrator
of William Savory. Sureties: Philip
Rickets, George Griffith. Date: 25
April 1739.

31:23
- inventory of Simon Wilmer.
- inventory of William Pell.
- inventory & LoD of John Phillips.
- inventory of William Wilson.
- accounts of Edward Diens
administrator of William Diens.
- accounts of Jackson Griffith
surviving executor of Benjamin
Griffith.
- accounts of Hanse Hanson & John
Young & his wife Elisabeth executors
of Hans Hanson.

Exhibited from AA:
- inventory of George Uriell.

10 May. Thomas Bullen (g, TA)
exhibited:
- additional inventory of William
Michael.
- inventory of Henry Bowdle.
- inventory of Edmund Fish.
- accounts of John Sherwood & Francis
Sherwood executors of Francis
Sherwood.
- accounts of Sarah Brown
administratrix of Nicholas Brown.
- accounts of John Pritchard & his
wife Jane administratrix of Patrick
Mulican.
- accounts of Sarah Mullikan & William
Mullikan executors of John Mullikan.

12 May. Exhibited from AA:
- accounts of John Iiams acting
executor of William Iiams.

15 May. Nehemiah King (g, SO)
exhibited:
- will of Jobe Shery. Also, bond of
Littleton Townsend administrator.

Court Session: 1739

Sureties: John Dennis, Jr., William
Catlin. Date: 3 January 1738.
- bond of Mary Jones administratrix of
  James Jones. Sureties: Robert
  Jones, Daniel Jones. Date: 26 April
  1739.
- inventory of John Hunter.
- inventory of Jobe Shery.
- accounts of Peris Chapman
  administrator of John Hunter.
- accounts of Robert Hodge
  administrator of Ezekiel Denning.
- accounts of Elisabeth & William
  Walton executors of Fisher Walton.
- accounts of Mary Lockwood
  administratrix of Richard Lockwood.
- accounts of Jane Gilliland acting
  executrix of John Gilliland.
- accounts of William Kibble
  administrator of John Stevens.

Joseph Allen vs. Barbara Allen
administratrix of Joseph Allen.
Exhibited bill of costs for each.

17 May. Exhibited from BA:
- bond of Joshua George administrator
  of Francis Holland. Sureties (CE):
  William Rumsey, John Baldwin. Date:
  17 May 1739.

31:24   William Rumsey (g, CE) exhibited:
- will of Samuel Young, constituting
  Elinor Young executrix. Said Elinor
  was granted administration.
  Sureties: Benjamin Chew, John Young.
  Date: 13 March 1738.
- will of Thomas Johnson, constituting
  Rebecca Johnson executrix. Said
  Rebecca was granted administration.
  Sureties: William Wye, Benjamin
  Pearce. Date: 14 March 1738.
- will of Alexander Ewing. Also, bond
  of James Porter & Nathaniel Ewing
  acting executors. Sureties: William
  Mitchell, Joshua Ewing. Date: 15
  March 1738. Also, renunciation of
  A. Barry. Date: 15 March 1738.
  Also, renunciation of Samuell Ewing.
  Date: 6 March 1738/9.
- will of William Douglas,
  constituting Mary Douglas executrix.

Page 206

Court Session: 1739

- bond of John Rickets administrator of John Thomas Rickets. Sureties: Thomas Rickets, James Roberts. Also, renunciation of Thomas Rickets (eldest son), recommending his next eldest brother. Date: 30 April 1739.
- inventory of Martha Mounts.
- inventory of James Husband.
- inventory of Fouch Davis.

Exhibited from SO:
- inventory of Daniel Brown.
- additional accounts of William Kibble administrator of John Stevens.

18 May. Exhibited from DO:
- accounts of Huett Nutter executor of Sarah Nutter.

21 May. Thomas Bullen (g, TA) exhibited:
- will of Thomas Pamphilon, constituting Margaret Pamphilon executrix. Said Margaret was granted administration. Also, widow's election. Sureties: Richard Aletem, John Valiant. Date: 11 April 1739.
- will of Denis Hopkins, constituting Eliza Hopkins executrix. Said Eliza was granted administration. Also, widow's election. Sureties: George Prouse, John Guy Williams. Date: 4 May 1739.
- will of Sarah Calk, constituting James Calk executor. Said James was granted administration. Sureties: Peter Calk, Bartholomew Roberts. Date: 8 May 1739.
- will of James Dawson, constituting Mary Dawson & Impey Dawson executors. Said executors were granted administration. Sureties: Risdon Bozman, William Hambleton. Date: 8 May 1739.
- 31:25 • will of William Bush. Also, widow's election. Also, renunciation of 1 executor.
- bond of Elisabeth Davison administratrix of John Davison.

Court Session: 1739

Sureties: Thomas Williams, Thomas
Higgins, William Whaley. Date: 6
April 1739.
- bond of John Batcheldor & his wife
Elisabeth administratrix of John
Burgess. Sureties: Samuel Dunning,
Andrew Banning. Date: 18 May 1739.

Exhibited from PG:
- will of Richard Bevan, Sr.,
constituting Richard Bevan executor.

22 May. Exhibited from QA:
- accounts of Solomon Clayton
administrator of Thomas Poole.

Exhibited from PG:
- will of Edward Holmes. Also, bond
of Edward Holmes surviving executor.
Sureties: Samuel Brassher, Garrett
Fitzgerald. Date: 22 May 1739.

24 May. Mr. Thomas Bullen (TA) to
examine accounts of:
- Elisabeth Michael executrix of
William Michael (TA).
- Edward Neal & Park Webb executors of
Richard Wiles (TA).
- Robert Newcam & his wife Ann
executrix of John Dawson, Jr. (TA).
2nd additional accounts.
- Robert Newcam & his wife Ann
administratrix of John Price (TA).
Additional accounts.

Mr. John Pitt (DO) to examine accounts
of:
- Elisabeth Campbell, Adam Muir, &
Thomas Muir executors of Walter
Campbell (DO).

25 May. Joseph Ennalls & his wife Mary
executrix of Thomas Haskins (DO) vs.
Elisabeth Holland, William Holland, &
Thomas Holland executors of William
Holland, Esq. (AA). Sheriff (DO) to
summon said Elisabeth to render answer.
Sheriff (CV) to summon said William &
Thomas to render answer.

28 May. Exhibited from AA:
- bond of Philip Syng administrator of

Court Session: 1739

Philip Syng. Surety: Hon. Levin Gale, Esq. (SO). Date: 28 May 1739.

29 May. Exhibited from PG:
• bond of William Murdock administrator of Henry Buttler. Sureties: Turnor Wootton, Osborn Sprigg. Date: 29 May 1739.

31:26 Exhibited bond of William Tilghman as Deputy Commissary (QA). Sureties: Robert Lloyd (g, QA), Edward Lloyd (g, TA). Date: 29 May 1739.

31 May. Exhibited from SM:
• accounts of Dryden Forbes administratrix of John Forbes.

Exhibited from AA:
• inventory of Robert Reynolds.

Mr. H. Wells Stokes (BA) to examine accounts of:
• Hannah Simmans, George Simmans, & Charles Simmans executors of Charles Simmans (BA).

2 June. Mr. Thomas Aisquith (SM) to examine accounts of:
• Ann Smith administratrix of Charles Smith (SM).

8 June. Mr. John Pitt (DO) to examine accounts of:
• Elisabeth Cole administratrix of John Cole (DO).

9 June. Exhibited from CV:
• LoD on estate of Col. John Smith.
• 11 June. accounts of Joseph Hall executor of Col. John Smith.

12 June. Mr. Thomas Bullen (TA) to examine accounts of:
• John Weymouth administrator of John Halsey (TA).

Mr. William Rumsey (CE) to examine accounts of:
• John Currer administrator of John Currer (CE).
• Elisabeth McManus executrix of John

Court Session: 1739

McManus (CE).
- Sarah Pearce administratrix of William Pearce (CE).

Mr. Charles Hynson (KE) to examine accounts of:
- Henry Ramsey & his wife Catherine & Edward Mitchell, Jr. administrators of John Hankin (KE).
- Jane Frisby administratrix of William Frisby (KE).

Samuel Hanson (CH) to examine accounts of:
- John Theobalds & his wife Elisabeth acting administratrix of Dr. Daniel Jenifer (CH). Additional accounts.
- Thomas Mitchell executor of Richard Wheeler (CH). 2nd additional accounts.

31:27 Mr. William Tilghman (QA) to examine accounts of:
- Hannah Killiow administratrix of William Killiow (QA).

14 June. Exhibited from AA:
- additional accounts of Mary Towgood & Richard Lane executors of Col. Josias Towgood.

15 June. Exhibited from CE:
- additional accounts of William Alexander & his wife Araminta executrix of Col. Joseph Young.

Exhibited from BA:
- additional inventory of William Wheeler. Also, accounts of Martha Wheeler executrix.

16 June. Exhibited from AA:
- bond of Mary Thorp administratrix of George Thorp. Sureties: Edward Fottrell, Thomas Lynn. Date: 16 June 1739.

18 June. Mr. Gabriel Parker (CV) to examine accounts of:
- John Skinner executor of William Skinner (CV).
- Rebecca Day executrix of William Day

(CV).

<u>21 June</u>. Gabriel Parker (g, CV)
exhibited:
- bond of Catherine Orm administratrix
  of John Orme. Sureties: George
  Lawrence, John Yoe. Date: 5 May
  1739.
- inventory of John Brome.
- inventory of Elisabeth Sedwick.
- inventory of Charles Bowen.

Exhibited from AA:
- will of John Gaither, constituting
  his wife Elisabeth & his son
  Benjamin Gaither executors.

Peter Dent (g, PG) exhibited:
- will of Joseph Coleman, constituting
  Thomas Coleman & Mordica Coleman
  executors. Said Thomas & Mordica
  were granted administration.
  Sureties: George Scott, Charles
  Burgess. Date: 27 March 1739.
- will of Mrs. Martha Greenfield.
  Also, bond of Martha Warring
  executrix. Sureties: Leonard
  Covington, Francis Waring. Date: 30
  March 1739. Also, renunciation of
  Ann Wright (executrix with Mr.
  Henry Hawkins & her sister Martha
  Waring), recommending Francis
  Waring. Date: March 1739. Also,
  renunciation of Hen. Hawkins
  executor. Date: 25 February 1738/9.
- will of Henry Ward, constituting
  Margaret Ward & Elisabeth Ward
  executrices. Said Margaret &
  Elisabeth were granted
  administration. Sureties: John
  Stoddart, Henry Acton. Date: 4 June
  1739.
- will of John Taylor, constituting
  Unice Taylor executrix.
- will of John Abington, exhibited by
  Dr. Andrew Scott & his wife Mary
  executrix. Also, widow's election.
- bond of Michael Jones administrator
  of Daniel Freeman. Sureties: Mathew
  Markland, James Willson. Date: 28
  March 1739.
- bond of Thomas Brown administrator

31:28

of Thomas Winder. Sureties: Edmond
Carthidge, Stephen Renfrow. Date:
20 April 1739.
- inventory of Roger Matthews.
- inventory of Humphry Sawyer.
- inventory of John Turner.
- inventory of Nicholas Brumley.
- accounts of Henry Acton & his wife
  Johanna executrix of Thomas
  Millstead.
- additional accounts of William
  Decregar & his wife Ann executrix of
  John Jones.
- 3rd additional accounts of Mary
  Offutt administratrix of William
  Offutt.
- accounts of John Beall administrator
  of Joshua Calvert.
- 2nd additional accounts of John Boyd
  administrator of Isaac Hyde.

22 June. Exhibited from CH:
- accounts of Andrew Scott
  administrator of Capt. John Watts.

Mr. Peter Dent (PG) to examine accounts
of:
- Ann Pottenger executrix of Robert
  Pottenger (PG).

25 June. Sheriff (BA) to summon Jane
Partridge wife of Dr. Buttler Partridge
(BA) to prove will of William Wheeler
(BA). Said Jane is one of witnesses.

26 June. Exhibited from AA:
- will of Humphrey Meredith
  (cordwainer, Annapolis). Also, bond
  of Elisabeth Meredith acting
  executrix. Sureties: William
  Ghiselin (AA), Richard Snowden (AA),
  Andrew Farrell (Philadelphia).
  Also, renunciation of Patrick Creagh
  (Annapolis), recommending Elisabeth
  Meredith widow. Date: 26 June 1739.
  Witnesses: Richard Burdus, Josh.
  Hopkinson.

31:29 Gabriel Parker (g, CV) exhibited:
- additional accounts of Martha
  Lingham executrix of Thomas Lingham.

Court Session: 1739

Mr. Peter Dent (PG) to examine accounts of:
- Joseph Chapline administrator of Samuel Fenley (PG).

27 June. Exhibited from AA:
- bond of Sarah Brown administratrix of John Brown. Sureties: John Franklin, Joseph Brown. Date: 27 June 1739.

2 July. Samuel Hanson (g, CH) exhibited:
- will of John Thompson, constituting Thomas Thompson & William Thompson executors. Said executors were granted administration. Sureties: John Beal, Sr., John Thompson. Date: 8 May 1739.
- will of Peter Villet, constituting Celia Villet executrix. Said Celia was granted administration. Sureties: John Moran, John Parker. Date: 16 May 1739.
- will of Edward Gilpin, constituting his wife Elisabeth Gilpin executrix.
- inventory of Marmaduke Simes.
- additional inventory of Zachariah Wade.
- inventory of John Glaze.
- inventory of Mark Penn.
- accounts of Samuel Adams & his wife Charity administratrix of Zachariah Wade.
- accounts of Benjamin Adams administrator of John Mackey.
- accounts of Charles Adams & his wife Mary executrix of Joshua Ratcliffe.

Mr. Nehemiah King (SO) to examine accounts of:
- Mary Hall administratrix of Alexander Hall (SO).
- James Peterkin & his wife Elisabeth administratrix of William Nutter (SO).
- Edmond Cropper administrator of Godfry Sprogle (SO).
- Mary Bozman administratrix of George Bozman (SO).

Court Session: 1739

8 July. Mr. Charles Hynson (KE) to examine accounts of:
* Barbara Corse administratrix of William Corse (KE).
* Marton Potter & his wife Susannah executrix of John Johnson, Esq. (KE). Additional accounts.

9 July. Nehemiah King (g, SO) exhibited:
* will of Peter Fitchgarrill, constituting John Woolford executor. Said Woolford was granted administration. Sureties: Thomas Brown, David Brown. Date: 4 June 1739.
* will of Jacob Waggaman, constituting Ephraim Waggaman executor. Also, widow's election. Said Ephraim was granted administration. Sureties: David Wilson, Bowd. Robins. Date: 19 June 1739.
* will of John Brittingham. Also, widow's election. Also, bond of Elijah Brittingham administrator. Sureties: James Baker, John Parsons. Date: 1 June 1739.
* will of John Larramur. Also, widow's election.
* will of Mathew Parremore.
* will of William Freeman. Also, widow's election.
* bond of Alexander Buncle administrator of John Johnston. Sureties: James Martin, Edmund Hough. Date: 20 April 1739.
* bond of Rachel Stevens administratrix of Richard Stevens. Sureties: John Parson, William Kibble. Date: 1 June 1739.
* bond of William Jarman administrator of Henry Jarman. Sureties: Henry Turner, Samuel Parker. Date: 8 June 1739.
* bond of Absolom Beszix administrator of John Allison. Sureties: Benjamin Turvile, Alexander Linch. Date: 19 June 1739.
* bond of Mary Fimmons administratrix of Samuel Fimmons. Sureties: John Fimmons, Dennis Hudson. Date: 19 June 1739.

31:30

Court Session: 1739

- inventory of Mathew Nutter.
- inventory of Thomas Howard.
- inventory of Henry Jarman.
- inventory of John Brittingham.
- inventory of William Beasey.
- inventory & LoD of George Lanck.
- inventory of William Simpson.
- inventory of James Rownds.
- inventory of Richard Simpson.
- inventory & LoD of Edward Short.
- accounts of Mary Tingle executrix of John Tingle.
- accounts of Rebecca Taylor (alias Rebecca Smith) administratrix of Thomas Taylor.
- accounts of Presgrave Turvile administrator of Thomas Howard.

Court Session: 10 July 1739

Docket:
- E.J. for James Maxwell, et.al. (BA) vs. R.F. & W.C. for William Savory administrator dbn of Col. James Maxwell & administrator of James Maxwell. Libel, answer
- Christopher Gardner son of Christopher Gardner (BA, dec'd) vs. William Cumming, Esq. procurator for Lloyd Harris (BA) administrator dbn of said dec'd. Summons to defendant to show cause why he conceals effects of dec'd.
- 31:31 • Benjamin Young, Esq. procurator for Charles Digges for self, et.al. (PG) vs. E.J. for William Digges acting executor of Edward Digges. Summons to take testimony of John Digges.
- John Hall executor of Johanna Hall (BA) vs. Edmund Jennings, Esq. procurator for James Phillips (BA) son of said Johanna. Sheriff (BA) to render attachment to defendant to show cause why he conceals effects of dec'd. Said Phillips deposed that Benjamin Deaver gave him the summons. Said Phillips is indisposed & not capable to ride to Annapolis. Signed: T. Sheredine.
- B.Y. for John Levett (PG) vs. E.J. for George Buchanan & his wife Margaret & Edward Sprigg

Page 215

administrators dbn of Robert Levett.
Petition. Edm. Jenings, Esq. is
procurator for said Spriggs.

- Edward Fottrell (AA) vs. W.C. for
surviving executors of Samuel Young,
Esq. & William Alexander & his wife
Araminta executrix of Joseph Young.
Libel. Richard Young & William
Cumming, Esq. procurator for Samuel
Young exhibited answer. Col.
Thomas Colvill & Mr. William Rumsey
to take answer from said Alexander &
his wife.

- Maybery Helm who married one of
daughters of Edward Parish (AA,
dec'd) vs. Mary Warman wife of
Stephen Warman & Edward Parish
acting executors of dec'd. Sheriff
(AA) to summon defendants to render
final accounts. Accounts exhibited.
Discontinued.

- E.J. for Thomas Fisher (QA) vs. Mr.
James Calder procurator for John
Baynard. Libel. Robert Norr.
Wright (sheriff, QA) to render
attachment to defendant to produce
pretended will of Richard Fisher
(QA, dec'd).

31:32
Said sheriff exhibited "cepi
corpus".

- W.C. for Roger Peele for self & his
2 brothers Robert & Samuel Peele vs.
William Peele administrator of
Samuel & Robert Peele. Zach.
Maccubbin (sheriff, AA) to render
attachment to defendant to pay
plaintiff.

- Martha Wheeler executrix of William
Wheeler (BA) vs. Jane Partridge
wife of Dr. Buckler Partridge (BA),
one of witnesses to will of dec'd.
Sheriff (BA) to summon defendant to
prove will. Said Jane is unable to
attend the Office. Mr. H. Wells
Stokes (BA) to take her probate of
the will. Struck off.

- B.Y. for Joseph Ennalls & his wife
Mary executrix of Thomas Haskins
(DO) vs. William Cumming, Esq.
procurator for William Holland,
Thomas Holland, & Elisabeth Holland
executors of William Holland, Esq.

Court Session: 10 July 1739

Libel. Sheriff (DO) & sheriff (CV)
to summon defendants to render
answer.

GENERAL INDEX

(no surname)
Alice 120
Elisabeth 196
Peggy 167
Samuel 14

Abbott
Samuel 180
Abell
John 123
Samuel 102, 123
Abington
John 211
Acton
Anne 41
Henry 41, 66, 179,
211, 212
Johanna 179, 212
Adair
Alexander 7
Adams
Archibald 119
Benjamin 149, 213
Betty 144
Charity 163, 187,
213
Charles 213
Lodowick 113
Mary 213
Richard 173
Roger 144
Samuel 163, 187,
213
Addams
Archibald 138
Betty 120
David 6, 10, 159,
177
Isaac 10, 30, 159,
177
Roger 120
Summar 138
Thomas 10, 30
Adderton
Jeremiah 16
Addition 68
Aisquith
George 85, 110
Susanna 102

Thomas 4, 12, 14,
27, 35, 39, 51,
59, 64, 74, 82,
85, 102, 105,
109, 121, 123,
135, 145, 146,
148, 159, 162,
166, 169, 179,
181, 187, 191,
193, 200, 209
William 102
Akinson
Joan 197
John 197
Albert
Elisabeth 201
Alburt
Elisabeth 200
William 200
Alder
Elisabeth 180
George 161, 180,
194
Aldern
Richard 57
Aldred
John 101, 112
Aldridge
Johny 104
Aletem
Richard 207
Alexander
Agnes 151
Andrew 44
Araminta 187, 191,
203, 210, 216
John 156
Listian 38, 63, 151
Robert 8
William 8, 38, 63,
145, 187, 191,
203, 210, 216
Alford
Aaron 126
Joseph 31, 120
Allder
Elisabeth 116
George 116
Allen
Barbara 33, 47, 51,

53, 76, 88, 99,
111, 128, 142,
157, 206
Charles 119, 149
Elisabeth 49, 139
Francis 162, 163
John 157, 162
Jos. 133
Joseph 33, 47, 49,
51, 53, 76, 88,
99, 111, 128,
139, 142, 157,
206
Alles
William 102
Alley
John 64, 95, 131,
154
Allford
Joseph 93, 94
Margaret 94
Allfree
Thomas 40
Alliband
Thomas 175
Alling
Ann 31
John 31
Allison
John 214
Alman
Abraham 164
Alvey
John 15
Ambrose
Abraham 1
Amos
Thomas 33
Anderson
Elisabeth 139
James 34, 63
John Baptes 27
Margaret 27
Mary 7, 20, 21,
103, 130, 201
Rebecca 34, 63
William 139, 201
Andrew
Collan 175
Cullen 197
Andrews
John 14, 32
Thomas 69
Angel

James 15, 64, 135
John 64, 135
Angell
Barnaby 201
Anglin
Barbara 133
Cornelius 133, 172,
173
Angling
Cornelius 116
Arano
Margaret 80
Arbuthnot
Hugh 58
Arbuthnott
Hugh 11
Armsby
Sarah 38
Thomas 38
Armstrong
Francis 34
James 4
Asbeston
Mary 124
William 83, 124
Asbestone
Mary 59
William 59
Ashman
George 82
John 82, 113, 185
Atcheson
James 25
Atchison
William 119, 149
Atkinson
Joseph 35
Timothy 130
Attwell
Margaret 106
Atwell
John 106
Austin
(A) 87
(N) 27, 42, 53, 75,
98
Henry 27, 42, 53,
75, 87, 98
Robert 39, 63
William 78, 115
Aydelott
Benjamin 108, 151
Sarah 108
Thomas 108

Ayres
  John 55

Bab
  Thomas 18
Babb
  Peter 113
Bacon
  John 127
Bagford
  James 50
Bailey
  John 82, 83
Baily
  George 131
Baker's Delight 73
Baker
  Amelia 2
  Charles 2, 21, 200
  James 96, 182, 201,
    214
  John 35
  Priscilla 182
Baldwin
  John 45, 67, 117,
    124, 169, 186,
    206
  Thomas 42, 145
Bale
  Anthony 45
Ballard
  Henry 27, 195
Balley
  Ann 59
  John 59
Banan
  Mary 198
  Philip 198
Baning
  Andrew 198
Bankson
  Joseph 86, 109, 134
Banning
  Andrew 208
Barber
  Thomas 32, 33, 93
Barbutt
  William 115, 155
Bare Ridge 70
Barker
  John 3
Barkhurst
  James 13, 33

Jane 13, 33
Barkhust
  James 12
Barnard
  John 194, 203
  Samuel 76, 190
Barncclough
  John 197
Barnes
  Ford 81
  James 50
Barnett
  Thomas 198
Barney
  Fran. 21
Barret
  Philip 7
Barrett
  joseph 135
  Philip 45
Barry
  A. 206
Bartlet
  Joseph 35
Barton
  James 46
  Martha 33
  Samuel 33
  Temperance 46
  Thomas 190
Barwell
  Justinian 11, 28,
    77, 87, 94
Barwick
  James 77
  John 5
Bass
  John 78, 79, 90,
    118, 187
  Joseph 90, 117,
    118, 187
  Sarah 78, 90, 117
Batcheldor
  Elisabeth 208
  John 208
Bateman
  Benjamin 23
  Chris. 154
  Christopher 91,
    154, 155
  Henry 17, 19, 52
  Lawrence 102, 124
  Mary 23
  Michael 11, 154

Bates
William 70
Bath
Elisabeth 115, 155,
198
John 11
Battson
Thomas 28
Baucum
Nicholas 172
Bavington
John 79
Thomas 17, 79
Baxter
John 110, 160
William 110
Bayard
James 164
Peter 164
Bayley
Esther 124
Luke 124
William 21
Baynard
Esther 78, 107, 155
George 78, 107, 155
John 78, 107, 155,
216
Thomas 78, 107, 155
Beal
John 213
Beall
Charles 174
Jane 70, 71
John 71, 144, 212
William 144
Beanes
William 2
Beard
Lewis 129, 151,
177, 196
Rebbecca 196
Rebecca 129, 177
Beasey
Elisabeth 195
William 108, 195,
215
Beasman
Elisabeth 192
Joseph 192, 200
Beaston
Thomas 143
Beatty
James 193

Thomas 193
Beaucham
Isaac 22
Robert 22
Sarah 22
Beauchamp
John 63
Beavans
William 176
Beck
Edward 40, 101,
126, 204
George 24
Mathew 61
Beckett
John 50, 56
Priscilla 50, 56
Beckingham
William 18
Beckwith
Charles 56, 81
Elisabeth 144
Francis 5
William 144
Beddeson
Thomas 116
Beedle
John 186
Beesley
Thomas 156
Beezley
Elisabeth 132
Thomas 132
Belgrave
Andrew 196
Bell
Addam 29
Jane 26, 52, 70
John 174
Margaret 154, 160,
176
William 54, 154,
155, 160, 176
Bellos
Francis 205
Mary 205
Bellus
Francis 171
Belt
Joseph 51, 144
Margery 51
Bennett
Isaac 66, 139
Katherine 103, 107

Susanna 66, 139
William 57, 103,
107, 198
Benson
Mary 29, 134, 152
Thomas 5, 29, 62,
134, 152
Benton
Comfort 44
Cumfort 29, 39, 64
Berry
James 154, 176
John 32
Margaret 154
William 122
Besswick
George 114, 129,
168
Sarah 114, 129, 168
Besswicke
George 168
Richard 132
Beswicke
Richard 147
Beszix
Absolom 214
Betenson
John 36, 60, 132,
137
Beuges
Henry 198
Bevan
Richard 208
Beverly
George 35
Bibby
Lucas 106
Biddeson
Thomas 133
Biddison
Thomas 133, 173
Biggs
John 37
William 15
Biglands
Richard 85, 103
Robert 85, 103
Birch
George 77
Thomas 95
Birkhead
Nehemiah 17
Solomon 42
Bisco

John 159
Jonathon 109, 147,
170, 191
Margaret 109
Bishop
William 115, 175
Bissco
James 15, 35
Jonathon 15, 35
Black
Alexander 4
Blackiston
Ebenezar 21
Mary 165
Blackman
Ann 182
Thomas 182, 201
Bladen
William 28
Blake
John Sayer 153
Blakistion
William 80
Blakiston
Ann 80
Anne 48
Ebenezar 80, 165
Vincent 165
William 48, 80
Blanchett
John 66
Bland
Mary 6
Blunt
Mary 55, 77, 149
Robert 55, 77, 149
Samuel 153
Boddy
Stephen 199
Bodien
Francis 2
Francis Ludolph 21
Boling
Edmund 4
Bolton
Elisabeth 163
James 163
John 196
Bond
Benjamin 61, 200
Benson 36
Hester 192
Isabella 200
John 200

Peter 192, 200
Thomas 17
William 64, 102
Bonner
Francis 78
Boon
Jacob 55, 154
Margaret 55
William 55
Boone
Jacob 153
Bootes
William 126
Bordley
Thomas 74, 152
Boreing
James 18, 133, 172
Rebecca 133
Thomas 18
Bosman
George 176
Mary 176
Boswell
James 140
Bouchelle
Peter 17, 85, 118
Sluyter 85, 118
Bould
John 59
Bouldin
Thomas 44
Boulding
Thomas 118
Boules
John 39
Boult
Eliza 193
John 82
Thomas 74, 193
Bourne
Alice 10, 24, 105,
122
Jesse Jacob 10, 24,
105, 122, 171,
193
Bowdle
Henry 198, 205
Loftis 7, 9, 16,
20, 27, 42, 53,
75, 76
Thomas 103
Bowen
Ann 192
Charles 192, 211

James 192
Bower
Barbara 197
James 197
Bowie
John 140
Bowland
Elinor 6
William 6
Bowlen
Edmond 146
Bowles
George 201
James 184
Bowling
Edmond 166
John 113
Bowyer
Hester 46, 79
Peter 46, 79
Boyce
James 23, 51, 152,
173
Roger 17, 143, 161
Boyd
Abraham 61, 140,
192
Deborah 61
John 29, 36, 179,
212
Bozman
George 195, 213
Mary 213
Mr. 167
Risdon 43, 53, 54,
75, 77, 86, 88,
96, 99, 100,
111, 114, 128,
129, 142, 146,
147, 157, 167,
193, 198, 207
William 97
Braban
John 171, 193
Bradford
William 134
Bradly
Ann 56
Brady
John 36
Brahaun
Hannah 23
Patrick 23
Thomas 23

Brahawn
  Hannah 38, 121
  Patrick 38, 121,
    138
  Thomas 38
Bramble
  Elisabeth 7, 31
  John 7, 31
Branklin
  Henry 204
  Mary 204
Brassher
  Samuel 208
Brawdee
  Alexander 174
Bredell
  Isaiah 130, 151,
    177, 196
  James Stephen 130,
    177
  Stephen 196
Breeman
  James 30
  Katherine 30
Brereton
  Thomas 105
Bresshear
  Samuel 174
Brett
  George 85, 95
Brewer
  John 8, 28, 182
  Joseph 8
  Richard 27
Brice
  John 194
Bright
  Francis 77
Brittain
  Thomas 160
Brittingham
  Elijah 214
  John 214, 215
Broad Creek 73
Broadaway
  Nicholas 32, 55,
    77, 85, 116
Brocklehouse
  Anthony 191
  Martha 191
Brodey
  Alexander 161
Brogden
  William 184, 187

Brome
  Ann 180
  Henry 6, 24, 84
  John 6, 84, 170,
    180, 211
  Thomas 6, 180
Bromwell
  Jacob 64
Brooke
  Clement 86, 136
  Jane 87
  Leonard 2
  Walter 81, 174
  William 113
Brookes
  John 37
Broome
  Henry 65
  John 65
Broughton
  Daniel 27, 35, 110
  Sarah 27, 110
Brown & Clark   72
Brown's Increase 74
Brown
  Ann 186
  Benjamin 106, 120,
    150, 188
  Charles 120, 132
  Daniel 207
  David 34, 63, 214
  Edward 32, 115
  Elisabeth 3, 101
  Fra. 84
  Francis 113
  George 192
  James 77, 107, 200
  John 72, 74, 93,
    139, 213
  John Elliot 3, 101,
    145
  Joseph 213
  Mager 120
  Margarett 186
  Martha 144
  Mary 55, 106
  Matthew 196
  Nicholas 122, 156,
    181, 205
  Robert 186
  Sarah 44, 122, 181,
    205, 213
  Thomas 211, 214
  William 144

Browne
  Charles 4, 74
  John 44
  John Elliett 28
  John Elliot 91
  John Elliott 28
  Mary 44
  Matthew 44
Brownstone   72
Bruce
  Charles 148, 158,
    168
  John 23, 51, 119,
    139, 148, 158,
    163, 168, 173
  Sarah 23, 119, 139,
    148, 158, 163,
    168, 173
Bruff
  Thomas 93
Bruffitt
  Daniel 138
Brumley
  Nicholas 140, 212
Brumwell
  Jacob 103
Bruner
  William 68
Bruton
  William 54
Brutons Hope 69
Bryann
  Daniel 125
Buchanan
  George 5, 11, 18,
    58, 90, 104,
    185, 191, 203,
    215
  Margaret 203, 215
  Margarett 185, 191
Buck
  John 162
Buckingham
  Hannah 73
  John 73
Bullen
  John 42, 121
  Mr. 167
  Thomas 137, 147,
    149, 156, 159,
    167, 180, 181,
    198, 199, 205,
    207, 208, 209
Bullock

Catherine 15
John 15, 59, 201
Richard 15
William 27, 59
Buncle
  Alexander 43, 152,
    214
Burch
  George 77
  Lucas 106
  Thomas 157
Burchfeild
  Adam 116
Burdus
  Richard 212
Burge
  Thomas 45
Burgess
  Charles 211
  Edward 25
  John 25, 50, 208
  Samuel 25, 145
  Sarah 25
Burk
  John 196
  Thomas 196
  Ulrick 192
Burkett
  Abigail 56
Burley
  John 61
Burn
  Ann 39
  Arthur 153, 155
  Dennis 39, 59, 124
  James 124
  Margaret 153
  Patrick 124, 147
Burne
  Dennis 124
  James 102, 124
Burney
  Daniel 82
Burntwood 69
Burntwood Common 70
Burroughes
  Benjamin 105, 162
  John 105, 162
Burroughs
  Benjamin 15, 160
  George 11
  John 15, 35
  Lilley 11
  Lylly 95

Mary 13
Thomas 13
William 11, 33, 95
Burrows
John 21
Burton
Martha 184
Thomas 76
Bury
Humphry 10
Bush
William 207
Butler
Rupert 50
Butterworth
Isaac 192
Buttler
Henry 209
Byus
William 204

Cadle
Benjamin 104, 199
Cage
William 37, 139
Calder
James 106, 114,
134, 183, 216
Calk
James 207
Peter 207
Sarah 207
Callaghan
Margaret 167
Callahane
Margaret 168
Callahaune
Margaret 168
Callahawn
Margaret 111
Callawhan
Margaret 100, 111
Calvert
Charles 4, 65, 66
Joshua 2, 212
Rebecca 65
Cammel
Samuel 15
Campbell
Elisabeth 127, 208
Esther 118
John 45, 117
Joshua 118

Walter 104, 112,
126, 129, 172,
208
William 66
Campell
William 51
Camperson
Frances 100, 111,
167
Canaan 69
Cannaday
Matthew 123
Canner
Thomas 58, 93, 107
Cannon
Henry 150
John 82, 121
Canons' Delight 68
Caphaw
Jane 23
John 23
Capshaw
Ann 10
John 3, 10
Card
William 49
Carey
William 156
Carman
Hannah 2
John 77
Joseph 2, 21
William 11, 77, 153
Carmichaell
Walter 74
Carney
Robert 43, 130
Carpenter
John 32, 71, 117
Carr
Francis 182
John 101, 148
Carroll
Charles 4, 11, 19,
26, 28, 70, 71,
72, 87, 92, 94,
184, 185
Dominick 79, 85,
118
James 37, 72
Mary 70, 71, 85,
118, 149
Carslake
John 34, 96, 123,

132

Carter
  Charles 108
  Hercules 117
  John 108, 130
  Richard 122, 129
  Valentine 122, 129,
    131
  William 1, 80
Carthidge
  Edmond 212
Carvill
  John 204
Cassey
  James 92
Caswell
  Richard 17, 55, 173
Catlin
  William 206
Cavenaugh
  William 14
Cavenough
  William 59
Cawood
  Mary 14, 24
  Stephen 14, 24
Cay
  Dorothy 49, 65, 84
  Jonathon 49, 65, 84
Cearsey
  Peter 6, 38, 63
  William 38, 63
Certain
  Robert 153
Chairs
  Thomas 154
Chamberlain
  Samuel 49
Chamberlaine
  Catherine 201
  John 200
  Thomas 200, 201
Chambers
  George 123, 147
  Richard 29
  Samuel 132
Chandler
  Ann 66
  John 41, 66
Chaplin
  Joseph 101, 104,
    112
Chapline
  Joseph 213

Chapman
  Edward 108, 131
  Peris 43, 206
  William 42, 48, 135
Charles Hills 69
Charlscroft
  Elisabeth 58
  John 58
Charlton
  Edward 109
  Jane 109
Cheney
  Susanna 136
  Thomas 136, 158,
    185
Chetham
  Edward 55, 93
  Sarah 55, 93
Chew
  Benjamin 206
  Henrietta Maria 49,
    147, 158
  John 8
  Mary 36, 121, 137,
    140
  Nathaniel 36, 121,
    137, 140
  Samuel 17, 21, 49,
    91, 121, 137,
    140, 148, 158
Chezeldine
  Kenelm 74
Child
  Abraham 122, 123
  Henry 14, 74
  Margaret 14
Childs
  Benjamin 44
  Henry 169
Chilton 68
Chilton
  Stephen 146
Chinoworth
  Jane 86, 152
  John 86, 152
Chinton
  Elenor 67
Chipley
  Elenor 126
  Elinor 78
  John 78, 126
  William 78, 126
Chocke
  George 91

John 91
Chunn
    Joseph 15
    Samuel 185
Clagett
    Charles 180
    Mary 81
    Sarah 81
    Thomas 140
Clanning
    Dennis 115, 155
Clark
    Caleb 122, 156
    Jane 118
    Mary 169, 191
    Rebecca 122
    Robert 4, 169, 191
    William 2, 40, 97
Clarke
    Abraham 204
    Caleb 198
    Hezekiah 139
    Jane 44
    Joshua 168
Clarks Enlargement 69
Clarks Purchase 68
Clarkson
    Elisabeth 2
    Thomas 2, 96, 140
    William 2, 25, 96,
        140
Clarvo
    Bridgett 141
    Elisabeth 141
    Francis 141
    John 9, 19, 26, 41,
        53, 75, 87, 98,
        110, 127, 141
Clary
    Mary 84, 95
    William 84, 95
Clayland
    Harris 132, 159,
        181
    John 32
    Roger 132, 156,
        159, 181
Clayton
    Solomon 32, 33,
        154, 196, 208
Cleaver
    Elisabeth 20, 118,
        166
    John 20, 118, 166

Cleaves
    Nathaniel 196
Clegett
    Ann 97
    Mary 97
    Thomas 97
Clemans
    John 196
Clements
    Edward 37
    Joseph 37
Clift
    Elisabeth 12, 35
    Henry 12, 35
Clink 74
Clouds
    Richard 116
Cloyd
    Elisabeth 25
    Robert 25, 163
Clyd
    Elisabeth 36
    Robert 36
Coade
    Richard 4
Coale
    Thomas 81
    William 14
Cobb
    James 56
Cock
    Edward 65
Cockey's Addition 72
Cockey
    Elisabeth 98
    John 89, 92, 105,
        148, 158, 162
    Thomas 89, 90, 92,
        98, 105, 132,
        148, 150, 158,
        162
Cockran
    William 4, 5, 51
Cockshutt
    Thomas 39, 179
Cod
    St. Leger 21
Codd
    St. Leger 2, 64, 91
Coffeny
    John 4
Coffin
    Thomas 43, 129
Colbatch

Joseph 132, 179
Cole
 Charles 19, 70, 71
 Elisabeth 12, 35,
  127, 209
 Frances 124
 Jacob 64, 123
 John 127, 150, 209
 Mary 124, 160, 175
Coleman
 Joseph 211
 Mordica 211
 Thomas 211
Coles
 Rachel 138
Colk
 Peter 181
Collier
 Betts 5
 George Betts 62
 Robert 5, 130
Collins
 John 115, 122, 129,
  131
 Price 159, 184
 Rebecca 122, 129,
  131
 Richard 11, 153
Collison
 George 57
Collisson
 Elisabeth 34, 65,
  93, 131
 George 34, 35, 65,
  93, 131
Colston
 John 92
Colvill
 Thomas 186, 216
Combs
 James 21
Comegys
 E. 115
 Edward 1, 40, 84,
  126, 152, 171
 William 1, 80, 84,
  91, 126
Coming
 Malachi 189
Compton
 James 124
Conaway
 John 51, 62, 169
Connell

William 33, 50
Conner
 John 135
Connolly
 Christopher 156,
  181, 199
 Margaret 156, 199
Conwell
 Elisabeth 92, 103
 John 92
 Richard 92
Conwill
 Elisabeth 161
 John 161
 Richard 161
Coody
 Henry 37, 173
Cook
 Cornelius 47, 79
 Margaret 189
 Mary 5
 Samuel 196
Cooke
 Mary 38, 58
 Thomas 81
Cooksey
 Justinian 185
Cooley
 James 17, 49, 109
 Nathaniel 165
Coombes
 William 10, 24, 31,
  66
Coomes
 Sarah 25, 31
Cooper
 Ann 64, 105, 162,
  182
 Edward 143, 194
 Gabriel 96, 108
 Grace 196
 John 54, 117
 Mark 160
 Mary 5, 35, 64, 74,
  83, 105, 162,
  182, 194
 Richard 82
 Sarah 96, 100, 167
 Thomas 96
 William 51, 96,
  100, 167
Coots
 Robert 97, 140, 175
Copley

Roger 147
Coppen
    Elisabeth 183
    George 183
Copson
    John 17, 186
Cordary
    Abraham 130
    Daniel 108, 130
Cordery
    Abraham 43
Corkett
    Althea 192
Cornish
    Elenor 104, 112
    Elinor 129
Corse
    Barbara 125, 214
    James 1, 125
    John 125
    William 125, 166,
      214
Corwardine
    Abraham 204
Cosden
    Alfonso 164
    Alphonso 187
    Elisabeth 164
Costin
    Amy 130
    Isaac 29, 39, 63,
      130
Cotten
    Mary 171
Cotter
    William 14
Cotterell
    Samuel 61
Cottrell
    Samuel 4, 136
Coulson
    Thomas 119, 138
Coulter
    Michael 74
Coursey
    Henry 54
    John 32
    William 77
Courson
    Rebecca 58
    Thomas 58, 94
Courts
    Charles 37, 66
    John 37, 185

Michael 132
Coutanceau
    John 17, 20
    Peter 182
Covell
    Jeremiah 195
    Jonathon 195
    Mary 195
Covington
    Henry 77, 153
    Leonard 211
Cowman
    Joseph 91, 92
Cowper
    Mary 64
Cox
    Abraham 124, 164
    Albert 124
    Ann 23, 118, 124,
      132, 150
    Daniel 22, 23, 118,
      132, 150
    Edward 104, 134
    Elisabeth 133
    Henry 91, 144, 161
    Jane 104
    John 143
    Joseph 133, 172
    Lazarus 32, 33
    Mary 32, 46, 60,
      144, 161
    Thomas 60
    William 45, 62
Coxon
    Anarah 204
    Edward 204
Coy
    Edmund 126
Cozens
    Edward 1
Crabb
    Priscilla 65
    Ralph 65
Crabin
    Alexander 7
Craen
    John 94
Cragh
    Archibald 1, 33, 80
Craghill
    George 15
Crane
    David 91
Crapper

Edmund 96
Crauford
   David 97
Craycroft
   Clement 140
   Jane 140, 172
Creagh
   Neomy 152
   Patrick 90, 212
   William 152
Creagie
   Thomas 144
Crockett
   Gilbert 55
   John 18
Crofford
   John 44
Cromwell
   John 48, 54, 76,
      82, 88, 92, 99,
      101, 170
   William 48, 82
Croneen
   John 196
Crooke
   Charles 104
   Sarah 100, 104
Cropper
   Edmond 213
   Edmund 177
Crosby
   Burden 10
Cross
   Hannah 73
   Robert 73
Crouch
   Mary 7, 174
   Wedge 7, 20, 174
   William 73
Crow
   John 144
Cruckshanks
   James 183, 204
   Mary 183, 204
Crudgenton
   Roger 28
Cuckholdspoint   73
Cullason
   Joseph 102
Cullen
   Andrew 197
   James 204
   William 120, 121,
      204

Cullin
   Thomas 45, 62
Culverhouse
   John 35
Cumming
   Robert 100
   William 9, 18, 19,
      20, 26, 41, 42,
      52, 53, 67, 70,
      74, 141, 145,
      157, 162, 169,
      178, 182, 188,
      190, 191, 202,
      203, 215, 216
Cunliff
   Foster 198
Cunningham
   Arthur 44
   Barbara 44
Currer
   John 143, 209
   William 143, 186
Currey
   John 164
Currick
   Hugh 66
Cutchin
   Robert 105, 151
   Winifred 105
Cutler
   William 159

Dale
   John 130
Dallam
   William 17, 81, 151
Dallas
   Walter 49, 74, 77,
      104, 112, 129
Daniel
   Charles 49, 181
   Rachell 49
Daniell
   Charles 109
Darby
   John 9, 19, 20, 26,
      27, 41, 52, 75,
      87, 98, 110,
      127, 141
   Walter 107
Darnall
   Henry 2
   John 13, 14, 190

Mary 190
Rachel 13
William 2
Darnell
    Charles 82
    Rachel 82
Dashiel
    Christopher 60
    James 131
    Joseph 60
    Robert 63
Dashiell
    George 6, 30
    James 60, 63, 108
    Joseph 60
    Robert 6, 30
    Sarah 60
    Thomas 60
Dashiells
    Bridget 43
    George 43
    James 43
    Joseph 43
    Robert 29
Dashiels
    George 39, 63
    Joseph 130
    Robert 39
    Sarah 130
Daugheday
    John 46
David
    John 171
    Sarah 124
    William 124
Davidge
    John 42
Davidson
    Capt. 72
Davie
    Ann 133
    John 133
Davis Pasture 68
Davis
    Edward 13
    Elisabeth 39, 40,
        47, 63
    Fouch 143, 164, 207
    John 16, 39, 63
    Mary 40
    Peter 180, 199
    Richard 20, 33, 40,
        80, 163, 184
    Thomas 143, 187

William 40
Davison
    Elisabeth 207
    John 207
Daviss
    William 172
Dawkins
    James 180
Dawson
    Edward 174
    Impey 207
    James 207
    John 3, 208
    Mary 3, 207
Day
    Daniel 7, 10, 150,
        161
    Elinor 7, 10
    Francis 145
    Nicholas 33, 116
    Rebecca 60, 210
    Robert 60
    Sarah 33, 62, 116
    Thomas 54, 77, 155
    William 60, 92, 210
Deacon
    Mary 15, 16, 145,
        166
    William 15, 16,
        145, 166, 189
Deal
    John 43
Dean
    Thomas 189
Dearing
    Redmon 33
Deaver
    Benjamin 215
Debron
    John 180
Decregar
    Ann 212
    William 212
Deep Creek 73
Deep Creek Neck   72
Dehinoyosia
    Alexander 68
Delap
    George 94
Demmitt
    John 50
Denney
    Ann 92, 115, 154
Denning

Ezekiel 6, 30, 206
Dennis
  John 206
Denny
  Ann 178
  Joseph 122
Dent
  George 53, 157
  Peter 2, 3, 9, 10,
    13, 24, 25, 29,
    31, 34, 36, 38,
    44, 50, 61, 65,
    81, 85, 86, 87,
    96, 97, 114,
    116, 137, 139,
    144, 146, 150,
    161, 163, 171,
    172, 174, 179,
    180, 185, 194,
    197, 211, 212,
    213
Denton
  Vachel 19, 26, 70,
    71, 172, 181,
    192
Denune
  James 173
  Rebecca 173
Denwood
  John 103, 130
Deoran
  James 125
Deoreger
  Ann 163
  William 163
Deroachburn
  Joseph 196
Devene
  Edmond 23
  Edmund 113
Devenish
  Ishmael 155
  John 171
  Mary 171
Deveron
  Elenor 97
  Elinor 24, 85
  William 24, 85, 97
Devonish
  Ishmael 153
  Mary 153
Dewlin
  George 156
Deye

Penelope 157
Thomas Cockey 157
Dial
  John 187, 191, 201
  Sarah 187, 201
Diass
  Henry 82
  Thomas 82
Dicas
  Edward 1, 134, 174
  William 1, 134, 174
Diceas
  Edward 40
Dickenson
  Elisabeth 96
  James 96
Dickinson
  Hannah 180
  James 180
Dickison
  Frances 141
Diens
  Edward 205
  William 205
Digges
  Charles 22, 27, 42,
    53, 75, 134,
    180, 190, 202,
    215
  Edward 180, 190,
    202, 215
  John 190, 202, 215
  William 87, 180,
    190, 202, 215
Dines
  Robert 138
Disharoon
  Lewis 163
Disheroon
  Michell 176
Disney
  Ann 48, 104, 114
  James 48, 104, 114
Ditto
  William 192
Dixon
  Benjamin 161, 171
  Isaac 34, 35, 57,
    131, 156
  James 161, 171
  John 13
  Joice 108
  Obed 161
  Sturgis 108

Dobson
   Hannah 65, 83
   Isaac 65, 83
   William 65, 83
Dockery
   Matthew 92, 175
Docwra
   John 161
   Matthew 54
   Salome 161
Dodd
   Thomas 115
Dodson
   James 24, 65, 84,
     170
   John 24, 65, 84,
     170
Donahoe
   Sarah 62, 133, 152
   Teague 62, 133, 152
Donaldson
   Bridget 56
   Bridgett 145
   James 56, 149, 197
   John 145
Donawen
   Thomas 61
Donelson
   John 29, 30
   Katherine 29
Donohoe
   Teague 97
Doran
   James 183
   Jane 183
Dorington
   William 120, 164
Dorrumple
   Elinor 119, 148,
     149, 170
   John 119, 148, 149,
     170
Dorsett
   Thomas 81
Dorsey
   Bazil 197
   Caleb 197
   John 33, 57, 105,
     145
   Richard 197
   Samuel 69, 197
Dorseys Addition 69
Dossey
   Ann 74

John 64, 74, 105,
   123, 162, 182
Dottson
   John 49
Douglas
   Mary 206
   William 16, 206
Douglass
   Joseph 139
Dowell
   John 48, 54, 55,
     137, 149
   Philip 48, 54, 55,
     137, 149
Dowen
   Dennis 23
Dowlin
   Murdock 26
Dowling
   Murdock 22
Downes
   George 108, 130
   John 54
   Margaret 108
   Robert 108
Downing
   Elisabeth 9, 19,
     26, 41, 53, 75,
     87, 98, 110,
     127, 141
   Nathaniel 141
   Nicholas 9, 19, 26,
     41, 53, 75, 87,
     98, 110, 127
Doyle
   Sarah 154
   William 154, 176
Doyne
   Jane 51, 114, 118
   Joseph 51
   Robert 51, 114, 118
Dozen
   Peter 21
Drew
   George 11, 24, 138,
     169
Driver
   Matthew 150
Droughton
   John 11
Drury
   Charles 135
   William 7, 21
Dryer's Inheritance 68

Dudley
   James 12, 35
   Mary 156, 159, 181
   Samuel 156
   Thomas 156
   William 156, 159,
     181
Duhamell
   Peter 92, 154, 178
   Rachel 92, 178
Duke
   Christopher 104,
     133
   James 170
Dulany
   Daniel 74
   Sarah 199
   Thomas 199
Dunn
   John 29, 36
   Mary 165, 171
   Robert 183
Dunning
   Samuel 208
Durbin
   Christopher 49
Dutton
   Robert 79
Duvall
   Marren 116
Dye
   Penelope 148
   Thomas Cockey 148
Dyson
   Thomas 139, 157

Eager
   Hannah 72, 73
Eagleson
   Brian 118
Earle
   James 11, 13, 32,
     44, 47, 54, 55,
     64, 77, 78, 85,
     89, 92, 95, 101,
     105, 107, 110,
     114, 119, 131,
     141, 153, 154,
     160, 175, 178,
     179, 196, 198,
     200
   John 11, 115, 153
   Joseph 193, 203

Early
   William 40
Eaton
   Andrew 27
Ebtharpe
   Thomas 117
Eburnethy
   Ann 119, 139
   John 119, 139
Eccleston
   Margrett 58
Edelen
   Christopher 2
   James 150
   John 2
   Margaret 159
   Philip 160
   Richard 159, 201
Edgar
   John 25, 50, 85,
     116
Edmondson
   James 46
   John 9, 19, 46, 147
   William 122, 132
Edmonston
   James 48
   Ninian 48
Edny
   Ann 73
   Robert 73
Edwards
   Richard 7
   Sarah 32
   William 32, 55, 85,
     115, 116
Edzard
   Esdra Theodore 13
Egerton
   Charles 123, 147,
     193
   James 123, 193
Egon
   John 175
Eilbeck
   William 25, 85, 97,
     116
Elbert
   Frances 16
   William 16, 154,
     156
Elgate
   William 176, 184
Elliot

Benjamin 78
Mary 78
Mathew 62
Monica 102
Robert 4, 102
Elliott
   Benjamin 13, 55
   George 54
   John 151, 153
   Joseph 154
   Mary 13, 55
   Robert 182
Ellis
   Owen 25
Ellit
   Francis 43, 151,
     152
Ellt
   Elinor 84
   Rebecca 84
Elston
   Ralph 198
Elt
   Elinor 60
   Robert 60
Eltington
   Martha 67
Elwood
   Richard 44
Emerson
   John 54
Emory
   John 77, 153
   Will. 115
   William 93, 114
Ence
   John 40
England
   Sarah 194
English
   Thomas 21
Ennalls
   B. 22
   Bartholomew 22, 38,
     58, 60, 82
   Elisabeth 60, 120
   Henry 22, 30
   J. 38
   Joseph 22, 27, 38,
     42, 53, 75, 87,
     98, 110, 127,
     135, 141, 144,
     150, 182, 208,
     216

   Mary 135, 150, 208,
     216
   Thomas 22, 37, 38,
     42, 58, 120
   William 22, 27, 42,
     53, 75, 87, 98,
     110, 127, 141,
     144
Enoch
   Henry 84, 101, 104,
     112
Ensey
   Catherine 24, 31,
     66
   John 10, 24
   Katherine 10
Erwin
   Anne 65, 83
Estep
   John 94, 186
Etherington
   Bartholomew 186
Eubanks
   Edward 103
Evans
   Ann 108
   Edmund 10, 56
   Edward 49
   Evan 21
   John 2
   Rebecca 2, 40, 91,
     152, 166
   Richard 69, 171
   Sarah 21, 204
Everett
   James 154
   Joseph 40, 80, 84,
     107, 166
   Katherine 40, 84,
     107, 166
Ewing
   Alexander 206
   Joshua 206
   Nathaniel 206
   Samuell 206

Facer
   Henry 67
   James 67, 68
   Martha 68
   Thomas 9, 19, 26,
     41, 52, 67, 68
Fairbrother

William 14
Fairfax
  John 13, 186
Falcom
  John 12
Falconar
  Gilbert 84, 166,
    174
  Hannah 84, 165, 174
  Margaret 165
Fallin
  Redmond 11
Fannen
  John 2
Fanning
  John 1, 21, 59, 78
  Mary 59
Farlow
  Elisabeth 74, 76,
    88, 99, 111,
    128, 173
  Little 128
  Thomas 74, 76, 88,
    99, 111, 128,
    173
Farmer
  John 28, 126, 166
  Mary 126
  Sophia 28
Farqua
  Allen 193
  William 193
Farquar
  Allen 194
Farquhar
  Allen 177
  William 177
Farr
  John 185
Farrell
  Andrew 212
Farthing
  Ann 16, 187, 201
  James 124
  William Maria 16
  William Mariea 187
  William Meriea 201
Fearson
  Percival 113
  Ruth 113
  Walter 66
Feethold 72
Feilder
  John 146

Nicholas 28
Susanna 146
Fell
  William 157
Fendall
  Elisabeth 10, 13,
    24
  John 149
Fenley
  Samuel 213
Fenwick
  Ellen 102, 110,
    121, 147
  Ignatius 102, 121,
    124, 147
Fernandes
  Peter 3
Ferrell
  Daniel 1
  Elisabeth 1
Fielder
  John 160
Fimmons
  John 214
  Mary 214
  Samuel 214
Finley
  Samuel 101, 112,
    144
Finnicum
  Mary 154
Finnley
  Samuel 104
Finnly
  Samuel 84, 104
Finshaw
  Elisabeth 191
Fish
  Edmund 147, 198,
    205
Fisham
  Elisabeth 200
Fisher
  Abigail 119, 155
  Barkley 130, 177,
    196
  Bartley 29
  John 119, 154, 155
  Richard 194, 203,
    216
  Sarah 29
  Thomas 194, 203,
    216
Fitchgarrill

Peter 214
Fitzgerald
  Garrett 208
  Patrick 125, 126,
    174
FitzJeffery
  Joseph 59
Fleearty
  Stephen 204
Fleming
  John 43, 130
Fletcher
  Michael 34, 43, 53,
    75, 148, 157,
    168
Fling
  John 1
  Mary 1
Flinn
  Ann 204
  Daniel 204, 205
Flower
  William 27
Floyd
  Thomas 121
Flynn
  Ann 183
  Daniel 183
Follows
  John 43, 198
Fooks
  Benjamin 108
Foothold 73
Forbes
  Dryden 123, 209
  George 4
  John 4, 123, 147,
    209
Ford
  Ann 144
  Edward 37
  Jane 92
  John 87, 89, 92,
    99, 144, 145,
    147
Fordham
  Benjamin 69
Forest
  Patrick 102
Forster
  James 44, 118
Foster
  Elenor 201
  Ellenor 123

James 44, 118, 123,
  144, 147, 201
Fottrell
  Edward 14, 55, 76,
    88, 110, 112,
    129, 142, 187,
    191, 192, 194,
    203, 210, 216
  Sarah 187
Foulars
  Edward 63
Foulkes
  Joseph 116
Foulks
  Joseph 133, 151
Foulston
  Richard 106, 134
Fowke
  Gerrard 31, 51
  Sarah 31, 51
Fowlar
  Ann 84
  John 84
Fowler
  Edward 39
Foxley
  Elisabeth 66
  Joseph 66
Foy
  Andrew 4
  Barbara 4
  Frances 7
Framan
  John 6
Frame
  Major 65
  Richard 65
Francis
  Joseph 21
  Richard 9, 18, 19,
    70, 76, 89, 99,
    111, 127, 142,
    156, 157, 167,
    177, 190, 202
  Tench 5, 12, 16,
    22, 31, 34, 42,
    46, 57, 64, 65,
    83, 85, 93, 96,
    103, 104, 107,
    122, 131, 132,
    137, 156
Franklin
  John 213
  Richard 14

Fraser
  Alexander 73
Frasher
  John 135
Frasier
  John 160
Frazer
  Barbara 4
  George 150
  John 2, 4, 59, 150,
    194
Freeborn
  Rachel 73
Freeman
  Ann 117
  Daniel 211
  Isaac 117
  James 24
  John 69
  Thomas 114, 121
  William 117, 143,
    187, 214
Freshwater
  Robert 86, 90
Friends Choice 72
Friendship 73
Frisby
  Elisabeth 124
  Jane 126, 210
  Peregrine 124
  William 126, 149,
    166, 210
Fuller
  John 133
Fulston
  Richard 1

Gadd
  Christiana 192
  Thomas 192
  William 192
Gaither
  Benjamin 211
  Edward 8, 179
  Elisabeth 211
  John 211
  Margarett 179
Gale
  Betty 184
  George 43, 198
  James 125, 166
  John 125
  Levin 130, 209

Galle
  Grace 39, 59
  Laurence 59
  Lawrence 39
Galloway
  Charles 12, 41
  Elisabeth 73
  James 21
  John 9, 19, 26, 41,
    52, 67, 70, 91
  Joseph 91
  Peter 17, 21, 73
  Richard 24, 91
  Sarah 91
Gally
  Lawrence 35
Galshiott
  Laurence 47, 79
Games
  John 57
Gardiner
  Anne 31, 85, 95
  Chris. 112, 169
  Christopher 96,
    117, 158, 169
  Christopher (AA)
    112
  Francis 31, 85, 95
  Joseph 101, 113
  Robert 46, 116
  Thomas 4, 12, 35
Gardner
  Christopher 178,
    190, 202, 215
  Martha 6
  Matthew 49
Garey
  George 34, 132,
    156, 159
  Jane 132, 159
  Lawrence 14
Garnett
  George 2, 86, 91,
    106, 126, 184
  Jonathon 2
  Joseph 40
  Thomas 2, 86, 106,
    184
Garrett
  Amos 9, 19, 26, 41,
    52, 67, 71, 72
  Elisabeth 67
  James 67
  Peter 82

Sarah 67, 69, 71
Seth 67
Garrettson
  Elisabeth 200
  Garrett 200
  George 200
  James 200
  John 200
Garrott
  Henry 192
Gary
  Everard 92
  Everett 92
  Mary 92
Gasken
  Elisabeth 198
  John 198
Gasle
  Richard 30
  Tabitha 30
Gassaway
  John 14, 24
  Nicholas 8
  Thomas 8, 28
Gault
  Patrick 21
Geary
  George 181
  Lawrence 92
Geaves
  George 184
Gellett
  John 198
  Samuel 198
Gentle Craft 68
George
  Joshua 8, 46, 90,
    132, 206
  Robert 2
Ghiselin
  William 77, 100,
    169, 212
Gibbens
  Anne 63
  Thomas 63
Gibbins
  Ann 34
  John 34, 63
  Thomas 34
Gibson
  Richard 149, 193,
    199
  William 82, 102,
    201

Giddens
  Morris 103
Gilbert
  John 101, 126
Giles
  Jacob 118
  Johanah 118
  John 192
  Richard 7, 9, 20,
    27, 42, 53, 75,
    76
Gill
  William 157
Gilleland
  John 6
Gillett
  John 176, 195
  Samuel 176
Gilliland
  Jane 162, 198, 206
  John 162, 176, 198,
    206
Gillingham 68
Gillis
  Ezekiel 26, 52
Gilpin
  Edward 213
  Elisabeth 213
Giltrap
  Peter 195
Gin
  Elisabeth 71
Ginn
  (N) 71
  Elisabeth 9, 19,
    26, 41, 52, 67,
    70
Gist
  Richard 48
Gladen
  Mary 137
  Robert 137
Glanvill
  Stephen 20
Glashon
  Eleanor 65
  John 65, 94
Glass
  Francis 66
Glaze
  John 186, 213
  Sarah 186
Gleaves
  George 21, 165

John 165, 184
Joseph 80, 165, 184
Sarah 165, 166
Glen
  Nicholas 64
Goddard
  John 161
Goff
  John 132
Gold
  James 178
  Richard 178
Goldsborough
  J. 42, 75, 111,
    128, 129, 157,
    203
  John 99
  Robert 45
Gooding
  Elinor 48, 80
  Samuel 40, 80
  Samuell 1, 48
Gordon
  Robert 42, 48, 54,
    76, 82, 88, 99,
    121, 147
Goslee
  Richard 6
  Tabitha 6
Gostwick
  Thomas 81
Gott
  Richard 151, 191
Gough
  Benjamin 4, 39, 59
  Jane 39, 59
  Joseph 32
  Stephen 102
Gould
  James 77, 115, 175,
    197
  Richard 77, 115,
    197
Gourney
  Capt. 189
Gover
  Elisabeth 56
  Robert 56
  Samuel 56
Grace
  Nathaniel 46, 64
  William 46, 64
Graham
  Margarett 45

Tarance 45
Grainger
  John 81, 132
  Mary 132
  William 30
Granger
  Benjamin 150
  John 56
  Mary 56, 150, 172
Grant
  Alexander 191
  Elisabeth 191
  John 166
Grantham
  William 203
Graves
  John 15, 27
  Thomas 27
Gray
  Jane 181
  John 165, 166
  Joseph 108
  Leon 197
  Mary 103
  Thomas 103, 130
  Waistcoat 103
  Westcoat Gray 130
  William 180, 193
Greason
  Joshua 181
  Sarah 198
Great Brushey Neck
  68
Green
  Ann 154
  Bowles 20, 205
  Charles 133
  Elisabeth 107, 135,
    150
  John 133, 196
  Jonas 173
  Nicholas 16
  Robert 20, 33, 40,
    80, 163, 165,
    184
  Susannah 16
  Thomas 151
  William 107, 135,
    138, 150
Greenfield
  Eleanor 179
  James 179
  Martha 211
Greenwell

John 181
Greenwood
Daniel 194
Gregory
John 151
Simon 18, 62
Gresham
John 20, 125, 165
Grey
Elinor 175
Leon 175
Greys Sands 69
Griffin
James 31
Griffith
Ann 78
Benjamin 1, 78,
174, 205
Daniel 32, 93, 196
George 22, 205
Jackson 40, 78,
174, 205
John 119
Matthew 119, 175
Samuel 61, 110, 155
Griges
John 109
Grimes Enlargement 68
Grimes Stone 68
Grimes
Ann 73
William 73
Groome
Amey 25
Amy 13
Richard 13, 25
Samuel 204
Grover
John 36, 49
Groves
George 34
John 13
Mathew 13
Matthew 37
William 23
Guy
William 138
Guyther
John 109
Gwin
James 197
John 175
Tabitha 197
Gwinn

Ann 12, 37
Anne 41
Benjamin 12, 41
Joseph 12, 41
Ralph 37

Hackleberry Forest 69
Haddaway
William Webb 57
Haddock
Elisabeth 106
James 106
Hagan
Ignatius 3
Haile
Frances 34
Nicholas 34, 199
Thomas 66
Haith
Abraham 63
Ann 103, 152
William 103, 152
Hale
Frances 21
Nicholas 21
Hales
Edward 1
Philip 1
Half Solomons Hill
69
Hall's Palace 68
Hall
Alexander 29, 63,
213
Ann 50
Anne 46
Catherine 169
David 80, 171
Edward 81, 109,
134, 202
Elihu 8, 143
Elisabeth 8
Francis 22, 27, 42,
53, 75, 140
Hannah 86, 100,
112, 128, 142
Henry 61
Johanna 24, 182,
190, 202, 215
John 7, 81, 86,
100, 109, 112,
128, 134, 182,
190, 202, 215

Joseph 96, 130,
131, 177, 209
Katherine 51, 62
Mary 29, 213
Parker 81, 109
Richard 17, 21
Thomas 51, 62, 147,
169, 176
Halsey
John 156, 209
Hambleton
Arthur 121
William 207
Hamilton
Arthur 82, 147
Hans 45
Thomas 139, 186
Hamm
Elisabeth 90
Ephraim 90
Hammond
Charles 8
John 8, 54, 196
Mordecai 48, 89,
123
Sarah 196
Thomas John 185
W. 89
William 14, 76, 89
Hampton
Mary 55, 78
Richard 122, 123
Thomas 55, 78
William 55, 78
Hance
Benjamin 17, 21, 57
Handey
Thomas 62
Handley
Elinor 107
Marmaduke 107
Handly
Elinor 138
Hugh 60
Marmaduke 58
Susannah 60
Hands
Bod. 183
Handy
Jane 62
John 195
Samuel 10, 30
Thomas 10, 30, 97,
133, 176

Hankin
John 125, 126, 210
Katherine 125
Hanna
Alexander 139, 160,
187, 199
Mary 139, 187, 199
Hanson
Benjamin 61, 105,
173, 192
Elisabeth 20
Frederick 12, 165,
166
George 12
Hannah 174
Hans 1, 2, 20, 174,
205
Hanse 165, 205
Mary 165
Robert 13, 23, 119,
139
Samuel 3, 10, 12,
14, 23, 31, 33,
36, 41, 51, 65,
66, 79, 84, 94,
95, 100, 101,
113, 114, 118,
119, 137, 139,
145, 148, 149,
152, 160, 163,
173, 185, 187,
199, 210, 213
Sarah 61, 173, 192
Harbert
William 32
Harding
Edward 34
John 102
Joseph 46, 58
William 46, 58
Hardisty
Francis 61, 97
Hardman
Elisabeth 187, 199
Thomas 187, 199
Hardy
William 146, 160,
166
Harper
Francis 130
Richard 6
Samuel 5, 23, 82
Sarah 5, 48
William 5, 48, 82,

132, 159, 181
Harraut
  Peter 66
Harrington
  Jane 122
  Joseph 122
  Richard 11, 122,
    133
  William 122
Harris
  Benjamin 57
  George 57, 170, 193
  James 84
  John 12, 37
  Joseph 170, 192
  Lloyd 96, 112, 117,
    158, 169, 178,
    190, 202, 215
  Margaret 158, 169,
    178, 190, 202
  Thomas 55
  William 42, 53,
    158, 169, 170,
    178, 190, 202,
    204
  Workman 13, 78
Harrison
  Benoni 23, 118
  Dorcas 61, 97
  Elisabeth 160
  John 160, 191
  Joseph 181
  Robert 93, 181
  Thomas 61, 97
  William 15, 109,
    160
Harryman
  George 104
Hartley
  Joshua 147, 166
  Mary 147
Harvey
  Samuel 106
  Thomas 175
  William 191
Harwood
  Frances 58
  Grace 22, 57
  Peter 22, 34, 57
  Robert 34, 123,
    131, 156
  Samuel 58
Haseler
  Elisabeth 201

Richard 201
Haskins
  Aaron 4
  Thomas 5, 135, 150,
    208, 216
Hasswell
  Dr. 31
Hastings
  Oliver 154
Hatcheson
  Vincent 20
Haw
  Daniel 37
  John 51, 101, 113
  Mary 37, 101, 113
Hawkins
  Alexander 66
  Elisabeth 105, 153
  Ernault 105, 153,
    175
  Hen. 211
  Henry 211
  John 56, 116, 139,
    161, 175, 192
  Rebecca 56
  Thomas 37
Hayes
  Ann 12, 35
  John 4, 12, 13, 36
  Sarah 13
Hayns
  Hezekiah 68
Hays
  John 33
  Peter 66
  Sarah 33
Hayward
  Francis 38, 59
  John 38, 58, 59
  Thomas 120
Heard
  John 181
  Mark 59
Heart
  Gilbert 109
Hebb
  Thomas 102
  William 182
Hebron
  Elisabeth 90
  John 90, 126, 152
  Thomas 90
Heighe
  James 17, 24, 121,

192
Rober 105
Robert 121
Helm
  Ann 193, 203
  Mayberry 193
  Maybery 203, 216
Hemsley
  Anna Maria 11, 78, 116
  William 11, 55, 78, 115, 116
Henderson
  Robert 129
  Thomas 82
Hendon
  Hannah 151
  Josias 33, 151
Hendrick
  John 35, 83, 159
Hening
  Jedidah 182
Henley
  Robert 4
Henny
  Sarah 158, 187
  Thomas 158, 187
Henry
  John 195
Hepbourn
  Thomas 40
Hepburn
  John 190
  Thomas 171
Hereford 69
Herman
  Ephraim 136
Hernley
  Darby 133
  Edmond 133
  Edmund 133
Herrington
  John 122
Herron
  Frances 45
  Francis 45
Hewett
  Robert 67, 70
Hewitt
  Richard 106
Hewling
  Jonas 18, 39, 96, 109
Hickcock

Sarah 68
Hickman
  Margaret 36, 119, 136
  William 36, 56, 119, 136
Hicks
  John 14, 182
  Joseph 122
  Levin 4, 31, 114, 120, 138
  Patience 184
  Thomas 120, 127, 150
  William 184
Hickson
  John 198
Hicory Ridge 69
Higgens
  Dorothy 4
  Thomas 4
Higgins
  Alice 93
  Dorothy 61, 136
  James 34, 93, 123, 131, 156
  Stephen 145
  Thomas 61, 136, 208
Higginson
  Ann 172
  John 76, 172, 189, 190
Higgs
  Aaron 16
Higton
  Bathea 199
  Bathia 37
  John 37, 51, 199
Hill
  Ann 15
  Henry 140, 186
  John 15
  Levin 14, 17, 19, 52
  Richard 43, 97, 130
Hilleary
  John 54
Hillery
  John 48
Hillton
  Francis 102
Hindman
  Jacob 75, 110, 112, 127, 141

Hinkson
  Ann 16
  John 16
Hinsley
  Mary 175
  Nathaniel 175, 197
  Peter 175
Hitchcock
  Ann 192
  William 192
Hitcherson
  William 61
Hix
  John 1
  Sarah 1
Hobbs,
  Joy 43
Hobbs
  Absalom 44, 62
  Absolam 163
  Absolom 184
  John 4, 61, 136
  Joy 62, 97, 163,
    184
Hodge
  Robert 6, 206
Hodgkin
  Thomas 81
Hodgshon
  William 119, 137
Hodgson
  Elisabeth 24
  Johannah 24
  Richard 24
Hodson
  Charles 120
  Margarett 108, 131
  Roland 108, 131
Holding
  Elisabeth 175, 179
  Richard 175, 179,
    197
Holland
  Elisabeth 208, 216
  Francis 162, 169,
    178, 206
  John 45, 133, 152
  Susannah 162, 169,
    178
  Tabitha 133, 152
  Thomas 2, 208, 216
  William 29, 60,
    133, 152, 182,
    208, 216

Holliday
  Edward 171
  Francis 171
Hollis
  William 61
Hollock
  John 138, 164, 193
  Martha 138, 193
Holmes
  Edward 208
  Mary 19, 70, 71
  Richard 65, 107,
    133
Holton
  James 46, 58
  Martha 46, 58
Honest Mans Lott   69
Hood
  Alice 117
  Will. 117
  William 117
Hoodt
  John Caspar 164
  John Casper 187
Hook
  James 144
  Margaret 144
Hooper
  Henry 127, 204
  Mary 120, 150
  Sarah 97
  Thomas 150, 164
Hopewell   72
Hopewell
  Francis 59, 182
  hugh 182, 201
  Joseph 102, 191
Hopkins Forbearance 72
Hopkins
  Benjamin 12, 118
  Comfort 9, 19, 26,
    41, 52, 87, 98,
    110, 127, 141
  Denis 207
  Dennis 34
  Elisabeth 63
  Eliza 207
  Jane 64, 97
  John 9, 19, 26, 41,
    52, 75, 87, 98,
    110, 127, 141
  Joseph 93
  Robert 25
  Somfort 75

Stephen 64, 97
Hopkinson
   Josh. 212
Hopper
   William 32, 175
Horney
   James 16, 46, 83,
      198
   Jane 96
   Jefferey 156
   Jeffery 123
   Margaret 16, 46
   Solomon 16, 34, 46,
      83, 96, 123, 181
Horsey
   John 41, 43, 62, 97
   Nathaniel 5, 9, 19,
      20, 26, 27, 41
   Samuel 5, 30
   Sarah 9, 19, 20,
      26, 27, 41
   Smith 5
   William 9, 19, 26,
      41, 63, 97
Hosier
   Hannah 47, 80
   Henry 12, 47, 80
Hoskins
   Aaron 105, 124,
      162, 182
   Robert 8
Houfington
   John 107
Hough
   Edmund 214
Houlden
   Richard 196
Houlton
   Ann 59
   William 39, 59
Houston
   Benjamin 152
   Joseph 152
Howard's Search 72
Howard
   Benjamin 72, 145,
      162
   Catherine 145
   Cornelius 69, 89,
      146, 159
   Edmund 159
   Ephraim 89, 146
   George 96, 177, 195
   Henry 44, 89, 146

John 8, 145
Joseph 8, 10, 16,
   89, 146
Joshua 159, 179
Katherine 72
Mary 1, 40
Mathew 1
Michael 74
Nehemiah 96
Sarah 14, 37
Thomas 60, 195, 215
Howards & Porters
   Range 69
Howards Interest 69
Howards Mount 70
Howell
   John 141
   Thomas 106, 120
   William 102
Howison
   Ann 3, 66
   John 3, 23, 66
Hoxton
   Capt. 72
   Hyde 170
   Susannah 170
Hoy
   James 81
Hoye
   Tabitha 81
Hudson
   Dennis 162, 214
   Philip 79
   Richard 24
   Thomas 23
Huett
   Richard 82
Hugell
   Honnor 100
   Robert 100, 132
Hughes
   Hannah 86, 109
   Mary 77, 89
   Samuel 172
   Thomas 77, 89
   William 86, 109
Hughs
   Hannah 134
   William 134, 192
Huitts
   Mary 183
Hukill
   John 44, 79, 144
   Mary 44

Hull
    Daniel 196
    Hannah 196
Hulse
    Elisabeth 94, 113
    Meverel 113
    Meverill 94
Hume
    William 101, 126
Humphries
    Mary 6
    Thomas 6
Humphrys
    Mary 11
Hungerford
    Barton 95
    John 49
Hunt
    Thomas 59, 64, 102
Hunter
    Eleanor 65, 94
    John 43, 206
Hurlock
    George 103
Hurt
    Capt. 71
    Morgan 20, 165, 183
    William 20
Husband
    Alice 186
    James 187, 207
    John 143
    William 44, 143,
        164
Hutchins
    Elisabeth 136
    Francis 136, 149
    Nicholas 39, 62
    Thomas 39, 62, 151
Hutchinson
    William 186
Hutson
    John 15
Huttson
    John 35
Hyde
    Isaac 29, 36, 180,
        212
Hynson
    Charles 1, 7, 12,
        33, 40, 47, 48,
        64, 78, 79, 80,
        84, 86, 90, 101,
        106, 107, 114,

        118, 125, 134,
        145, 152, 163,
        165, 171, 174,
        183, 184, 188,
        194, 199, 204,
        210, 214
    Nathaniel 165
    Thomas 64, 91, 165,
        183
    W. 165
    William 64, 91,
        165, 204

Iiams
    John 205
    William 205
Ijams
    Elisabeth 136
    John 134, 136
    Thomas 134
    William 134, 136,
        147
Inch
    John 80
Iniskern 72
Ireland
    Thomas 36
Irving
    George 43
Isgate
    Francis 58
Ivey
    Elinor 150, 161
    John 150, 161

Jackson
    Edward 17, 90
    Geo. 32
    Jacob 104
    James 162, 172
    Joshua 120
Jacobs
    Walter 108
Jadwin
    Jeremiah 11
James
    Charles 182
    John 165
Jarman
    Henry 214, 215
    Richard 21
    William 214

Jarrard
  Elisabeth 84
  James 84
Jarvis
  Philip 121
Jenifer
  Daniel 210
  Mary 73
  Michael 73
Jenings
  Ariana 152
  Edm. 52, 216
  Edmond 19, 26, 52,
    194
  Edmund 9, 19, 41,
    53, 67, 70, 72,
    76, 88, 98, 111,
    127, 142, 152,
    156, 157, 167,
    177, 190, 191,
    203
Jenkins
  Ann 141
  Enoch 141
  Francis 141
  Richard 47, 62, 64,
    81, 152, 173
Jennifer
  Daniel 31
Jennings
  Edmund 188, 202,
    215
Jerman
  Richard 21
Jobson
  Ann 72
  Daniel 47, 79
  Thomas 72
Joce
  Nicholas 21
John
  Elisabeth 45
  Joshua 45
Johns
  Benjamin 192
  Richard 50, 56, 94
Johnson
  Albert 32, 89, 116,
    141, 155
  Alburt 32
  Alexander 80
  Daniel 7
  Edward 79
  Elenor 154

  Francis 154, 175
  Henry 32, 33, 79,
    89, 93, 116,
    141, 155
  James 160
  John 1, 2, 79, 90,
    91, 145, 214
  Mary 32, 56, 79,
    153, 155
  Purnall 176
  Rebecca 206
  Susanna 2, 145
  Susannah 72
  Thomas 42, 44, 60,
    78, 125, 174,
    206
Johnston
  John 214
Jones
  Ann 96, 116
  Anne 25
  Arthur 121, 199
  Charles 119
  Daniel 206
  David 61, 172, 180
  Griffith 125, 183
  Henry 25
  Hugh 164
  Isaac 177
  Jacob 125
  James 206
  John 25, 50, 96,
    116, 121, 138,
    139, 163, 212
  Joseph 177
  Lewis 5
  Mary 28, 135, 160,
    206
  Michael 61, 211
  Philip 17, 50
  Richard 49, 50
  Robert 141, 178,
    206
  Sarah 120
  Solomon 109
  Theophilus 81
  Thomas 28, 45
  Vincent 132
  William 15, 16, 27,
    123, 135, 160,
    176
Jordan
  Alexander 83
  Elisabeth 64, 102

Justinian 200
Margaret 83
Theodoras 102
Theodorus 64
Jowles
    Kenelm 123
Joyner
    William 55, 95,
        115, 200
Jump
    William 54

Kacey
    Philip 5
Kankey
    John 44, 79
Kear
    James 183
Keare
    James 125
    John 199
Keech
    James 101, 113, 201
    Mary 101, 113
    Samuel 201
Keen
    James 36, 51
Keene
    Nicholas 37
Kellam
    Sarah 63
Kelld
    Thomas 168
Kelley
    Edmond 26
    Elinor 26
    Nicholas 63
    Rachel 186
    Sarah 63
    Thomas 143
Kemey
    Elisabeth 8
    Walter 8
Kemp
    Mary 32, 85, 116
    Matthew 119
    richard 32, 55, 85,
        116
Kempton
    Margarett 189, 190
Kendall's Delight 68
Kennard
    P. 80

Philip 21, 126, 165
Kennett
    William 129, 177
Kenning
    Joseph 44
Kenslagh
    Dominick 104, 125
Kent
    Jannet 136
    Jannett 119
    John 119, 136
Kerr
    John 92
Kerrick
    Patrick 37
Kersey
    Jane 123
    John 96, 123
Key
    Philip 67, 170
Kibble
    William 206, 207,
        214
Killiow
    Edward 154
    Hannah 154, 210
    William 154, 176,
        210
Kimber
    John 90
Kimey
    Elisabeth 31
    Walter 31
King
    Alexander 115
    Benjamin 30
    Capell 30, 43, 108,
        131
    Charles 102, 201
    Elisabeth 123
    Francis 2
    James 15
    John 31, 66, 114,
        148, 173
    Joseph 16, 79
    Mary 41
    Nehemiah 5, 6, 10,
        29, 34, 38, 43,
        47, 62, 64, 96,
        103, 107, 108,
        129, 133, 134,
        144, 151, 159,
        162, 163, 176,
        177, 184, 195,

198, 205, 213, 214
Planner 176
Robert 6, 41, 62, 84, 95
Thomas 36, 123, 147
Whittington 29
William 2
Kininmont
Andrew 16
Samuel 16
Kinnimont
Ambrose 122, 156
Joseph 132
Katherine 122
Kirby
David 122
Matthew 122
Thomas 27
Kirk
James 36
John 85
Joseph 36, 59, 109
Mary 36
Sarah 85
Kirke
John 107
Sarah 107
Knight
Peter 2, 3
Richard 130
William 124, 186
Knott
Ann 123
George 123, 182
Thomas 123
William 147
Knotts
James 153
Knowles
John 54, 83, 86, 88, 96, 99, 100, 111, 112, 114, 128, 129, 142, 146, 147, 157, 167, 168, 193
Mary 43, 53, 75, 77, 167, 168
Mrs. 167, 168
Knowlman
Jane 12

Ladyman

Priscilla 36
William 36, 49, 84, 143, 149
Lamar
John 161
Lamb
Edward 126
Elisabeth 94, 147, 172
Francis 205
Lambden
Ann 153
George 153
Lamberson
Abraham 184, 195
Sarah 184
Lamden
William 57
Lancaster
Thomas 61, 82
Lanck
George 215
Land of Goshen 68
Landman
Daniel 34
Lane
Alexander 125
Francis 176
Richard 136, 143, 210
Thomas 147
Langfitt
Frances 120
Lank
George 195
Mary 195
Lansdale
Isaac 82
Larey
Dennis 198
Large
Mary 71
Larkin
Elisabeth 24, 92
Larramur
John 214
Larrance
William 83
Lashley
Alexander 66
Latham
Aaron 44, 118, 143
Laton
William 94

Laurence
  John 97
Lavell
  John 24
Lawrence
  Benjamin 44
  George 211
  John 44
  Levin 44
  Peter 153, 154
Laws
  Panther 38, 63
  Robert 108
Lawson
  George 158, 169,
    178, 190, 202
Lay
  John 62
Layfield
  George 10, 30, 96
  Katherine 10
  Thomas 10, 30
Layton
  Alice 22, 38
  Thomas 22, 38
  William 38
Lea
  Alice 64
  John 62, 64
League
  John 105
Leate
  Jonathon 200
Lee
  Arthur 101, 126,
    183
  James 144, 194
  Luke 102, 110, 135,
    160
  Mary 11
  Phebe 101, 126
  Richard 42, 75, 141
  Sarah 102, 135, 160
  Thomas 175
Legg
  John 115
Leigh
  Dorothy 14, 85,
    121, 147
  John 14, 35, 85,
    121, 147
Lemee
  Elisabeth 4, 31,
    114, 138

Lenard
  John 156
Lenord
  Patrick 27
Leonard
  John 54, 77, 93,
    101, 131, 155
Lester
  Alice 109
  George 109, 116
Levett
  John 185, 191, 203,
    215
  Robert 185, 191,
    203, 216
Lewin
  John 3
Lewis
  Charles 137, 161
  Elisabeth 137
  Francis 33, 184
  John 46, 79
  Richard 23
Linch
  Alexander 195, 214
  John 30
Lindow
  James 29
Lindsey
  Sarah 176
  Thomas 176
Lingham
  Martha 212
  Thomas 212
Linthicum
  Francis 23
  Gideon 87, 89, 99
  Jane 87, 89, 99
  Rebecca 23
  Thomas 23
Lisay
  Alexander 139
Litherland
  John 182
  William 182
Little Piney Next   72
Little
  Elisabeth 74, 76,
    88, 99, 111
  James 74, 76, 111,
    128, 173
  John 88, 99
Littleton   68
Lloyd

Edward 153, 209
Elisabeth 81
James 166
John 81
Philemon 147
Rebecca 166
Richard 51, 139,
    166
Robert 49, 209
Lloyde
    Richard 37
Lock
    Meverill 15
Lockerman
    Elisabeth 193
    Jacob 193
Locklin
    Margaret 61
Lockwood
    Mary 108, 159, 184,
        206
    Richard 108, 151,
        159, 184, 206
Lomas
    John 19, 43, 70,
        71, 121
Lomass
    John 28
Long Venture 72
Long
    Samuel 43, 62
    Solomon 43
Loockerman
    Dorothy 9, 18
    Elisabeth 88, 96,
        99, 100, 111,
        112, 114, 128,
        129, 142, 146,
        147, 157, 167
    Govert 18, 144
    Jacob 8, 9, 18, 19,
        89, 96, 99, 100,
        111, 114, 128,
        129, 142, 144,
        146, 148, 157,
        159, 167, 168
    John 18, 35
    Nicholas 18
    Thomas 18
Lord
    Francis 5
    Henry 5
Love
    Samuel 139

Loveday
    John 5, 46, 58, 181
    Sarah 46, 58
Lovelin
    William 117
Low
    Jacob 120
Lowe
    Nicholas 22, 27,
        42, 53, 75, 134
    Samuel 18
    William 34
Lowman
    Letitia 95, 124,
        125
    Samuel 95, 124, 125
Lowry
    Robert 5
Lucket
    Ignatius 161
    Jane 160
Luckett
    Ignatius 3, 145
    Jane 145
Lunns Addition 73
Lurtey
    John 64, 122
Lusby
    Ellenor 52
    John 9, 17, 18, 19,
        26, 41, 52
    Mary 52
    Robert 14, 169
    Samuel 52
    Thomas 14
    Zachariah 181, 192
Lynch
    Patrick 39, 96, 109
Lyngan
    Martha 25
    Thomas 25
Lynn
    Aaron 108
    Thomas 210

Macclannahan
    Thomas 197
Macclester
    Randal 43
Maccnemara
    Margarett 184, 185
Maccoy
    John 37

Page 253

Maccubbin
  Nich. 52, 67, 70
  Nicholas 17
  Samuel 133
  Zach. 19, 26, 27,
    42, 52, 53, 54,
    70, 88, 89, 112,
    143, 188, 203,
    216
  Zachariah 48
Macdaniel
  Bryan 137
  Charles 113
Mackall
  John 57
Mackatee
  William 10, 66
Mackeel
  Clare 31
Mackelfresh
  David 132, 146
Mackellfresh
  David 110
  Martha 110, 132
Mackemys
  Morriss 58
Mackey
  John 213
Mackgraw
  James 120
  John 120
Mackmory
  John 144
Mackormick
  Michael 94
Maclendon
  Hannah 34
  James 34
Macnemara
  M. 67
  Michael 14, 19, 23,
    49, 91, 92, 110,
    145, 197, 201
Maconchie
  William 37
Macoy
  John 113, 149, 160
MacWilliams
  Mary 201
  Thomas 201
Madden
  Daniel 91
Maddox
  Notley 13, 37, 158,

    168
  Notly 3, 148
Maddux
  Bell 38, 63
  Thomas 38, 63
Madsley
  James 81
Magee
  John 39, 63
Maggatee
  William 24, 31
Maglammery
  Edward 162
Magrah
  John 82
Magruder
  John 144, 174
  Robert 10, 50, 61
  Samuel 55
  Sarah 50, 61
  William 50
Mahaun
  John 119, 138
Mahone
  Thomas 2
Maiden Fancy 68
Major
  Andrew 121
Majors Choice 69
Majors
  Andrew 82
Malden
  James 170
Maldin
  James 148
Mankin
  Stephen 3, 37, 113
Manning
  John 23, 83
  Margrett 138
  Mary 23
  Nathaniel 38, 58,
    138
  Richard 138, 172
  Victorious 83
Mannying
  Thomas 6
Mannyng
  Joshan 51, 84, 150,
    161
  Thomas 51, 84, 150,
    161
Mansfield
  Paul 189

Robert 79, 80, 145, 166
Samuel 79, 145, 166
Manson
John 32
Lilley 115
Lylly 32
Marbury
Francis 13, 114, 150
Leonard 13, 25, 114, 150
Luke 13, 114, 150
Mariarte
Ninian 25
Markland
Mathew 211
Matthew 61
Marling
Isaac 5, 46, 58
Marsey
John 129
Marsh's Forest 72
Marshall
Ann 115, 119, 155
Jane 63
Richard 139
Thomas 10, 24, 25, 63, 87, 140
William 36, 87, 140
Marshment
Mary 97, 175
Philip 97, 175
Marten
John 95
Martin
Ann 103, 133
James 29, 214
Thomas 57, 65, 83
William 103
Martindale
John 50
Martindall
John 36
Mason
Anne 23
Frances 17
George 23
John 17
Joseph 40, 153, 205
Mathew 197
Matthew 32, 77, 153, 155
Rachel 153

Massey
Elisabeth 33, 80
William 33, 80
Mastin
Richard 12, 37
Mathews
Ann 86
Elisabeth 12
John 86
Roger 45
Thomas 131
William 12
Mattershaw
George 115
Matthews
Alice 171, 193
Hugh 117, 194
Mary 194
Roger 100, 109, 112, 128, 142, 174, 212
Thomas 191
William 171, 193
Mattingley
Thomas 123
Mattison
Hugh 165
Maxfield
Thomas 7
Maxwell
Asael 86, 128, 142
James 56, 86, 89, 99, 100, 104, 112, 128, 142, 143, 157, 158, 168, 169, 178, 190, 202, 215
Thomas 97
McCabe
James 47, 79
Mccalister
Patrick 138
McClain
Alexander 165
McClammey
Elenor 133
Woney 133
McClane
William 21
McClean
Abigail 155
Ann 11, 93, 115, 155
Daniel 45, 175

Daniell 115
James 11, 33, 93
Jane 45
McClemey
 Elinor 163
 Woney 163
McClemmey
 William 176
McClendon
 James 57
McCollough
 John 117, 187
 Mary 117
 Tole 117, 118, 187
McCoy
 John 51
McCubbin
 William 70
McDaniel
 Charles 3
 Daniel 160
McDermot
 John 16
McDowell
 John 6
 William 7, 45
McGachan
 Alexander 1
McGraw
 John 124
McKeel
 John 203
McKeele
 John 204
McKown
 Francis 12
 Sarah 12
McLeod
 Robert 90, 145
McManus
 Elisabeth 117, 118, 209
 John 44, 117, 164, 210
McPherson
 Alexander 95, 149
McWilliams
 Mary 4, 179
 Thomas 4, 82, 179
Mead
 Joseph 104, 151, 199
Mears
 Robert 107

Thomas 107
Mecotter
 Hezekiah 103
Medcalf
 Mary 107
 Thomas 107
Medcalfe
 William 103
Medcalfs Chance 69
Medcalfs Mount 69
Medford
 Mary 56
Medkin
 John 138
Meek
 Francis 31, 173
Meeke
 Francis 114, 148
Meekes
 Francis 20
 Robert 20
Meekins
 Isaac 57
 James 57
Meeks
 Robert 21, 126, 165
Meglenin
 William 183
Melegue
 Samuel 197
Mellor
 Nehemiah 195
Melogue
 Hannah 175
 Samuel 175
Melson
 Samuel 182
Melton
 Elisabeth 159, 181
 James 159, 181
Mercer
 David 14, 92
 Mary 14
 Robert 186
 William 186
Meredith
 Elisabeth 212
 Humphrey 173, 212
Merreday
 Henry 73
 Sarah 73
Merrell
 Catherine 160
 Philip 160

Merrick
  James 147
Merridith
  John 54
Merrill
  Catherine 182
Merriott
  Elisabeth 105, 145
  George 145
  William 121, 145,
    179, 180
Merritt
  John 102
Merryman
  John 191
Metcalf
  Joseph 101, 104,
    112
Metcalfe
  Mary 65, 133
  Thomas 65, 133
Michael
  Elisabeth 122, 208
  William 122, 156,
    205, 208
Middle Neck 68
Middleland 72
Middlemore
  Josias 47, 64, 81,
    152, 172
Middleton
  Susanna 85, 95
  Thomas 36, 85, 95,
    140, 161
Midford
  Bullman 1
Milbourne
  Caleb 29
  Samuel 171
Milburn
  Stephen 201
Miles
  Elisabeth 61, 200
  Evan 61, 81, 200
  Henry 130
Mill Land 69
Millain
  Henry 109, 116, 151
Miller
  Jacob 95, 113, 173,
    186
  James 182
  John 32, 153
  Martha 183

Mary 28
Michael 183
Sarah 95, 173, 186
William 149
Millford 73
Millford & Taylors
  Lott 69
Millington
  Alembey 168
  Elisabeth 86, 88,
    96, 100, 111,
    112, 114, 128,
    129, 146, 148,
    157, 167, 168
  Grace 100, 111, 167
  Oliver 100, 111,
    167
Millman
  John 201
  Mary 201
Mills
  Charles 35, 64, 102
  James 24, 82
  John 126
  Jonathon 176
  Joseph 138
  Mary 126
  Moses 176
  Smith 184
Millstead
  Joanna 97
  Thomas 97, 171,
    179, 212
  William 66
Milton
  Abraham 21
Minskie
  John Samuel 174
Mitchell
  Benjamin 62
  Edward 125, 210
  Thomas 6, 81, 145,
    161, 210
  William 206
Moale
  John 45, 157
Mockbee
  William 8
Moffett
  John 175
Mohone
  Thomas 78
Money
  Francis 38, 58, 109

Mary 38, 58, 108
Robert 7, 45, 78
Ruth 7, 45
Monk
WIlliam 151
Monroe
William 92
Monrow
William 67
Montoe
Charles 23, 118
Montoes
Charles 51
Moody
James 8, 46, 90
Sarah 46
Thomas 196
Moor
William 43
Moore
Henry 61, 81
James 80, 90, 91,
165, 199
Jannet 100, 112
Jennett 167
Josias 167, 168
Margaret 66, 76,
88, 94, 99, 106,
177
Mary 90
Mordecai 66, 76,
88, 94, 99, 106,
177
Richard 66, 76, 88,
99, 106, 177,
179
Samuel Preston 66,
76, 88, 94, 99,
106, 177
Sarah 61, 81
Morain
Jonathon 57
Kezia 57
Moraine
Jonathon 58
Kezia 58
Moran
Gabriel 94, 113
John 94, 113, 213
More
Andrew 18
Morgan
James 122, 124
Morrett

John 64
Morrice
Jacob 85, 148
Morris
Elisabeth 94
Isaac 47, 63
Jacob 4, 166
Randolph 15, 94,
118
Robert 198
Morristen
Ann 22
George 22
John 22
Morriston
John 82
Mosley
James 204
Motherby
Charles 200
Mouatt
James 8, 17
Mounts
Christopher 186
Martha 186, 207
Mudd
Elisabeth 3, 84, 95
Henry 3, 23, 85, 95
Thomas 3, 149
Muir
Adam 208
Thomas 208
Muire
Adam 127
Thomas 127
Mulican
Patrick 205
Mullican
John 149, 181
Patrick 22, 181
Sarah 149, 181
William 149, 181
Mullikan
John 205
Sarah 205
William 205
Mulliken
John 83
Mullikin
Thomas 139
Mullon
Mary 35, 36
Mumford
James 39, 97

Thomas 39, 97
Muncaster
  James 3
Murdock
  John 36
  William 170, 190,
    191, 209
Murfey
  Margaret 91
Murfy
  William 121
Murphey
  Alice 11
  John 102
  Margaret 64
  William 196
Murra
  David 43
Murray
  Dr. 22, 30
  Duncan 130
  Dunkin 62
  John 40, 101, 103,
    126, 130
  Josephus 159
  Sarah 103
  William 18, 22, 30
Murry
  John 6

Nabb
  John 197
Nairne
  Robert 29
Neal
  Edward 208
Neale
  Charles 79, 139,
    190
  Henry 160
  William 139, 160
Neall
  Francis 57
Negroes
  Bess 52
  Charles 52
  Great James 168
  Jemmey 168
  Jenny 52
  Moll 141
Nellson
  John 62
Nelson

Anne 43
Hugh 103, 131
John 43
William 10, 103,
  131
Nevett
  Thomas 204
Nevill
  Walter 153, 154
Newbold
  John 62, 108
Newcam
  Ann 208
  Robert 208
Newcom
  Anne 31
  Robert 31, 35
Newell
  Mary 69
Newman
  John 37, 51, 119,
    139
  Priscilla 37, 119,
    139
Newton
  Edward 93
  Thomas 32
Nicholls
  Benjamin 204
  Edward 89
  John 42
  Joseph 31, 94
  Mary 42, 89
  Solomon 23, 152,
    173
Nicholson
  Elisabeth 39, 63
  Hannah 163, 171
  John 39, 63, 134
  Joseph 84, 114,
    163, 171
Nicolls
  John 57
  Mary 57
Nilson
  William 43
Noads
  Ann 69
Noakes
  George 124
Noaks
  George 102
  Mary 102
Noble

George 140
Isaac 6
Mark 42, 57
Susanna 6
Norman
  James 40, 80, 166
  Nicholas 92, 148
Normansell
  Katherine 47
  Richard 21, 47, 84,
    114
Norris
  John 29, 50
  Mary 29, 50
North
  Robert 24
Norwood
  John 33, 49
  Rachel 33
  Samuel 69
  Sarah 69
Norwoods Fancy 69
Noyes
  Nicholas 189
Numbers
  Catherine 78, 135,
    144
  Peter 78, 90, 135,
    143, 144
Nuner
  John 127
Nutter
  Charles 93, 119,
    120, 138, 150,
    183
  Christopher 119,
    129
  Elisabeth 130, 144
  Huett 119, 120,
    183, 207
  Mathew 129, 215
  Sarah 120, 138, 207
  William 22, 38,
    130, 138, 145,
    151, 213

Obryan
  Thomas 115
Odall
  Ann 144
  Henry 144
Odear
  Stephen 97

Odell
  Henry 25
  Thomas 25, 31
Offutt
  Jane 55, 180
  Mary 29, 38, 61,
    185, 212
  William 29, 38, 55,
    61, 171, 180,
    185, 212
Oldson
  Abraham 47, 78
Oliver
  John 174
One Third Timber Neck
  69
Oneal
  Hugh 101, 126
Onorton
  Isabella 176
  John 176, 195
Orgin
  Elisabeth 56
Oriel
  Edward 85, 148, 166
  Elenor 85, 166
  Elinor 148
Orm
  Catherine 211
Orme
  John 211
Orrick
  John 82
Oryon
  Mallygo 16
Othoson
  Garratt 45
  Garret 16, 47
  Garrett 79
  Sarah 16, 47, 79
Outerbridge
  Burr 30
Outon
  John 63
  Sarah 63
Outten
  John 38
  Sarah 38
Overard
  Peter 106
Owen
  Thomas 150
Owens
  Joseph 146

William 33, 138

Paca
  Aquila 109
  John 134, 157
Painter
  Edward 81, 134
  Margaret 81
Pamphilon
  Margaret 207
  Thomas 207
Parish
  Edward 193, 203,
    216
Parker
  Abraham 14, 31, 51,
    137
  Ann 51
  Elisabeth 146, 175
  Gabriel 6, 7, 10,
    17, 24, 36, 39,
    49, 50, 51, 56,
    60, 65, 84, 91,
    92, 103, 105,
    109, 114, 119,
    121, 131, 136,
    137, 143, 144,
    146, 148, 149,
    150, 159, 161,
    170, 171, 179,
    180, 192, 193,
    199, 210, 211,
    212
  George 174
  John 213
  Mary 14, 31
  Samuel 214
  William 116
Parkinson
  Abraham 3, 48, 106,
    137
Parnham
  Francis 139
  John 113, 139, 160
Parratt
  Aaron 122
Parremore
  Mathew 214
Parres
  Edward 97
Parrish
  Edward 3
  John 3

Parson
  John 214
Parsons
  Benjamin 80
  Francis 29, 138
  John 214
  Mary 165
  Solomon 165
  Thomas 154
Partridge
  Buckler 116, 133,
    216
  Buttler 212
  Jane 212, 216
Patchall
  John 124
Patridge
  Isaac 127
Patten
  Edward 126
  Elliott 166
Pattison
  Jacob 56, 57
  St. Leger 56
Patton
  Robert 44
Paul
  Elisabeth 30
  Nicholas 30, 38,
    107
Paulson
  Ann 81
  James 81, 94
Pavett
  Isaac 170, 191
  Margaret 170
  Margarett 191
Payte
  John 6
Peacock
  Richard 126, 188
Pearce
  (N) 25, 27
  Benjamin 7, 45, 206
  Gideon 1
  John 31
  Margaret 7
  Margarett 45
  Nathaniel 1, 40
  Sarah 164, 210
  Thomas 78, 164
  William 25, 27, 42,
    53, 75, 87, 98,
    164, 187, 210

Peard
   Sarah 189
Pearkins
   Daniel 1
Pearson
   Justine 138
   Noah 58, 81, 138
   Richard 58
Peat
   Capt. 71
Peden
   John 176
Peele
   Ebenezar 189
   James 3
   John 111, 127, 142,
      156, 167, 177,
      188
   Robert 46, 53, 75,
      76, 88, 98, 111,
      127, 141, 142,
      156, 166, 177,
      188, 189, 203,
      216
   Roger 46, 53, 75,
      87, 98, 111,
      127, 141, 156,
      166, 177, 188,
      189, 203, 216
   Samuel 46, 53, 75,
      76, 88, 98, 111,
      127, 141, 142,
      156, 162, 166,
      169, 177, 178,
      188, 189, 203,
      216
   William 46, 53, 75,
      88, 98, 111,
      127, 142, 156,
      162, 166, 168,
      177, 178, 188,
      203, 216
Peiree
   Mary 194
Peirpoints Lot 73
Pell
   Mary 183
   William 183, 205
Peney
   Catherine 83
   John 83
Penington
   John 16
   Rachel 137

Robert 137
Penn
   Jane 185
   Mark 37, 185, 213
   William 37, 51, 66,
      119, 139
Pennell
   Caleb 18
Pennewell
   Richard 30
Pennington
   Henry 117
   Mary 79
   Rachel 44, 164
   Robert 44, 79, 164
   William 79
Pent
   Mr. 140
Pepper
   William 195
Perkins
   Daniel 80, 205
   Ebenezar 183
Perren
   John 84
Perrie
   Samuel 2, 186
Perry
   John 154
Peterkin
   David 5, 38, 58
   Elisabeth 213
   James 164, 204, 213
   Mary 38, 58, 164,
      204
Pettycoat
   John 69
Phelpes
   Walter 136
   William 136
Phelps
   Walter 8
Pherson
   Percival 84
   Ruth 84
Philips
   Ann 19
   James 118, 190
   John 19
Phillips
   Ann 9, 26, 75, 87,
      98, 110, 127,
      141
   Anne 41

James 119, 138,
    182, 202, 215
Jane 53
John 9, 26, 41, 53,
    75, 87, 98, 110,
    127, 141, 171,
    205
Mary 35
Robert 35, 59
Thomas 196
Phillpot
    John 186
Phillpott
    John 13
Phipps
    Solomon 174
Pickering
    Dinah 28
    Elisabeth 28
    James 28
    Margaret 54
    Robert 54, 77
Pickring
    Jeremiah 182
Piggott
    John 143, 187
    Samuel 143
Pile
    William 146, 175
Piles
    Francis 174
    John 3, 11
    Mary 3, 11
Pinar
    James 40
Pinder
    Margaret 47, 54,
        78, 119, 155
    William 32, 33, 47,
        78, 119, 155
Piner
    James 40
    Thomas 1
Piney Neck 72
Piper
    Christopher 130
Pitchfork
    Frances 5
    Thomas 5, 35
Pitt
    John 4, 5, 7, 11,
        22, 23, 30, 37,
        38, 48, 56, 58,
        65, 81, 85, 93,

        106, 108, 114,
        118, 119, 126,
        132, 135, 137,
        138, 144, 150,
        159, 164, 172,
        182, 185, 188,
        193, 203, 208,
        209
Plafay
    Catherine 197
    Philip 197
Plaisted
    Ichabod 76, 190
Plater
    George 65, 184
    Rebecca 184
Plummer
    Elisabeth 2, 25, 60
    Jerome 74, 169
    John 2
    Margaret 74, 159,
        169
    Micajah 2, 60
    Samuel 2
    Thomas 159, 191
    Yate 2, 60
Poilloun
    John 164
Poleson
    Powell 78
Pomroy
    John 15
Poole
    Sarah 32
    Thomas 32, 93, 208
Pope
    John 43
Porter
    Francis 6, 103
    James 206
    John 198
    Joshua 176
    Lawrence 103
    Thomas 121
    William 6
Poston
    John 157
Pottenger
    Ann 212
    John 28
    Robert 28, 172, 212
    Samuel 28
Potter
    Marton 214

Susannah 214
Pottinger
   Anne 140
   Robert 139, 140
Powell
   Alice 8
   Charles 204
   Howell 180
   James 65, 83
   Richard 154
   T. 154
   William 8
Powson
   Patience 107
   William 107, 130,
    184
Prather
   Catherine 61
   Edward 61
   John 61
Pratt
   John 196
Presbury
   George 134
   Mary 134
Preston
   Thomas 119, 137
Price
   Ann 119, 155
   Hyland 78, 98, 101,
    125
   James 78, 126
   Jane 7, 15, 45
   John 15, 31, 103,
    123, 208
   Joseph 7, 45
   Mary 78, 101, 125
   Sarah 78, 126
   Thomas 154, 175
   William 54, 77
Prichard
   John 90
Primrose
   George 115
   Violet 115, 198
Prindowell
   Elisabeth 105, 121
   John 17, 105, 121,
    192
Prior
   Edmund 114, 176
   William 114
Prise
   John 176

Pritchard
   Jane 181, 205
   John 181, 205
Proffee
   James 23, 113
Proffiy
   James 113
Prouse
   George 207
Providence 69, 74
Pryor
   Catherine 114
   Edmond 155
   William 114
Pullin
   John 56
Purdee
   Elisabeth 101
   William 101
Purnall
   William 154

Quary
   Robert 68
Quidly
   Mary 110
   William 110
Quin
   Elisabeth 156
   John 156
Quinn
   Elisabeth 57, 135
   John 57, 93, 133,
    135

Rackliff
   Charles 43
Rackliffe
   Charles 130
Raisens
   Mary 9
   Thomas 9
Raisins
   Mary 19, 20, 26,
    27, 42, 53, 75
   Thomas 19, 20, 26,
    27, 42, 53, 75
Rakestraw
   John 92
Raley
   Grace 181
   Michael 181, 201

Ramesy
  Andrew 30
  James 30
  Thomas 30
Ramsey
  Ann 173
  Catherine 210
  Henry 210
  John 137, 173, 186
  Thomas 121
Randall
  Augustine 92, 148
Randolph
  Thomas 147
Range 68
Ranters Ridge 72
Raper
  Richard 59
Rasin
  John 125, 199
  Mary 80, 87, 163,
    183
  Thomas 80, 87, 125,
    163, 166, 183,
    199
Ratcliff
  James 35
  Joseph 113
  Joshua 113, 187
  Mary 113, 187
Ratcliffe
  Joshua 152, 213
  Mary 152
Rathell
  Elisabeth 65, 83
  John 65, 83
Rattenbury
  John 18
Raven
  Luke 46
Rawles
  John 196
Rawlings
  Daniel 10
  Deborah 72
  Elinor 169
  Isaac 10
  John 158
  Richard 72
Ray
  George 13, 137, 140
  Joseph 116, 139
  Susanna 137, 140
  Susannah 13

William 116, 139,
    144
Raymond
  Susannah 72
Razolini
  Onorio 65
Read
  George 183
  James 29, 36
  John 102, 123
  Joseph 165
  Nathaniel 54
Readey
  Nicholas 152
Reading
  John 1, 7, 78, 126
Readman
  John 4
Realey
  Ann 191
  Robert 191
Reas
  William Philip 72
Recards
  Phillip 93
Redemption of Iniskern
  72
Redgrave
  John 91
Reding
  Sarah 1
Redman
  John 35, 105, 124,
    182
Redmon
  John 162
Reed
  Mary 2
Reeder
  Benjamin 160
Reeves
  Thomas 200
  Ubgate 200
Register
  Henry 78, 90
Reiley
  Bryan 65, 87
  Mary 65, 87, 171
Reily
  Bryan 161, 171
Rencher
  Thomas 73
  Underwood 29
Renfrow

Stephen 212
Reyley
    Bryan 140
    Mary 140
Reynolds
    Edward 98
    John 5, 34, 83, 90,
        93, 98
    Mary 98
    Robert 90, 209
    Thomas 17, 109
    William 90, 185
Rhoads
    Elisabeth 38, 63
    Henry 61
    Timothy 38, 63
Rhodes
    Henry 116
Ricaud
    Benjamin 40, 125,
        183
Rich
    Joseph 47, 79
    Mary 175
    Stephen 175
Richardson
    Ann 152, 174, 183
    Antho. 180
    Isaac 93, 127, 138
    Jane 22
    John 22
    Joseph 106
    Mary 62, 89
    Solomon 93, 127,
        138
    Thomas 64, 95, 131,
        152, 174, 183
    William 91, 106,
        191
Rickards
    William 108
Rickets
    John 207
    John Thomas 207
    Philip 205
    Thomas 207
Ricketts
    David 143
Riddle
    Walter 35
Ridgeleys Beginning 70
Ridgely
    Charles 82, 106
    Elisabeth 106

Henry 8
Ridgeway
    Richard 194
Ridgley
    Henry 14
Rigbie
    Nat. 112, 128, 169,
        191, 202
Riggin
    Charles 62
Riley
    Thomas 195
Rimer
    Hugh 164
    Mary 164
Rimmar
    Hugh 93
    Mary 93
Rimmer
    Hugh 172
    Mary 172
Rind
    Alexander 171
Ringgold
    Elias 91
    James 80, 125, 126,
        165
    Mary 91
    William 42
Rippon
    Robert 186
Risteau
    John 90, 131
Ritchie
    Robert 39, 74, 77,
        104, 112, 129
Roach
    Samuel 29
Robbins
    Bodwin 47
    Elisabeth 47
    Thomas 47
Roberson
    Andrew 129, 176
Roberts
    Bartholomew 207
    Edward 200
    Elisabeth 135
    James 207
    John 17, 18, 55,
        95, 105, 200
    Richard 39, 84
    Robert 39, 84
    Roberts 114

Samuel 135, 158
William 145
Robertson
  Robert 61, 134
  William 37
Robey
  Michael Hinds 186
  Peter 113, 186
Robins Camp 68
Robins
  Bowd. 214
  Bowdoin 63
  Elisabeth 63
  George 196
  John 168
  Thomas 63
  William 172
Robinson
  Alice 92
  Charles 191
  John 121
  Mary 121
  Peter 14, 92, 172
  Richard 134
  Sarah 14, 61
  Thomas 93
  William 115, 149,
    172
Robison
  Andrew 177
  William 74, 76, 88,
    99, 111, 128
Robson
  Charles 7, 31
  David 138, 185, 204
  Elisabeth 138, 164
  John 57
  Mary 7, 31
  William 66
Roby
  Michael Hyns 95
  Peter 95
Roch
  Gregory 175
Rochester
  Francis 175
Rock
  Gregory 197
Rockhould
  Charles 105
Roe
  Edward 77
  John 77, 93
  Martha 77

Thomas 77
Roger Grey 68
Rogers
  Edward 165
  Elisabeth 165, 183
  John 66
  William 3, 11, 33,
    89, 189
Rokey
  Jane 32
Rolph
  Glanvill 1
  Margaret 1
Ronald
  James 139
Roper Gray 73
Rose
  William 17, 50
Ross
  Thomas 138, 164
Rosser
  John 45
Roth
  Mary 54
  William 54
Rouls
  Ann 40
Round
  Catherine 195
  James 195
Rowles
  Ann 73
  Jacob 18
  John 32, 148, 154,
    174
  Martha 153
  William 73
Rowlls
  John 40
Rownds
  James 215
Ruley
  William 92
Rumsey
  Edward 164
  William 7, 8, 12,
    16, 44, 46, 47,
    78, 85, 90, 95,
    98, 101, 117,
    118, 124, 135,
    137, 143, 158,
    164, 186, 187,
    206, 209, 216
Russell

John 123, 147
Thomas 16
Ruth
  Jane 119, 155
  John 119, 155
Ryan
  Abigail 47, 53, 76,
    88, 98, 111,
    127, 142, 156,
    167, 177, 190,
    202
  Cornelius 47, 53,
    76, 88, 98, 111,
    127, 142, 156,
    167, 177, 190,
    202
Rycroft
  Richard 97
Ryland
  John 164
Ryley
  John 32

Saide
  Elisabeth 107
  John 107
Salemon
  Elisabeth 102
  Robert 102
Salmon
  Robert 193
Salmond
  Robert 124
Salsbury
  James 175
Sampson
  John 50
Sanders
  Eleanor 37, 66, 149
  Eleonar 94
  James 62
  Jane 14
  Joseph 51, 66, 114,
    118
  Thomas 10, 37
  Verlinda 37
  Virlinda 10
Sands
  Robert 34
Santee
  Ann 202
  Christopher 202
Sapenton

Margaret 7, 45
Nathaniel 7, 45
Saser
  Elisabeth 3
  John 3
Satur
  Henry 131
Saunders
  Jane 92
Savory
  William 56, 86, 89,
    99, 100, 112,
    128, 142, 143,
    157, 158, 168,
    169, 178, 190,
    202, 205, 215
Sawell
  Peter 170, 199
Sawyer
  Humphrey 174
  Humphry 212
Scarborough
  John 30, 43, 151
Schee
  Harmanus 21
Scott
  Andrew 29, 62, 79,
    211, 212
  Day 29, 62
  Edward 163, 171
  George 79, 174,
    190, 211
  John 120, 159, 182
  Mary 211
  Nathaniel 47, 78
  Thomas 8, 25, 61,
    130
  Walter 16
  William 122
Scotten
  John 92
  Richard 92
Scotton
  John 154
Scrogen
  John 13
Scroggen
  George 139
Seager
  John 15
Sedgwick
  Elisabeth 192
Sedwick
  Benjamin 149, 192

Elisabeth 211
Seeney
  Elisabeth 181
  William 181
Seeny
  Elisabeth 147
  Joshua 147
Sellman
  William 8
Selman
  John 132
Semmes
  Ignatius 23
  Juliana 23
  Marmaduke 37
Seney
  Solomon 32
Seon
  Jane 133, 176
  Thomas 133, 176
Serjent
  Elisabeth 81
  John 81
Seth
  Charles 54, 77, 197
  Elisabeth 54, 77
  John 54
Sewall
  Charles 59, 135
  Clement 59, 87
  Mitchel 189
  Nicholas 59, 83,
    135
  Peter 193
Sewell
  Henry 73
  Mary 73, 80
  Peter 149
  Richard 20, 80
Sewells Fancy 73
Sewells Increase 68
Shaghunsy
  William 31
Shanks
  Thomas 82
Sharp
  George 176, 195,
    198
  Mary 176, 198
  Peter 103
  Solomon 103, 180
  William 103
Sharpe
  Peter 85

Solomon 85
William 85
Sharples
  William 49, 171
Shaw
  Daniel 50
  John 103
  Jonathon 29, 44
  Joseph 153
  Sarah 44
Shawhun
  Daniel 165
Sheapard
  Christopher 161
  Rowland 162
Sheen
  Robert 38
Shehawn
  Darby 12
Sheild
  William 34, 57
Sheldon
  John 103, 130
  Mary 103, 130
Shemwell
  Isaac 95, 163, 173
Shener
  Christopher 27, 201
Shepard
  Christopher 135
  Rowland 135
Sheperds Chance 73
Sheperds Grove 73
Sheperds Range 72
Shepherd
  Christopher 39, 151
  Rowland 39, 151
Sheredine
  T. 104, 215
  Thomas 5, 133
Sherreden
  William 97
Sherwood
  Daniel 180, 198
  Francis 93, 181,
    205
  Hugh 12, 46, 58
  John 93, 181, 205
  Mary 12, 46, 58
Shery
  Jobe 205, 206
Shield
  Lambert 34, 85,
    103, 131, 156

William 1, 86, 103, 131, 156
Shierclieffe
  Moma 182
  Thomas 182
Shiles
  Thomas 43
Shipley
  Adam 50, 148
  Peter 50, 82, 145
  Richard 50, 145
  William 11
Shirley
  Richard 102, 110, 201
  Sarah 102
Shirly
  Richard 187
Shivers
  John 17, 19, 26, 52
Shockley
  John 29
Shoebrook
  Thomas 153
Short
  Ann 195
  Edward 195, 215
  John 195
Shropshire
  Alice 131, 156
  Edward 131, 156
Sim
  Patrick 97, 140, 170
Simco
  George 143
Simes
  Marmaduke 213
Simkin
  John 199
  Priscilla 200
Simmans
  Charles 133, 134, 172, 209
  George 134, 209
  Hannah 133, 209
Simmes
  George 28
Simmonds
  James 15
Simmons
  Andrew 38
  George 3, 28, 29, 101

James 59
Simms
  Marmaduke 185
  Mary 185
Simpson
  Archibald 203
  Elioner 203
  Richard 195, 215
  Thomas 195
  William 195, 215
Simson
  Eliza 194
  Joseph Green 194
Sindall
  Elisabeth 151
  Philip 151, 172
Singleton
  John 29, 151, 152
Sinners
  Capt. 71
Sisson
  William 113
Skeen
  Robert 63
Skeine
  Robert 6
Skillington
  Elijah 122
  Kenelm 122, 198
  Lidia 122
Skillirn
  Thomas 82
Skinner
  Andrew 42
  John 149, 210
  Nathaniel 10, 25
  Richard 5, 34
  Robert 10, 25, 161
  William 149, 179, 210
Skirven
  George 1, 40
  Sarah 1
Slade
  Josiah 82
Slater
  Ellis 49, 192
Sligh
  Thomas 17, 104
Slye
  Charles 83, 170
Smallwood
  Benjamin 10, 50
  James 9, 23

Pryor 9
Thomas 9
Smart
    Alexander 73
    Elisabeth 58, 120,
      159, 182
    Margaret 73
    Richard 58, 120,
      159, 182
Smith's Range 72
Smith
    Abraham 159, 184
    Andrew 127, 150
    Ann 109, 209
    Anthony 15
    Benjamin 13, 34, 50
    Charles 109, 126,
      147, 209
    Charles Som. 185
    Charles Somerset 24
    Charles Somersett
      94
    Daniel 175
    Elias 186
    Elisabeth 4, 150
    George 196
    Henry 6
    James 1, 20, 80,
      84, 114
    Jane 135, 160
    John 33, 59, 73,
      81, 92, 95, 116,
      131, 135, 149,
      209
    Joseph 180
    Magdalen 6
    Margaret 185
    Mary 13, 34, 50,
      192
    Philip 48, 55, 90,
      106, 135, 173
    Rachell 127
    Rebecca 215
    Richard 107, 133,
      150
    Samuel 21, 24, 26,
      52, 94, 101
    Sarah 1, 91
    Thomas 122, 125,
      126, 197
    Walter 170
    William 4, 6, 160,
      192
Smithers

Mary 204
William 1
Smithson
    Ann 4, 59
    Owen 4, 59
    Sarah 186
Smullin
    Randall 29
Smyth
    Thomas 80
Snowden
    Richard 99, 212
    William 182
Sollars
    Sabrett 121
Sollers
    Sabret 21
    Sabrett 17
Somervell
    James 180
Sont
    Thomas 160
Sparkes
    Cornelia 54, 115,
      155, 197
    George 115, 153
    John 54, 77, 153,
      155
Sparks
    George 200
    John 200
Spearman
    Ann 126, 188
    Philip 126, 188
    William 166
Spencer
    Jervis 1
    John 20, 21, 118,
      166
Sprigg
    Edward 104, 185,
      191, 203, 215
    Osborn 209
    Thomas 51
Sprogle
    Godfrey 96, 130,
      177
    Godfry 213
Spry
    Thomas 35
St. Lawrence
    Nicholas 62
St. Tee
    Christopher 193,

203

Stacey
  William 34
Stallings
  Jacob 36
  Joseph 36, 132, 137
  Samuel 36, 132
  Sarah 137
Standiford
  Samuel 200
  William 200
Standly
  Alexander 56
Stansbury
  Luke 5, 89
Stanton
  Jonathon 130, 133,
    163
Starkey
  Joshua 61
Steivenson
  William 100, 145,
    173
Stephens
  Sarah 73
Stevens
  Dorothy 5
  Elisha 5
  Francis 96, 100,
    167, 168
  John 6, 34, 109,
    206, 207
  Rachel 214
  Richard 214
  Walter 31
  William 127, 163
Stevenson
  Edward 133, 151
  Francina Augustina
    193, 194
  Hugh 195
  John 91
  Richard 18
  Robert 184
  William 43, 92,
    130, 193, 194,
    201
Stevinson
  William 63
Steward
  Catherine 195
  Katherine 39, 177
  William 39, 177,
    196

Stewart
  Catherine 47
  Charles 140, 174
  George 20
  John 94, 106, 120,
    138, 188, 200
  Monaca 200
  William 47
Stievenson
  William 145
Stifin
  John 51
Stiles
  John 109
Stimpson
  Benjamin 13
Stimpton
  Benjamin 34
Stimton
  Benjamin 50
Stinchcomb
  Ann 61
  Nathaniel 61
Stockett
  Thomas 132, 179
Stocking
  Ralph 147
Stoddart
  John 87, 98, 211
  William 87, 98
Stoddert
  John 25
  William 25, 36
Stokes
  H. Wells 142, 191,
    199, 209, 216
  Hump. Wells 133
  Humphrey Wells 33,
    47, 49, 50, 61,
    64, 80, 86, 96,
    104, 109, 116,
    128, 135, 151,
    152, 172, 173
  Humphry Wells 17,
    21, 39, 45
  Mary 185, 204
  William 185, 204
Stone
  Elisabeth 50
  Hugh 119
  Margaret 189
  Mary 119
Stonestreet
  Robert 147

Story
Robert 17
Stout
Ann 64, 91
Anne 2, 21
James 2, 21, 64, 91
Stramat
Anne 41
Elisabeth 23
John 41
Peter John Baptist
24
Stromat
Ann 66
John 66
Studham
John 103, 169
Thomas 103, 123,
169
Sturtons Rest 69
Sudler
James 110, 154, 155
Mary Ann 154
Sulivant
Darby 126
John 126
Sullivan
Darby 183
Sullivant
Darby 165
John 165
Sumerlands Lott 68
Summers
John 56, 60, 81,
150
Mary 56, 150
Summerset
Thomas 25
Summersett
Thomas 10
Sumners
Isaac 204
John 107, 204
Sutton
Jane 145, 171
John 78, 145, 161,
171, 193, 203
Swallyivant
Catherine 72
Timothy 72
Swan Cove 73
Swan Neck 68
Swann Neck 73
Swann

Thomas 37
Sweatman
John 201
Sweeny
James 148
Sweetman
John 27, 35
Swift
Jane 55
John 11, 179
Theop. 133
Thomas 11
William 11, 55,
155, 179
Swillyivant
Katherine 72
Timothy 72
Sword
William 110
Syng
Deborah 173
John 173, 188
Philip 208, 209

Taite
William 17, 20, 182
Talbott
Daniel 92
Richard 92
Tall
Philip 150
Talton
James 36, 102
John 36
Tanner
Eleanor 160
Henry 160
Thomas 115, 200
William 115, 155,
200
Tarlton
James 124
Tasker
Benjamin 28
Tate
Thomas 6
Taylor
Bryan 17, 105, 173
Elinor 62
Everard 180
Henry 123
Hope 63
Hugh 140, 174

James 15, 123
John 17, 134, 151,
    211
Joseph 105, 124
Mary 15, 20, 105,
    124, 164
Peter 18, 31
Rebecca 163, 198,
    215
Robert 15, 28, 63,
    105, 124
Thomas 45, 46, 163,
    184, 198, 215
Unice 211
Walter 62, 97
William 7, 20, 60,
    164, 174
Temple
    John 123
Tenant
    Thomas 107, 132
Tench
    Francis 135
Teneson
    Abraham 191
    Justinian 82, 201
    Mary 191
Tennant
    Thomas 57
Tennison
    Abraham 109, 147,
        169
    Mary 109, 169
Terrill
    John 160, 173
Terring
    Robert 110
The Contest 72
The Enlargement 68
Theobalds
    Elisabeth 31, 210
    John 31, 37, 51,
        173, 210
    William 51
Thomas
    Ann 80, 119, 149
    Anne 47
    David 12, 47, 80,
        152, 174, 183
    Elisabeth 13
    George 185, 199
    Hannah 40
    Henry 204
    Jane 95, 116

John 40, 119, 149
Joseph 133
Philip 14, 49, 91
Robert 73
Simon 56
Thomas 13
Trustram 35, 42,
    95, 114, 116
W. 9
William 7, 9, 20,
    26, 35, 42, 53,
    56, 75, 76, 81,
    123, 132, 147,
    150, 204
Thomasman
    James 54, 77
    Tamer 54
Thompson
    Absalom 121
    Aug. 32, 117
    Augustine 79, 126
    Elinor 39, 59
    George 102
    Ignatius 102
    James 39, 59
    Jane 5
    John 5, 17, 28, 45,
        117, 213
    John Medly 39, 59
    Mary 28
    Richard 44, 117
    Robert 117, 124
    Susanna 103
    Thomas 31, 39, 85,
        102, 107, 213
    William 5, 213
Thorn
    James 95
    William 95, 118,
        163, 173
Thornton
    Catherine 183
    Elinor 170
    Posth. 142, 193
    Posthumus 170
    William 183
Thorp
    Catherine 45
    Edward 45
    George 28, 210
    Mary 210
Thorpe
    Catherine 62
    Edward 62

Thursby
  Ann 48, 106, 137
  Edward 48, 106, 137
Tidmarsh
  William 7
Tilghman
  Anna Maria 196
  John 35
  Richard 11, 196
  William 153, 209,
    210
Tillman
  Aaron 34, 63
Tillotson
  Christopher 153,
    160, 176
  Joan 153, 160
  John 153, 160
  Robert 92
Tillottson
  Christopher 197
  John 197
Timber Neck 69
Tingle
  John 108, 176, 198,
    215
  Mary 108, 198, 215
Tipet
  John 124
  Philip 59
Tipett
  John 200
Tippen
  Diana 55
  William 55
Todd
  Elenor 197
  Elisabeth 104
  Lance 104
  Thomas 33, 197
Todds Range 69
Tolle
  Timothy 15
Tolley
  Mary 35
  Thomas 18, 35
Tomlinson
  Abigail 10, 30
  Samuel 10, 30
  Solomon 10, 30
Tootell
  Richard 77, 100
Touchstone
  Henry 12, 45, 158,
    187
  Sarah 12, 45
Tounsand
  John 6
  Littleton 6
Tounsend
  James 62
  Littleton 6
  Rebecca 6
Tovey
  Samuel 125
Towers
  James 155, 197
Towgood
  Josias 92, 136,
    143, 210
  Mary 136, 143, 210
Townsend
  Benjamin 43, 130
  Charles 162
  John 97, 163, 184
  Littleton 163, 184,
    205
Train
  James 44, 177, 196
  Sarah 177, 196
Treeg
  James 204
  William 204
Trew
  Hannah 2, 21
  William 2, 21, 40,
    80, 166, 204
Tripp
  Henry 204
Trippe
  (N) 39
  Edward 58
  Henry 85, 107
Trotton
  Luke 24
Truelock
  Henry 40, 47, 53,
    76, 88, 98, 111,
    127, 142, 157,
    167, 177, 190,
    202
Trueman
  Henry 14, 37
Tryall
  Joseph 154
Tubman
  Richard 25
Tucker

Thursby
  Ann 48, 106, 137
  Edward 48, 106, 137
Tidmarsh
  William 7
Tilghman
  Anna Maria 196
  John 35
  Richard 11, 196
  William 153, 209,
    210
Tillman
  Aaron 34, 63
Tillotson
  Christopher 153,
    160, 176
  Joan 153, 160
  John 153, 160
  Robert 92
Tillottson
  Christopher 197
  John 197
Timber Neck 69
Tingle
  John 108, 176, 198,
    215
  Mary 108, 198, 215
Tipet
  John 124
  Philip 59
Tipett
  John 200
Tippen
  Diana 55
  William 55
Todd
  Elenor 197
  Elisabeth 104
  Lance 104
  Thomas 33, 197
Todds Range 69
Tolle
  Timothy 15
Tolley
  Mary 35
  Thomas 18, 35
Tomlinson
  Abigail 10, 30
  Samuel 10, 30
  Solomon 10, 30
Tootell
  Richard 77, 100
Touchstone
  Henry 12, 45, 158,
    187
  Sarah 12, 45
Tounsand
  John 6
  Littleton 6
Tounsend
  James 62
  Littleton 6
  Rebecca 6
Tovey
  Samuel 125
Towers
  James 155, 197
Towgood
  Josias 92, 136,
    143, 210
  Mary 136, 143, 210
Townsend
  Benjamin 43, 130
  Charles 162
  John 97, 163, 184
  Littleton 163, 184,
    205
Train
  James 44, 177, 196
  Sarah 177, 196
Treeg
  James 204
  William 204
Trew
  Hannah 2, 21
  William 2, 21, 40,
    80, 166, 204
Tripp
  Henry 204
Trippe
  (N) 39
  Edward 58
  Henry 85, 107
Trotton
  Luke 24
Truelock
  Henry 40, 47, 53,
    76, 88, 98, 111,
    127, 142, 157,
    167, 177, 190,
    202
Trueman
  Henry 14, 37
Tryall
  Joseph 154
Tubman
  Richard 25
Tucker

Henry 4
John 92, 175
Tull
    Richard 22, 38
    Thomas 62, 96
Tulley
    James 97
Tunney
    Isaac 34, 167
Tunny
    Isaac 57
Turbutt
    William 153
Turner
    Elisabeth 36, 60,
        84, 174
    Henry 214
    John 174, 212
    Thomas 122
Turpin
    Hannah 6
    John 6, 44
    William 6
Turvile
    Benjamin 214
    Presgrave 195, 215
    William 38, 39
Turvill
    William 29, 108,
        130
Tuttle
    John 123
Tyler
    Mary 161
    Robert 161
    William 97
Tylors Lot 72
Tyrea
    Henry 71
Tyschow
    Bastin 152
    Elisabeth 152

Underhill
    Ann 79
    John 79
Ungle
    Frances 131, 158
    Robert 131, 158
Upper Taunton 69, 70
Upton
    John 84
Uriell

George 162, 205
Helena 162
Urquhart
    John 200
Uscears
    John 31, 57, 135,
        150
    Mary 30, 135, 150

Valiant
    John 57, 207
Valliant
    John 103
Vandeaver
    Jacob 16
Vanderford
    Charles 93
    Thomas 153
    Vincent 93
Vandergrift
    Nicholas 117
Vansweringen
    Joseph 16, 35, 59,
        146, 166
    Martha 35
Vaudery
    George 64, 102
    Jane 64, 102
Vaune
    Abbraham 46
Veale
    Margaret 109
    William 109, 147
Veazey
    Robert 90, 143
Vennables
    John 30
Vennings Inheritance
    69
Veunables
    John 6
Vickars
    John 147, 181, 204
    Martha 147
    Thomas 204
Vickers
    John 121
Vigros
    Edward 29
Vigrose
    Edward 63
Villet
    Celia 213

Peter 213
Vincent
  Sarah 13
  William 13
Vowles
  Ann 39, 59
  Richard 4, 39, 59
Vuriell
  George 71

Waddell
  Robert 5
Wade
  Charity 37
  Zachariah 37, 79,
    163, 187, 213
  Zephaniah 2
Waggaman
  Ephraim 214
  Jacob 214
Wailes
  Helena 134, 152
  Helenor 43
  Joseph 5, 43, 134,
    152
Wails
  Joseph 130
Wainwright
  Pleasance 57, 90
Walker
  Daniel 32, 55, 95,
    155
  Elisabeth 194
  John 32, 34, 45,
    95, 155, 194,
    196, 197
  Thomas 30
  William 35
Wall
  Rebecca 81, 138,
    150
  Thomas 81, 107,
    138, 150
Wallace
  William 55
Walles
  George 102
Wallis
  Hugh 171
Walls
  William 79, 165
Walters
  John 103

  Mary Elisabeth 103
  Thomas 93
Waltham
  John 33, 41
  William 33, 40, 41
Walton
  Elisabeth 151, 177,
    206
  Fisher 151, 176,
    177, 206
  Stephen 151
  William 151, 177,
    206
Wamsley
  Thomas 79
Ward
  Ann 5, 34, 63
  Elisabeth 14, 103,
    211
  George 103, 156,
    159, 181
  Henry 7, 25, 45,
    211
  John 8, 14
  Margaret 37, 211
  Matthew Tilghman
    196
  Owen 31, 60
  Pereg. 70
  Stephen 5, 30, 34,
    63
  William 90
Ware
  Francis 23, 95
Warfield
  Alexander 73
  Richard 158
Waring
  Barton 139
  Basil 49
  Francis 211
  Marsham 44, 81, 83
  Martha 49
  Richard Marsham 44,
    81, 83
  Thomas 49
Waringford
  Benjamin 97
Warman
  Mary 193, 203, 216
  Stephen 193, 203,
    216
Warner
  Garey 56, 132, 150

Hester 44
Richard 44, 45, 118
Solomon 122, 132
Warren
  Mary 3, 50, 62
  Thomas 3, 50, 62
Warring
  Martha 211
Water
  John 130
  Mary Elisabeth 130
Waterman
  Nicholas 21
Waters
  Edward 176
  James 185
  Littleton 136
Wathen
  Elisabeth 113
  Henry 113, 139,
    187, 199
  Hudson 113
  John 113
Watkins
  John 14, 48, 94,
    104, 113
  Nicholas 94, 172
  Thomas 17, 19, 52
Watson
  Francis 107, 120,
    204
  Henry 144
  John 28
Watts
  Capt. 72
  John 79, 160, 183,
    212
Wattson
  Esther 15
  John 15, 124
Waughop
  Catherine 51, 83,
    124
  James 16, 51, 83
  Katherine 16
  Thomas 16, 51, 83
Webb
  Daniel 189
  John 57, 189
  Park 198, 208
  Perez 189
Webster
  Isaac 17, 18
  Richard 30

Samuel 151
Weeks
  Samuel 184
  Simon 184
Weems
  David 91
Welch
  John 15, 201
Wells
  Charles 192
  Elinor 9, 17, 18,
    26, 41, 52
  John 153, 176, 179
  Ruth 153, 179
  Thomas 9, 17, 18,
    26, 41, 52
Welsh
  James 162
  John 137, 155, 196,
    197
  Rachel 137
  William 110
Wenman
  John 137
West
  Capt. 71
  George 108
  Mary 91, 126
  William 108
Wetherall
  Henry 134, 151
Weymouth
  John 156, 209
Whaley
  Charles 96
  John 9, 19, 20, 26,
    27, 41, 52, 74,
    75, 87, 98, 110,
    127, 141
  William 208
Whayland
  Benjamin 38
Wheeler
  Clement 13, 25, 36
  Francis 13, 36
  Ignatius 13, 36
  John 100, 152
  Leonard 13, 36
  Martha 151, 210,
    216
  Richard 145, 161,
    210
  Thomas 13, 100, 152
  William 151, 172,

210, 212, 216
Wheyland
  Benjamin 127
Whiller
  Ann 186
  William 186
Whips
  John 148
Whitaker
  Robert 25
  William 196
White
  Catherine 60
  John 34, 51, 63,
    66, 195
  Joseph 89
  Samuel 146, 157,
    168, 178
  Stevens 60
  Thomas 34, 63, 109
  William 7, 30, 60,
    198
Whitehead
  Samuel 92
Whitley
  Thomas 5
Whitlowe
  John 4
Whitter
  Ann 23
  Anne 37
  William 23, 37, 94
Whittington
  Joseph 115
  William 60
Wickes
  Francis 12
  Joseph 77, 126,
    148, 153, 154,
    174, 196
  Samuel 12, 125
  Simon 125, 126
Wickham
  Nathaniel 161
Wicks
  Samuel 40
Wight
  Edward John 154
Wilds
  Mary 35
Wiles
  Mary 123
  Richard 208
Wiley

William 46
Wilkins
  Thomas 40, 152, 171
  William 90
Wilkinson
  John 170, 182
  Joseph 159, 170
  Mary 159, 170
  Rebecca 182
  Thomas 115
  William 182, 201
Willett
  Charles 140, 194
  Mary 140, 194
Williams
  Aaron 49, 143, 149
  Annion 35
  Benjamin 15, 179
  Charles 116, 144
  Christopher 92,
    115, 176
  David 116
  Elisabeth 15, 35,
    66
  Ennion 46, 58
  Esther 7, 60, 92,
    175
  Frances 46
  James 32, 66, 197
  Jane 30
  John 17, 30, 32,
    40, 60, 62, 97,
    130, 146, 197
  John Guy 34, 207
  Lew. 125
  Mary 118
  Richard 136
  Samuel 18, 161, 171
  Thomas 118, 208
  William 41, 66
Williamson
  Alexander 114
  William 92
Willis
  Andrew 164
  Elisabeth 24
  Rebecca 164
  Richard 93, 121,
    164, 172
Willitt
  Charles 163
  Mary 163
Willmore
  Mr. 40

Willmott
   John 82
Willson
   James 153, 211
   John 188
   Mary 188
   Peter 117
   Richard 186
   Samuell 43
Wilmer
   Lambert 80, 91,
     165, 199
   Simon 80, 91, 125,
     199, 205
   William 125, 165
Wilson
   David 43, 176, 214
   Frances 124
   George 125
   James 34, 35, 124
   John 124, 125, 173
   Joseph 124
   Samuel 176
   Sarah 125
   Thomas 124, 144
   William 14, 125,
     205
Wimsett
   Ann 15
   John 15
Winchester
   Jacob 77, 154
   Tabitha 46, 57
   Thomas 46, 57
Winde
   Allender 120
Winder
   Allender 120
   Thomas 120, 212
Winnall
   William 49
Winstanley
   Elisabeth 72
   Joseph 72
Winter
   John 23
Winterbury
   John 78
Wise
   Barbara 135, 160
   Margaret 32
   Matthew 135, 160
   Richard 32, 54, 77,
     155

Wiseman
   Elisabeth 59, 135,
     160
   Robert 59, 83, 110,
     135, 160
Wolter
   John 129
Wood
   Barbara 139, 197
   James 102
   John 46, 72, 139,
     144, 197
   Joseph 95, 124,
     125, 164, 187
   Letitia 95
   Martha 164
   Robert 96
   Samuel 200
   William 86, 152
   Winefred 170
   Winifred 170
Woodal
   John 54
Woodall
   John 101, 155
   Martha 101, 155
Woodcocks Nest 68
Wooden
   Joseph 24, 65, 84,
     170
Woodward
   Achsa 67
   Achsah 9, 19, 26,
     41, 52, 67, 72
   Amos 67, 68, 71
   Elisabeth 68
   Garrett 69
   Hannah 68
   Henry 67, 68, 69
   Mary 9, 19, 26, 41,
     52, 67, 68, 69,
     70
   William 19, 68, 70,
     71
Woodyard 70
Woolford
   (N) 39
   John 214
   Thomas 85, 107, 127
Woollford
   Thomas 18
Wootton
   Turner 48
   Turnor 209

Worthington
 Charles 157
 Hannah 48, 54, 76,
  88, 99, 101, 170
 Thomas 158
 William 48, 54, 76,
  82, 88, 99, 101,
  170, 172
Wrath
 Mary 155
 William 155
Wright
 Ambrose 153
 Ann 211
 Blois 172
 Bloys 105
 Edward 13, 33, 94
 Henry 66, 76, 88,
  99
 Jacob 49
 John 91
 Mary 13, 91, 141,
  178
 R. N. 88, 100
 Robert Norr. 112,
  129, 203, 216
 Samuel 12, 13, 55,
  77, 149
 Solomon 32, 141,
  164, 178
 Thomas 105
 Thomas Hynson 164
Wrightson
 John 57, 83, 103
 Rachel 57, 83, 103
Wroth
 James 78
 Kinwin 16
Wyatts Range 69
Wye
 William 206

Yates
 Robert 12, 41, 185
Yoe
 John 136, 211
Young
 Araminta 40, 42,
  136, 187
 Benjamin 141, 190,
  215
 David 198
 Edward 198

Elinor 206
Elisabeth 2, 174,
 205
Jehu 108
John 70, 71, 85,
 110, 174, 192,
 205, 206
Joseph 14, 40, 42,
 43, 70, 86, 136,
 187, 191, 203,
 210, 216
Parker 60
Rebecca 39, 179
Richard 14, 19, 26,
 52, 55, 70, 71,
 73, 76, 88, 110,
 112, 129, 131,
 136, 142, 146,
 157, 168, 170,
 178, 187, 216
Samuel 14, 39, 42,
 55, 70, 71, 76,
 86, 88, 90, 110,
 112, 121, 129,
 131, 136, 142,
 146, 157, 168,
 178, 179, 180,
 187, 188, 191,
 192, 203, 206,
 216
Younger
 Humphry 7, 20

Zelefro
 Andrew 186
 Jane 186
 Joseph 186

INDEX OF EQUITY CASES

Allen vs. Allen 47, 53, 76, 88, 99, 111, 128, 142, 157, 206

Bozman vs. Besswick 114
Bozman vs. Callawhan, et.al. 111
Bozman vs. Fletcher 157
Bozman vs. Loockerman 96, 99, 100, 111, 128, 129, 142, 146, 148, 157, 167, 193
Bozman vs. Millington 86, 88
Bozman vs. Moore 112

Carter vs. Collins 122, 129
Chaplin vs. Enoch & Metcalf 101, 112
Chezeldine vs. est. of Chezeldine 74
Cumming vs. Woodward 9, 19, 26, 41, 52, 67

Dallas vs. Campbell & Cornish 104, 112, 129
Deye vs. Cockey 148, 158
Digges vs. Digges 190, 215
Digges, et.al. vs. Digges 180, 202

Earle vs. Sutton 193
Edmondson vs. Loockerman 9, 19
Ennalls vs. est. of Ennalls 58
Ennalls vs. Holland, Holland, & Holland 208, 216

Fisher vs. Barnard 195, 203
Fisher vs. Baynard 216
Fisher vs. est. of Fisher 194
Fletcher vs. Bozman 43, 53, 75
Fottrell vs. Young & Young 55, 76, 88, 110, 112, 129, 142
Fottrell vs. Young, Young, & Alexander 187, 191, 203, 216

Gardiner vs. Harris 96, 112, 158, 169, 178, 190, 202
Gordon vs. Worthington 48, 54, 76, 88, 99

Hall vs. Digges 22, 27, 42, 75
Hall vs. est. of Hall 134, 202
Hall vs. Lowe 53
Hall vs. Phillips 182, 190, 202, 215

Harris vs. Lawson 158, 169, 178, 190, 202
Helm vs. Warman & Parish 193, 203, 216
Hilleary vs. Dowell & Dowell 48, 54

Levett vs. Buchanan & Sprigg 185, 191, 203, 216
Linthicum vs. est. of Linthicum 23
Loockerman vs. Loockerman 9, 18
Lusby vs. Wells 9, 17, 19, 26, 41, 52

Maddox vs. Bruce 149, 158, 168
Mathews, Hall, & Maxwell vs. Savory 86
Maxwell vs. Savory 178, 190, 202
Maxwell, et.al. vs. Savory 89, 99, 112, 128,
    142, 157, 168, 215

Parrish vs. est. of Parrish 3
Peele vs. Holland 162, 169, 178
Peele vs. Peele 46, 53, 76, 88, 98, 111, 127,
    142, 156, 166, 177, 188, 203, 216
Phillips vs. Downing 9, 19, 26, 41, 53, 75, 87,
    98, 110, 127, 141

Robison vs. Farlow 74, 76, 88, 99, 111, 128
Ryan vs. Truelock 47, 53, 76, 88, 98, 111, 127,
    142, 157, 167, 177, 190, 202

Savory vs. Hall 128
Savory vs. Matthews 128, 142
Savory vs. Matthews & Hall 100, 112

Thomas vs. Bowdle 20, 42
Thomas vs. Giles 7, 9, 27, 53, 75, 76
Thompson vs. Woolford & Trippe 39
Towgood vs. Towgood & Lane 136, 143

Wheeler vs. Partridge 216
Wright vs. Moore, Moore, & Moore 66, 76, 88, 99

Young & Young vs. White 157, 168, 178
Young vs. White 146

www.ingramcontent.com/pod-product-compliance
Lightning Source LLC
Chambersburg PA
CBHW061004280326
41935CB00009B/829